W9-APB-960

"In his sharp debut, Goza . . . writes with passion about the racist and classist roots of America's political and religious institutions. . . . Goza's ability to sharply discern and clearly explain ideas underlying American thinking will open important conversations about the nature of equality."

—***Publishers Weekly*** **Starred Review**

"An impressive analysis of the some of the religious and secular thinkers who inspired America's addiction to racist ideas—an addiction that continues to destroy America. *America's Unholy Ghosts* is for anyone daring to be anti-racist, daring to end racial inequity."

—Ibram X. Kendi

National Book Award-winning author of *Stamped from the Beginning: The Definitive History of Racist Ideas in America*

"This is a major and thoughtful contribution to the anti-racism movement."

—Gerald Horne

Activist and author of *The Fire This Time: The Watts Uprising and the 1960s* and *The Counter-Revolution of 1776: Slave Resistance and the Origins of the United States of America*

"Joel Goza could not have perceived how racism was and is imagined, institutionalized, and ingrained in U.S. American life had he not experienced the black church. *America's Unholy Ghosts* is a probing, spirited, edgy, ethical reflection on how both things happened, perceiving a baleful national legacy through the lens of black church faith and struggle."

—Gary Dorrien

Columbia University and Union Theological Seminary's Reinhold Niebuhr Professor of Social Ethics and author of *Breaking White Supremacy* and *The New Abolition*

"Joel Goza writes within the faith traditions of the Black Prophetic Church with the passion of a modern-day racial justice apostle, and with the mind of a philosopher unraveling some of the oldest ideas to justify racism and poverty. *America's Unholy Ghosts* is an urgent offering to its readers who seek exorcism and rebirth for a new nation."

—Khalil Gibran Muhammad
Harvard Kennedy School and author of *The Condemnation of Blackness: Race, Crime, and the Making of Modern Urban America*

"*America's Unholy Ghosts* is a paradigm shifter. This book fundamentally reorients our understanding of race, faith, politics, and our intellectual heroes. You will see the world differently after reading this book. A *tour de force*."

—Michael O. Emerson
Author of *Divided by Faith: Evangelical Religion and the Problem of Race in America*

"A wonderful read. . . . The depth of thought and writing are so savory that I find myself going over the lines again to make sure that I have received the full force of what *America's Unholy Ghosts* puts before us . . . this kind of book is the pause that refreshes my spirit!"

— Cleophus J. LaRue
Princeton Theological Seminary, author of *The Heart of Black Preaching*

"Joel Goza has done his homework and paid his dues. He is the best of all possible interpreters of the racial dilemmas facing America. He has read the books and, simultaneously, lived the life in Houston's challenging 5th Ward. *America's Unholy Ghosts* is the result of years of digging into the philosophical roots of American racism. Goza's easy, conversational style demystifyies the philosophers who helped shape our thinking. He skillfully reads the world they created through the lens of Martin Luther King's prophetic critique. This is a challenging and delightful essay on endurance and hope."

—Richard Lischer

Author of *The Preacher King: Martin Luther King, Jr. and the Word that Moved America*

"From the front lines of battling America's original sin, Joel Goza has written a truthful, immediately relevant book. Joel raises the ghosts of the genteel philosophical roots of our racialized thinking to show us how white supremacy required the assistance of some of Europe and America's most revered thinkers. Joel exposes the bad thinking that led to evil ideas and deeds, then ends with an eloquent call for us to move from hearing the truth to doing the truth in regard to race in America. We'll be coming to terms with and benefiting from this book for a long time, thank God."

—Will Willimon

Author of *Who Lynched Willie Earle: Preaching to Confront Racism*

"This book is an illuminating, challenging and well-written exploration into the hidden roots and unnoticed manifestations of racism. Reading it has helped me understand the frightening circumstances of our day in the light of our past. I recommend it enthusiastically."

—Justo L. González

Author of *The Story of Christianity* and *Mañana*

"Joel Goza introduces us to those respected intellectuals whose ideas became the DNA of white supremacy and American exceptionalism. He carefully and clearly documents his presentation with preciseness and ethical urgency that calls for an awakening from our apathetic slumbers. This book is a must read."

—J. Alfred Smith, Sr.

Past President the Progressive National Baptist Convention, Pastor Emeritus, Allen Temple, and Professor Emeritus American Baptist, Seminary of the West

"Joel Goza boldly and eloquently confronts white supremacy's sadistic presence. *America's Unholy Ghosts* insightfully strands together philosophy, politics, theology, race, and memoir to elucidate the contemporary predicaments of racial and economic inequality. It is an urgent and compelling call to action."

— Phillip Luke Sinitiere

Sections Editor at *The North Star* and author of *Protest and Propaganda: W. E. B. Du Bois, the CRISIS, and American History*

"In this book, Joel Goza explores the role that ideas can play in justifying and normalizing racialized injustice. In undertaking this type of intellectual archeology, Goza makes the case that racism is not an aberration but is buried deep in the DNA of our political and economic system. Goza's own active commitment to racial justice shines through in his prose. He makes a contribution here to a long-overdue conversation on the intellectual roots of racism, and inspires us not only to think but also to act."

— William Cavanaugh

Director of the Center for World Catholicism and Intercultural Theology and author of *Being Consumed* and the *Myth of Religious Violence*

America's Unholy Ghosts

America's Unholy Ghosts

The Racist Roots of Our Faith and Politics

By

Joel Edward Goza

CASCADE *Books* • Eugene, Oregon

AMERICA'S UNHOLY GHOSTS
The Racist Roots of Our Faith and Politics

Cascade Books
An Imprint of Wipf and Stock Publishers
199 W. 8th Ave., Suite 3
Eugene, OR 97401

www.wipfandstock.com

PAPERBACK ISBN: 978-1-5326-5143-4
HARDCOVER ISBN: 978-1-5326-5144-1
EBOOK ISBN: 978-1-5326-5145-8

Cataloguing-in-Publication data:

Names: Goza, Joel Edward, author.

Title: America's unholy ghosts : the racist roots of our faith and politics / Joel Edward Goza.

Description: Eugene, OR : Cascade Books, 2019 | Includes bibliographical references and index.

Identifiers: ISBN 978-1-5326-5143-4 (paperback) | ISBN 978-1-5326-5144-1 (hardcover) | ISBN 978-1-5326-5145-8 (ebook)

Subjects: LCSH: Racism—United States—History. | United States—Race relations. |

Race—Philosophy. | Race relations—Philosophy. | Racism. | Hobbes, Thomas, 1588–1679—Influence. | Locke, John, 1632–1704—Influence. | Smith, Adam,—1723–1790—Influence.

Classification: E185.61 .G69 2019 (paperback) | E185.61 .G69 (ebook)

Manufactured in the U.S.A. 03/21/19

Dedicated to:

The grandparents in 5th Ward who continue to fight for the future of their children.

War on.

God is with you.

There are several specific things that the church can do.
First, it should try to get to the ideational roots of race hate.

—Martin Luther King Jr., *Stride Toward Freedom*, 1957

Aren't ideas frightening?

—Ludwig Wittgenstein, *Remarks on Frazer's Golden Bough*, 1967

Contents

An Introduction

Born in a Bullet

America's Unholy Ghosts is a book about the frightening power of ideas and unearths the way brilliant philosophers ingrained racist instincts into America's religious and political life. This book is also about Martin Luther King Jr.'s fight to uproot racism and inequality from the American experiment by writing the conscience of the Prophetic Black Church onto American hearts, minds, and the laws of the land. *America's Unholy Ghosts* comes to a close exploring what Americans across racial and religious divides can learn from the Prophetic Black Church's ongoing struggle to continue King's mission to end America's addiction to racism and inequality—evils "lurking within our body politic from its very beginning."[1]

To begin, I need to share my story. Like many in white America, I received indoctrination into the virtues of the American heritage and believed radical change to the ideologies that shaped our way of life was neither needed nor possible. But convictions can change in the twinkling of an eye . . . or, as in my case, with the blast of bullets. In such a moment, one night in one of Houston's neglected inner-city communities, my life changed forever. In many ways, this book began with those bullets.

Three years before those bullets, I was home in the suburbs of Houston, Texas, during Christmas break of my senior year at Wheaton College. At the time, my father was a deacon at the nearby Southern Baptist church. He said he wanted to take me to breakfast the next day before heading to work and that made me antsy. College forced my faith and politics to evolve, and by my senior year the pillars holding up my evangelical worldview began to topple. It was not a conversation I desired to share. Coming from Texas, we are skeptical of anything involving evolution.

The next morning, we headed to Uncle Tom's Kitchen, our favorite breakfast spot in the area. He asked me how I was doing. I started cautiously, feeling my way along, but eventually arrived at the conversation concerning my evolving faith and convictions. Though my identity as a Christian was deepening, my commitment to evangelical ways of thinking was dying. He listened patiently as I talked the way college students talk. After I was done, he took his time. "Well, Joel," he said, "I don't know what you studied, but God's hand is on you, son. I expect you to follow him." And that was that.

When we shared breakfast that morning my dream was to head to Duke University's School of Divinity following graduation and pursue a life as a suburban pastor. And though Duke played a part, little did we know as we shared breakfast that morning that what lay before me in the not-too-distant future was a life in the inner city and in the Black Church. The evolution of my faith and politics was just beginning.

Measured by an odometer, the roads between where I was raised in Houston's suburbs and Houston's most marginalized inner-city communities are relatively short. In American cities, small distances between neighborhoods and zip codes regularly lead into entirely different worlds. When measured by a calendar, the three years between the morning with my father and the evening my life changed is a relatively short sliver of time. Yet, in that window, a whole lifetime seemingly passed me by.

After returning for my final semester at Wheaton College, I received acceptance and scholarships to Duke Divinity School, bringing my dream one step closer to reality. Yet, shortly after graduating from college and entering grad school, my body started becoming mysterious to me as my heart began beating with intense irregularities. The irregular heartbeats terrified me, and one day at a time life took the form of a perpetual anxiety attack inducing an emotional-spiritual-physical vertigo. It is strange how quickly some dreams become living nightmares.

At night, the only way I found to rest was to lay on the dormitory floor with my hands outstretched in the form of a cross. Somehow allowing my physical body to express the crucifixion taking place within me helped me to fall asleep. During those days and through those nights, I became intimate with my vulnerability, fragility, and brokenness. After one year of graduate school, I dropped out.

When classes let out, my mom flew to the Carolinas to pack up her baby boy and his few belongings and to take him back to Texas. Thankfully, two of my best friends from Wheaton—Justo and Stephen—joined me in Houston. A few months after arriving in Houston, a doctor diagnosed me as a diabetic through a routine physical. Apparently the graduate school diet of free pizza and donuts and the stress of graduate studies proved less than ideal for undiagnosed diabetes.

Yet putting my life together proved more difficult than diagnosing my disease. I found a church home that inspired me, was invited to join the staff, and was fired three months after beginning. Needless to say, the violent emotional-spiritual-physical vertigo rolled on, and I struggled to find my footing. In what felt like a miracle, after being fired from my church home, I found a job on the lower rungs of an elite accounting firm. I also found a new place to worship, and Sunday after Sunday I churched with thousands of other well-intentioned middle- and upper-class white folks. Slowly but surely stability replaced instability.

In the struggle to survive, I swapped the search for a meaningful life for a stable one. Sometimes that is what happens when we hit the dead-end of a life filled with good intentions. During this time, a mutual friend invited Justo, Stephen, and me to move to Houston's impoverished immigrant community of Denver Harbor, where he taught middle school. Often, I tried to understand our move to Denver Harbor in idealistic and sentimental terms. The deeper truth, however, was that I simply had little to lose.

Whatever the reason, we found ourselves renovating and moving into a house on the 6800 block of Laredo Street. Our block was rougher than we anticipated and often felt like the Wild West. Prostitution, drive-by shootings, and the remembering of those whom the cops had killed felt like weekly occurrences. Our community's families lived in the tragic limbo between hope in the American dream and the realities of our broken immigration, educational, economic, and criminal-justice systems. Our neighbors worked tirelessly to scratch out a life of dignity against great odds.

As the year went by, I straddled different worlds—working in Houston's skyscrapers, churching with wealthy white folks, and living with poor folks of color. We met our neighbor Beef after a drive-by one night. Beef was a DJ, and we began throwing block-parties together. Beef pounded out the music. Stephen, Justo, and I cooked the fajitas and invited our friends from the different worlds we inhabited to join us. Before too long most folks on the block started coming as well. The block parties provided a strange mix of immigrants and conservative Christians, gangsters and graduate students, yuppies, hippies, and my Southern Baptist parents and family.

Before long our intimacy with the families on our block shifted the center of our loyalties from America, its corporations, and evangelical churches to those our nation, corporations, and churches continued to fail. As we got to know our neighbors, our life integrated into their lives and families. We failed to meet people who fit a simplistic stereotype of either the demonized or idolized poor. We simply met people attempting to break the grip of poverty in a country and city that provided remarkably little help in their struggle for a sustainable life. Nonetheless, I witnessed daily folks with a deep intimacy with suffering find the courage to carve out very rich lives.

In time, the atmosphere on the block changed, but not overnight. Dangerous moments developed a familiar atmosphere to them. On the night my life changed, it was getting late as Justo and I watched a movie with some friends. Shots rang out in the street, and Justo and I looked out the window to see a mass brawl between some of the competing factions of the block. No longer were those fighting strangers to us. They were friends. Justo was the first one out of our front door, and I followed behind.

The fight that night began before the children escaped the crossfire and the ensuing brawl. Justo and I grabbed the three or four kids in the street and ran them into their grandparents' house. The front bedroom of the house provided a large bed, and we tucked them under the covers with their cousins. We smiled at them and promised them all would be well before heading back out into the streets where their fathers and uncles were fighting. Tucking the kids into bed only took a minute, but by the time we returned to the street much of the fighting was finished. We broke up the last remnants with the help of pleas from the children's mothers.

That night was not my first violent night—and certainly not the last—but there was something singular about it; something singular in my mental image of the children tucked in bed in the midst of a dangerous world; something singular about the brokenness of the mothers and the tears that rolled down their cheeks; something singular about the inability of families to break the cycles of violence and poverty that surrounded them and that shaped their lives. Something within me broke that evening, even as my personal struggles began to solidify into a steely form of quiet defiance.

Though I failed to see the interconnections between Denver Harbor and the larger American experiment, I knew the tragedy I witnessed that night was much larger than the violence of the 6800 block of Laredo St. Something was horribly wrong with our nation and city that made the 6800 block of Laredo a dangerous place to live and the cycle of poverty there nearly an impossible chain to break. I did not know if things could change, but I knew that things must change. That evening, this later truth—that things must change—began taking on a poignancy that rendered any questions about the possibility of change useless. Those bullets began a journey that committed me to a life in the inner city and to the pursuit of an understanding of the sickness of our nation that tied together Houston's communities of overabundance and desperation in such intimate proximity.

BETWEEN THE INNER CITY AND IVORY TOWER

Though I found fulfillment living in the inner-city, life was not getting any easier. I failed to flourish on my job and the company's patience was running out. I also knew another window was closing as Duke Divinity agreed to hold my scholarships for two years in case I decided to return. Returning to Duke for the final two years of my degree provided a unique opportunity to process all I experienced since dropping out of school and seemed less embarrassing than getting fired once again. With very mixed incentives, I made plans for one last block party and to return to Durham, NC.

When I returned to Duke, I brought with me a very different set of questions than the questions that began my graduate studies. I was infected with an itch to understand the racial inequities that America's ideologies of race, religion, and politics produced. I desired to understand how generational poverty went unchecked and unchallenged, why Christian leaders contended themselves with missionizing inner-city communities without committing themselves to altering a city's way of life to allow poor children a chance to thrive. I yearned to understand why Houston, America's most diverse city, a city of big businesses and big churches, a city with people who helped placed a man on the moon, proved unable to address the deepest needs of people in poverty.

Ironically enough, it was upon my return to the ivory tower that I was introduced to the spiritual and political genius of Martin Luther King. Before moving into Denver Harbor, I understood King as the source of inspiration for the integration of our nation and the uniquely American dream. After living surrounded by racialized poverty, I was better positioned to realize the revolutionary nature of King's genius. Within the fire of King's words concerning our nation's sins against black and brown folks, I saw the faces of my neighbors, and I realized that at the intersection of race, faith and politics in America, King is not Bill Nye the Science Guy. When it comes to race, faith, and politics, King stands with Copernicus, Newton, and Einstein; he stands with those whose revolutionary brilliance demanded we see our world through their eyes and unlearn all that we thought we knew of our world.

King provided my first introduction to the Prophetic Black Church[2] and began opening a door for me to enter into his tradition in a more meaningful way. Following Duke, I planned to re-enter the business world, move back to Denver Harbor, and find a church home in the inner city that spoke English. As the fall semester became spring, I started to search for a summer internship at a church with the potential to become a church home. The only churches I knew that spoke English in the inner city were black churches, and so I began looking for internships in Houston's Fifth Ward, an African-American community that bordered Denver Harbor.

Denver Harbor and Houston's Fifth Ward are separated by a train track. When Jim Crow ruled Houston, Denver Harbor was considered a white community and the train tracks made the racial line visible. Following integration, white flight, and decades of immigration, Denver Harbor grew increasingly Hispanic, and the train tracks continued to perpetuate a line of racial demarcation between the Latino and African-American communities. The Fifth Ward community originated after the Emancipation Proclamation to place freed slaves on expendable land near the heart of downtown Houston. Fifth Ward was where George Foreman grew tough and later carried with it a notorious reputation as the Bloody Fifth, producing the rap group the Geto Boys—"Damn, it feels good to be a gangster." It also nurtured the brilliance of Barbara Jordan, the first African-American woman to keynote the Democratic National Convention. I continued to learn there is more to communities than what appears on the surface of things.

Some of the troubling community statistics include: 43% of households have an annual income of less than $15,000 / Of residents over the age of 24, 4% have a college degree, 57% lack a high school degree, and 27% have a ninth-grade education or less / 48% of the housing stock is considered derelict / HIV rates are 600% and firearm related deaths are 318% higher than the Houston rate.

My search for internships initiated a series of holy accidents that put me in touch with a church that spearheaded wide-ranging efforts to revitalize the community, and I coordinated a call with the pastor of Pleasant Hill Missionary Baptist Church. In time, he welcomed me to intern with them for the summer and join their work within the church and community. My first black church experience took place within a small and intimate Wednesday night Bible Study. After a couple of songs—songs with the same lyrics but a different rhythm to the hymns I grew up with—the guest teacher failed to show. "Joel," the pastor announced with a smirk but without a warning, "you're on." It was training in living on your tiptoes and the beginning of a journey that transformed my life.

I can't tell you exactly what happened later that week when I attended my first Sunday worship service. I can only say how it felt through other experiences that felt similar. It felt like the first time I listened to Van Morrison's album *Moondance* and finally found the music I long desired but that I never knew existed. It felt like the first time at the optometrist when my vision, which I didn't realize was skewed, clarified. Those gathered to worship thanked God for the food on their plates, the roofs over their heads, and for his protection that guarded them through the night. They thanked God for food and shelter with the intensity of folks who knew mealtime and sleep-time often failed to ease hunger pains or provide rest. The music was brilliant, the preaching moved those gathered, and the congregation's hospitality provided palpable warmth to the atmosphere.

In time, I learned the Prophetic Black Church possessed all the human failures of other institutions, holy and otherwise. I know many who the Church's failures deeply wounded. And I know many of these wounds all too well. Yet what was clear to me from the first morning I worshiped in the Prophetic Black Church, and became clearer still with the passing of time, was that the Prophetic Black Church's intimacy with the broken and abused provided the Church a wisdom, a grace, a balm perfectly tailored for those who the American way of life fails. And the American way of life fails us all.

If the evening of the gang fight broke my peace with the status quo, that morning, in that sanctuary, a people gathered who began to stitch within me an incredibly different set of convictions regarding America's piety, politics, and vision for the future. I no longer felt like a sojourner. In their embrace, I felt at home in a church for the first time in a long time. When I received a job offer to join Pleasant Hill staff after I graduated Duke, it was not a complicated decision.

Yet one more year of studies at Duke awaited. In my final year, my itch to deepen my understanding of the intersection of race, faith, and politics flared with an intensity that felt like hunger pangs. During my final year, the intensity of that itch led me to begin studying and writing on the philosophers of the Enlightenment who provided the original paradigms through which America's ideologies flowed. I began studying these philosophers out of a desire to understand how the ideas and ideals that shaped our country—freedom and equality, democracy and the separation of church and state, reason and religious liberty, equality of man and free-market economics—were crafted to harmonize with slavery and perpetuated a nation divided along economic and racial lines. I attempted to work backwards by first reading what the writers of the Enlightenment philosophers wrote about slavery and then untangle how these philosophers harmonized enlightenment ideologies with "that peculiar institution."[3]

The study that was in its infancy when I graduated Duke continued on and off again for the next ten years as I worked in Houston's Fifth Ward. Over those years I became intimately familiar with the works of three philosophers in particular: the father of modern political philosophy, Thomas Hobbes, the father of Liberalism, John Locke, and the father of modern Economics, Adam Smith. By reading these philosophers backwards, I started to see how slavery acted as an invisible hand shaping the founding ideologies upon which we built our nation, its churches, corporations, and educational institutions. I learned that when we look at the architecture of the Enlightenment philosophers through the work taking place on the bodies of Africans and Indians, we see how their ideologies coalesced into paradigms that not only justified the genocide and slavery of yesteryears but that through which Americans *continue* to understand matters of faith and politics. The masterminds who harmonized enlightened ideologies with slavery are dead and gone, but their nifty philosophical footwork continues to shape our thinking and harden our hearts to our society's racial and economic inequities. While racial thinking evolved, the basic ideological architecture that produced slavery never went out of style.

During this time, however, my thinking was molded not only by my readings but also through the intimacies that developed when I joined Pleasant Hill's church family and their efforts to revitalize the Fifth Ward community. A year into our journey together, Sister Williams began praying for me to find a wife. What took me twenty-seven years of praying took Sister Williams two months. When my grandfather proved too frail to travel to our wedding, a Deacon from the church stood in his place. Later in the story, the church prayed for and accepted our children as their children. When two of our pregnancies led to death and not life, the church experienced our loss as their loss. Such is the power of family.

From the community's public apartments and churches, I processed with Fifth Ward students the murders—and our nation's responses to the murders—of Trayvon Martin,[4] Michael Brown, and the black Christians in the sanctuary of Mother Emmanuel AME Church in Charleston, South Carolina.[5]

The morning after the court acquitted George Zimmerman for the murder of Trayvon Martin, our students gathered at the church. The normal playbook for our summer gatherings disappeared as the students processed our nation's readiness to declare a racially motivated murderer innocent. The students already knew the difference between the America their teachers presented in social studies and the America they experienced in the Fifth Ward's streets. But that tension failed to prepare them for how our nation's courts continually declare racially motivated murderers innocent. As in the days of Emmett Till, with a whole nation watching, American courts of justice deemed young black life, their lives, justifiably expendable. Tears wetted cheeks, and a righteous anger simmered beneath quiet comments. As much as anything, heavy and heart-rending silences dominated. Those silences haunt me.

The church patiently brought me into the open secrets that haunt life in black America and partnered me with many of the city's leading practitioners and researchers committed to addressing urban inequality. I slowly learned to see how our shared history and current political arrangements perpetuate today's inequalities. I knew Rome was not built in a day, but I required patient tutorials to see how the chains of generational poverty shaping the Fifth Ward's struggles were forged and re-forged throughout our nation's ever-evolving history of oppressive practices; to see how national ideologies danced to different beats along lines of color; to see how the illusions within white communities crucify lives within black communities.

Denver Harbor stripped me of indifference, but it was the tutelage of the Prophetic Black Church that developed within me the capacity to see the interconnectivity of our deeply segregated city and nation. As Michael Eric Dyson word-smithed it: "America is far from simply black and white by whatever definition you use, but the black-white divide has been the major artery through which the meaning of race has flowed throughout the body politic."[6] By understanding *that* artery, one understands the very heart of the American experiment.

As we labored in the Fifth Ward, I witnessed firsthand how the inequities of our economic and educational systems formed a tragic partnership with a racist criminal-justice system. I did not learn from sociological studies how our culture fostered inequalities through the intimate interconnections of the cradle, classroom, and courtroom; I learned about the interconnections through my relationships with our community's families. I learned that the cycle of generational poverty contained many interlocking gears that worked together with the precision of a clock and the violence of a wrecking ball. And my eyes told no lies. After learning the statistics and working with our city's researchers and leading urban practitioners, I understood that the stories I witnessed were not the exceptions, but the epitome of how the racial world works in our nation.

At the intersection of race and place, religion and politics, I began seeing the different dimensions of the ideologies that shaped our religious, business, and political institutions. In Houston, we committed ourselves to small government and big prisons, to large churches commissioned to the salvation of souls and self-esteem, and to even larger companies whose focus on the bottom line often blinded them to the world fighting for survival in the shadows of their skyscrapers. Despite our ability to crack down on crime, save souls, and make money hand-over-fist, our powerlessness to break the Fifth Ward's generational poverty revealed haunting blind spots amidst our self-assuredness.

I came to see the very things that I received training from preschool through graduate school to deny: that the poverty of the Fifth Ward and the inequalities of its educational, economic, and criminal-justice systems were not aberrations of a just system, nor failures of individual folks to take personal responsibility, but the products of an intricately designed way of life. Eerily reminiscent of the "social predestination" pictured in Aldous Huxley's *A Brave New World*, our ideologies—our politics, economics, and religion—produced a system perfectly engineered to produce the results we reaped. Black babies, born into poverty, rightly anticipated spending their days in poverty, prison, and under the threat of police brutality. Despite our promises of opportunity and salvation, our systems operated with toxic precision and predictability for both the poor and the rich. The children of the rich stayed rich and the poor stayed poor, be they saved or damned.

One day at a time, as I churched and as I researched, I began seeing how the racial edges of American ideologies carved white superiority into American identity and racial inequality into American institutions.

REASONS TO READ & WHY I WRITE

One reason to read *America's Unholy Ghosts* is that it provides a deeply researched narrative that combines philosophy, history, and cultural analysis to deepen the understanding of race, religion, and politics in American life. Yet what separates this work is the location from which the research occurred and where the narrative was woven. There are truths of our nation that one only learns by living and working in places like the Fifth Ward, by watching too many of the community's children fall through the cracks of America's broken promises.

In such a context, I researched and wrote *America's Unholy Ghosts* as my heartbreak made me question the American way of life and trained me to think against the grain of our cultural common sense. The more clearly I saw the ways American politics and religion warred against my community, the more desperate I grew to see through the rhetoric that justified both our inequalities and our indifference. Understanding America's ongoing racial crisis cannot happen apart from oppressed people, for the power of racist ideas is only understood by standing in solidarity with those the American way crucifies.

In writing *America's Unholy Ghosts*, I seek to align myself with the Prophetic Black Church tradition to help readers understand how America's racial imagination was imagined, institutionalized, and ingrained. There is no better tour guide through the graveyard of racist illusions than the Prophetic Black Church. No institution understands the injustices that inspired the civil rights movement and brought Black Lives Matter to the streets more intimately than the church does. Historically, the Prophetic Black Church shaped both the heart and mind for much of the black community. With a big heart and beautiful mind, the Church labors for families made fatherless by an unjust criminal-justice system, for children left behind by a broken educational system, and for those attempting to create a life of dignity in a cruel world. American-made suffering acts as the historical whetting stone that sharpens the Black Church's prophetic edge, and it is this prophetic edge that I seek to provide for readers of *America's Unholy Ghosts* as we journey together.

I write because if our nation's racist instincts continue to haunt our land, so too does our desire for a faith and politics marked by mercy, justice, and equity. *America's Unholy Ghosts* embodies a hope that a deeper understanding of America's racist roots and learning from the Prophetic Black Church can empower those who labor to replace racial inequalities and enmity with equity and intimacy. I write to goodhearted white folks—whether spiritual or secular—desiring to break the grip of the generational sin that is white supremacy. White supremacy is the ever-evolving ways we justify racial inequalities and segregated lives, and it empowers a tragic indifference to the suffering of God's children. Generational sin is not an easy chain to break, for it is linked together by love and requires us to question the very things our mothers and fathers, pastors and teachers taught us to believe and to cherish. I write for white folks to understand that the problems of racism run much deeper than the matters of the heart and implicates the very way we imagine and manage our life together on America's blood-soaked soils.

I also write for those who know through experience our nation's racial sickness all too intimately. I write for those who sit in for-profit prisons for non-violent crimes, for black and brown children whose great giftedness is allowed too little room to thrive. I write for black mothers and grandmothers, fathers and grandfathers who give everything everyday and whose sacrifices too often fail to protect those they love from the cruelties of America's injustice. I write to help reveal the roots of our land's racist delusions and to join the work of breaking the hold of racist thinking on our shared lives.

America's Unholy Ghosts exists in this tension of prophetic dreams and the nightmare of our nation's ongoing racial crisis. It attempts to attack the ideological roots of America's racialized faith and politics that prevented us from hoping for a better way forward than segregated communities of a heartless law and order. Though slavery and Jim Crow laws are dead, the racist philosophies that spawned racial politics are alive and thriving and continue to empower America's ongoing racialization.

I wrote *America's Unholy Ghosts* under the little light I gained by living for the past decade at the intersection of race, faith, and politics amidst African-American and immigrant poverty. I see the light in churches coming together to worship and work for a new day. I see the light in inner-city schools where gifted students and teachers come together in great daring and sacrifice to end generational poverty. I see the light at block parties where folks laugh and dance and refuse to be broken.

Yet, nothing transformed me more than watching grandmothers, wearied by grandchildren and great-grandchildren, fight for a future worthy of their children's great giftedness. In their love, I see flashes of God's face and his Kingdom. For too long America's ideologies and paradigms of religious and political thinking implicitly questioned my church and community's humanity, brilliance, and beauty. The time has come to question our ideologies and uproot the racist ideas that continue to order America's faith and politics.

1

Prelude

Revolution, Evolution, and the Lies that Racialize Our Land

REVOLUTION

America lives amidst a cultural crisis at the intersection of race, religion, and politics. Cultural crises arise when a society's cherished illusions begin to die and force societies to re-examine their foundational principles, ideologies, and ways of life. New visions and ways of being always cost us the death of old illusions and ways of living.

In 1962, Thomas Kuhn released the groundbreaking book *The Structure of Scientific Revolutions.* In his book, Kuhn upends the illusion of science as a field of study that produces steady progress through a disciplined and religious devotion to the rationality of the scientific method. Instead, Kuhn argues that progress in science comes through the implosion of existing paradigms and worldviews. Copernicus, Galileo, Newton, Einstein: we know these geniuses' names not because they brought forward incremental change, but because when faced with a crisis they provided truthful and revolutionary ways to understand our world that changed how we lived.

What made Kuhn's book groundbreaking was how he framed his argument to use the history of science as a springboard to discuss the nature of revolutions that shifts society's paradigms and worldview at large. Perhaps what also made the work groundbreaking was the decade of the sixties in which Kuhn published his book—for if the sixties marked anything, the decade marked paradigm shifts that challenged traditional ways of life.

At the intersection of race, faith and politics, our lives find their shape in the unresolved strife and unfinished business of that era. If the sixties inaugurated a revolution, it never resolved the revolution it began. In fact, Martin Luther King, perhaps the only truly revolutionary political and spiritual genius our nation ever produced, thought that the revolution he helped inspire was just beginning and that the most important work lay beyond his own lifetime.

Martin Luther King divided the civil rights work into two eras. Phase one of the civil rights era marked a face-off regarding the rights of African Americans to participate fully in the life of our nation, confronting the realities of Jim Crow segregation and the racist restrictions of the South's voting booths. Part of the 1960s revolution was that for the first time televisions tied together living rooms across the nation by bringing ideas and images from around the world into the intimate confines of the American household. The leaders of the movement understood that it is within the context of the household that most Americans form their core convictions, and King and his allies manipulated this new instrument with remarkable success to display the violence of the American way of life. With striking brilliance, the movement replaced the images of race relations in the South crafted through movies like *Gone with the Wind* and *Birth of a Nation* with the images of Bull Connor releasing his ravenous dogs. America was not ready for what it witnessed within the intimate context of their living rooms, and the movement continued to labor until America could no longer stomach what it saw and proved ready to change the laws of the land.

Phase two of the civil rights movement involved the fight to translate the *rights* of African Americans into the *results* of racial equality in housing, wages, education, and opportunity. In the words of President Lyndon Johnson to the students of Howard University, the aim was to translate "equality as a right and theory" into "equality as a fact and equality as a result."[7] Though the hard-fought victories of the Civil Rights Acts of 1964 and 1965 brought phase one of the civil rights movement to a victorious close, phase two proved much more elusive and much less victorious.

The seeds of phase two's ambitions trace back to the earliest days of the movement. Within a year of the Montgomery bus boycott, King released his first book, *A Stride Toward Freedom,* wherein he called for an examination of "the ideational roots of race hate."[8] As the movement matured into its second phase, King increasingly called for confrontation with the founding ideologies of our nation. King believed our society was sick and that there was something singular about our nation's sickness that traced back to the very roots and ideologies that birthed the American experiment. In an essay published shortly after his assassination, King reflected on the status of the civil rights movement. "It is forcing America to face all its interrelated flaws—racism, poverty, militarism, and materialism." King wrote that the struggle exposed "evils that are rooted deeply in the whole structure of our society." The more intimate King grew with our racial sickness, the more ending Jim Crow and opening Southern voting booths felt like baby-steps rather than strides toward freedom. The more the movement revealed regarding the character of the relationships between race, faith, and politics, the more the movement revealed the need for a "radical reconstruction of society itself."[9]

Yet, the radical reconstruction—a revolutionary racial reformation—never took place. The push for rights to results was largely lost in translation and our cultural crisis roiled on. Rather than a revolutionary reformation that got to the roots of race hate and reconstructed society upon more equitable foundations, America embraced the status quo and pursued the politics of evolutionary racial progress. Evolutionary racial progress entails none of the risks inherent in radical revolution. Yet, when a revolution of ideas is required, an evolution of ideas only extends the life of thinking designed to fail.

THE AGE OF ILLUSIONARY INCLUSIVITY & THE EVOLUTION OF RACIST IDEAS

Though the Civil *Rights* Act failed to *result* in racial equality, America proved ready to turn the page on readjusting America's racial imagination. In 1968, the finger that helped turn the page from revolutionary racial reformation to patient evolutionary progress belonged to none other than Richard Nixon. In accepting the Republican nomination, Nixon declared: "We live in an age of revolution in America and in our world." But for Nixon, the only revolution we needed was "a revolution that will never grow old. . . . the American Revolution. The American Revolution was and is dedicated to progress, but our founders recognized that the first requisite of progress is *order*." He declared that King and the movement weakened the nation's laws and empowered "the criminal forces in this country."[10] The cure to the country's crisis resided in an evolutionary approach to progress and a religious recommitment to law and order. Nixon's rhetoric worked like a train-track switch that altered the direction of America's ambitions on race reform from the pursuit of King's beloved community to Nixon's land of law and order.

Assisting Nixon in law and order rhetoric was then California Governor Ronald Reagan. On the day of King's funeral, Governor Reagan mourned "a great tragedy that began when we started compromising with law and order, and people started choosing which laws they'd break." Rather than calling the nation to repent of racism, Reagan lamented King's refusal to submit to Jim Crow's authority over black lives.[11]

Rather than birthing a new racial rhetoric, Nixon declared his emphasis on law and order was a continuation of America's original revolution. That America's original revolution perpetuated—rather than healed—our nation's racial wounds was a reality that failed to subdue the speaker or audience's confidence in his logic. That night, Nixon effectively brought an end to the civil rights revolution without bringing racial equality. Rather than a racial reformation, America swapped Jim Crow segregation for Nixon's colorblind age of law and order. Despite colorblind claims, the new era proved an age equally rife with inequalities along racial lines.

From slavery to Jim Crow to the colorblind age, racism always required mythologies to provide the illusion of harmony and progress in the midst of the crisis. The foundation for keeping the illusion of racial progress in the colorblind age was the perpetuation of segregation. Though the color line proved every bit as entrenched as the days of segregation,[12] the lack of explicitly racial laws formed the illusion of racial inclusivity. And illusionary-inclusive, color-blind communities with loving families, sincere churches, and good schools proved fertile soils for racist ideas and worked to integrate a racial obliviousness all the deeper into the core of white identity.

Upon a foundation of segregation, education helped fortify the illusions of inclusivity and covered over the failures of our society's racial evolution. At school, children learned to celebrate the civil rights movement, memorized selective portions of King's "I Have a Dream" speech, and celebrated the accomplishments of exceptional black people. The celebration of exceptional black folks reinforced the conviction that our nation not only progressed in race relations but closed the book on racial injustice. Lost in the stories of *exceptional* black folks were the realities of the radical racial inequalities that shaped the life of *everyday* black folks.

As America entered the twenty-first century, white folks possessed three decades of education about how America's embrace of the civil rights movement had erased the lines of racial inequality. If unjust racial lines lived on, much of the education concerning our nation's racial equality that white folks received consisted of lethal white lies. The truth was that despite the civil rights movement, America's late-twentieth-century racism proved more subtle but not much less lethal.

At home, the education continued. If TV proved pivotal in opening the door to reconsidering race relations in the sixties, it proved equally critical in perpetuating myths about evolutionary racial progress in subsequent decades. TV sitcoms began contributing to such myths in the seventies, as shows like *The Jeffersons* featured a family moving on up in New York. A year later, *What's Happening* provided a taste of black swagger from Los Angeles's Watts neighborhood, without much taste of the rage that led to the Watts Riots only a few years before. The eighties introduced *The Cosby Show*, and America witnessed a black family living out the American Dream with just a little hard work and solid family values. The ninties unleashed the brilliance of Will Smith in *The Fresh Prince of Bel Air*. Yet rather than focusing on the realities of Philly's Westside, Will's story picked up in the home of a judge in the suburbs of LA. From the sixties to the nineties, the Jeffersons and Huxtables of New York and the Thomases and Bankses of LA were the black families white families knew best. More often than not, they were the only black families who entered white living rooms.

When TV programming moved from black fictions to black reality, from sitcoms to the news, their audiences witnessed news networks addicted to stories that focused on how the crack epidemic wrecked inner-city communities and stories of welfare abuse. Audiences learned the myth that the color of America's drug problem was predominately black rather than predominately white. The illusion about the color of addiction was then compounded through myths of an overfunded welfare system that black folk freely rode towards wealth without working.[13] Rounding out the myths on drugs and welfare were myths about the economy. The rapid exportation of well-paying jobs across the nation proved unable to upend the cherished illusion of a benevolent economy seeking to provide for the families of everyone and anyone ready to work. Welfare, rather than job exportation, became understood as the critical threat to both America's economy and morality. America's racial inequalities were understood as the failure of black folks, not the failure of the American way.

Yet as critical as the sitcoms and news anchors proved to be in distributing racist ideas, no one proved better at using the TV cameras to promote white illusions than politicians. Campaign seasons reinforced white mythologies as white folks listened to politicians from both parties who sought to secure their votes by saying what white ears itched to hear. Both parties ran on the law and order train tracks Nixon laid down. From Reagan to Bush to Clinton, politicians of the 1980s and 1990s demanded doubling down on the War on Drugs with tougher crime bills and reduction to welfare provisions.[14] All our politicians needed to protect the American dream from the threat of criminally lazy black folk was another vote for Nixon's vision of law and order.

Some white families complemented their vision with a spiritual lens. Yet since American churches are ten times more segregated than their communities, more often than not their spiritual lens provided a Christianity colored white.[15] Through this lens, faith filters through the fears and hopes of the white community making it impossible to determine where white culture ends and the Christian faith begins. From America's inception, white churches selected particular passages of Scripture and designed theological systems that posed no threat to racist logics. The systems simplified over time and convinced those in the church that soul salvation was the primary function of the gospel. In the age of illusionary inclusivity, memorizing the "Romans Road" and John 3:16's "for God so loved the world" was all that was needed for white redemption.

By limiting the focus to passages of Scripture involving piety, soul salvation, and obedience to rulers, the Bible's prophetic tradition, which concentrated on issues of inequality, race, poverty, and immigration, were spiritualized until their practical and political implications evaporated. Rather than identifying Christ in the poor, the marginalized, and the immigrant, Jesus took the form of what white people hoped to see when they looked in the mirror. Centuries before, Thomas Jefferson made Jesus look like a European rationalist and trimmed the New Testament accordingly to produce the Jefferson Bible. In the colorblind age, Larry Julian's *God is My CEO* became a bestseller. Perhaps white Christianity made white folks more fit for white life, but it certainly failed to provide depth perception concerning the interface of race, religion, and politics.

The racist secular lens produced a similar sentimentality to its racist spiritual counterpart as the vision of non-religious folks too often traveled through a liberal rationality colored white. It is not a coincidence that the styles of thinking deemed most rational by white elite circles was thinking crafted in white elite bubbles. Rather than the liberal's racist superiority residing in the morality of a white Jesus, liberals' racism expressed itself in self-confident "rational," "scientific," and "progressive" ways, ways that produce neither intimacy nor solidarity with black folk.

Throughout the twentieth century, progressive white folks harmonized liberal sentiments with racist instincts. From FDR to JFK and continuing on through Clinton, white liberals found more important fish to fry than the pursuit of equity for people of color. Beginning somewhere around JFK, racial equity was considered important but, with the notable exception of LBJ, the importance of racial equity was never urgent enough to illicit a self-sacrificial commitment that shifted the center of power away from white America.

Whether conservative or liberal, whether viewing the world through a spiritual or secular lens, the age of illusionary inclusivity and evolutionary racial progress rooted racial obliviousness all the more deeply into white America. It is no coincidence that the points of agreements between liberals and conservatives through the rest of the twentieth century proved most damning to black life. Reaganomics and Clintonomics were different in name but eerily similar in nature.[16] Beginning the War on Drugs and ending the War on Poverty eventually received bipartisan support. Whether spiritual or secular, liberal or conservative, in the politics of evolutionary racial progress white America trusted.

Learning in school that racial disparity ended after the civil rights movement, laughing with the Huxtables at home, watching the news and listening to our politicians and preachers framed white America's understanding of race. When folks with good hearts but racist ideas framed the picture of America's racial realities, it is little wonder that white America too easily believed a toxic combination of lethargy and criminality was the final barrier to achieving the American dream.

It is impossible to overstate how the ongoing segregation secured a dreamlike slumber for white America. For in the colorblind age, only intimacy with oppressed communities mutilated by American criminal-justice, educational, and economic systems could awaken white America to the failed mythologies of evolutionary racial progress. And in the colorblind age, no such intimacy between communities existed.

THE LAST DAYS & THE EMPIRE STRIKES BACK

After four decades of pursuing Nixon's path of evolutionary racial progress through law and order, it looked as though the little progress achieved provided America a bypass around King's demand for radical racial reformation. Ironically, it was when confidence in evolutionary racial progress rose to its highest that the myths of the colorblind era entered into their last days. With the election and re-election of President Barak Obama, America believed that it was transitioning from a colorblind to a post-racial age.[17] With a black President in America's White House, there existed a poignant hope that a movement was afoot for the translation of civil rights to equitable results, bringing to life the Declaration of Independence's rhetoric that "all men are created equal." And a movement was a foot, but it was not heading in the direction anyone anticipated. The Obama years did not bring about a reformation of racial results. Instead, the Obama years brought the nation to a point of a racial reckoning.

Like in the days of old, cameras played a pivotal role in forcing America to face realities it received elaborate training to deny. King and civil rights leaders captured the racial realities our nation longed to ignore by manipulating the worst impulses of Jim Crow's law and order before the news cameras. The reckoning we did not see coming would be different. No manipulation would be necessary. During the Obama years, the camera's eye was ever present and captured in graphic detail the truths our society desired to deny. Through small cameras on cellphones, the world witnessed the nightmare of lethal police brutality that too often haunts the black experience, as the eye of the camera placed flesh and blood on America's human sacrifices. The reality of police brutality was an open secret in black communities, but black testimony meant little until cellphone cameras proved police brutality to be more than the figment of the troubled black imagination.

Reminiscent of how Billie Holiday's beautiful and tortured song "Strange Fruit" etched the history of lynching rituals in the South on the American conscience, the camera lens made us unwilling participants in the "strange fruit" of the unarmed broken bodies for whom the criminal-justice system morphed into an angel of death. Truths that once only haunted the psyche of the black community began to haunt us all.

When Obama began his second term, the last people whose racially motivated deaths were written onto public memory were King and his contemporaries like Emmett Till of Chicago, Medgar Evers of Jackson, Jimmie Jackson of Selma, and the young girls dynamited in the Birmingham Church. During the Obama years, as videos continued to surface, the news could no longer ignore racially suspicious deaths, and an equally long list of names accumulated. The names of Trayvon Martin, Eric Garner, Sandra Bland, and the church of Mother Emmanuel AME where Dylann Roof slaughtered the Charleston 9 were etched onto national consciousness. Rather than the struggle for civil rights connecting these murders, the crime connecting these deaths often ran no deeper than their black skin.

The shockwaves of the videos and headlines reverberated throughout the nation. Communities tired of paying the price for the system's ability to justify any murder of a person discovered in black skin took their protests to the streets before a militarized police force with their hands held high. It is a tragic irony that African Americans most powerful ally in their fight for justice has been neither American ideals nor Christian principles, but rather smart phones with tiny cameras. These cameras allowed the world to witness the injustices Americans long denied and attempted to hide.[18]

Black Lives Matter was born in the aftershock of the innocent verdict pronounced in the trial of George Zimmerman following the murder of Trayvon Martin. It did not take long for the movement to provoke a white backlash that qualified the value of black lives in America. *All Lives Matter* masked racism as morality. Such instincts to qualify the value of black lives displayed just how flexible racial rhetoric in the colorblind age had become, especially in the minds of those who no longer knew they were racist. Nonetheless, due to the camera, as the Obama years progressed and tragedies continually surfaced, America's mainstream began losing grip on its illusionary inclusivity.

As the camera began helping America see through its illusions, it also started breathing life into statistics that continually revealed the failure of evolutionary racial progress. Through the research the racialized deaths inspired, we learned police killings of unarmed individuals occur multiple times a week, and between 2010 and 2012 federal statistics show young black males were twenty-one times more likely to be a victim than their white peers.[19] With new power, the statistics revealed more than the racialized violence of police. The statistics displayed an entire system that perpetuates violence on black people from the moment they are born on American soil. When we witness unarmed black people gunned down in the street, we witness only the tip of the iceberg of America's racial nightmare.

Inequality begins its haunting work in the cradles. Forty-five percent of young black children live in poverty.[20] When children move from cradles to the classroom, educational disparities only increase inequality's influence over our students of color.[21] In time, broken educational and criminal-justice systems couple to create schools whose incoming freshman are more likely to go to jail for nonviolent offenses than graduate college. Corporate America even learned how to profit from the school-to-prison pipeline as school districts throughout the nation began farming out students with disciplinary issues from poor communities to for-profit alternative schools. Rather than the for-profit alternative schools improving the trajectory of student's academic outcomes, these for-profit schools began operating as preparatory academies that fed their victims to for-profit prisons thus providing a school-to-prison pipeline in corporate form. Investing in children in poverty never proved more disgusting.[22]

When those who are born into poverty manage to pass through underfunded schools and avoid the criminal justice system, black and brown youth join an economic system where white men with criminal records secure more interviews than black men without records.[23] In America's economy, more often than not—as President Obama phrased it—"Johnny gets an interview but not Jamal."[24] Rather than our economy unleashing black and brown talent, it too often buries it.

When African Americans beat the odds to secure equitable education and employment, neither their education nor employment makes being black equitable. When the New Deal's reforms provided an infrastructure for middleclass white folks to develop wealth through housing policies, educational opportunities, and social security, almost all laws were crafted in such a way to leave black families out in the rain. Few card games proved more racist than the New Deal.[25] As public policies empowered white middleclass America to pursue the American Dream, other public policies redlined housing loans, schools, and Social Security benefits. White labor began to translate to real wealth, while black labor was restricted to the struggle to survive. Despite these racist policies, as racial inequalities increased, so too did myths that traced differences in racial wealth to differences in racial work ethics. Due to the endless list of racist edicts shaped by the White House, courthouses, and both houses of Congress, the median wealth of white households during the Obama administration was thirteen times the amount of black households.[26] Once we recognize how inequality haunts our babies from the cradle to the classroom, from the classroom to the courtroom, from the employment application to the unemployment line, from sweat to equity, we see how the "strange fruit" of broken black bodies represents only the tip of the iceberg of a system perfectly constructed to destroy black lives long before police lights ever flicker.

Complimenting the videos, headlines, and statistics that provided a more honest rendering of the reality of black lives, into the movement came some of the most talented intellectuals and writers of the young century—authors like Ibram X. Kendi, Michelle Alexander, and Ta-Nehisi Coates. Just as DuBois, King, and Baldwin labored in the twentieth century, these writers worked to give their audience new eyes through which to see their racialized world by painting with words the collective impact of six centuries of a land birthed, bred, and nurtured on racist ideas and racialized institutions. In *Stamped from The Beginning: The Definitive History of Racist Ideas in America,* Kendi writes "To the lives they said don't matter." As the stories of "Trayvon Martin and Rekia Boyd and Michael Brown and Freddie Grey and the Charleston 9 and Sandra Bland"[27] filled the airwaves, Kendi penned a book that details six centuries of racist ideas that formed America's heart, mind, and soul. Kendi writes with simplicity—a racist idea is simply any "concept that regards one racial group of people as inferior or superior to another racial group in any way."[28]

Kendi argues that we think about racist ideas all wrong. In his analysis, racist ideas are not birthed in hate and ignorance; they are birthed and nurtured by elites looking to pad their pocket or increase their political control. Rather than "ignorance/hate—>racist ideas—>racial discrimination," history teaches us it is the opposite: "racial discrimination—>racist ideas—>ignorance/hate."[29] A cycle forms where racist elites implement racist policies, and racist policies foster racist ideas and perpetuate indifference to racial inequities. As the cycle continues, race acts as an often-invisible hand forming our political and religious institutions and the very way we see and navigate the world and its inequalities.

Kendi argues that for too long we attempted to educate white folks out of racism, as if white folks' ignorance was the problem; for too long black folks attempted to assimilate to white culture, as if white culture was the solution. In page after page, Kendi details the ideas concerning black people that have haunted our nation, so convincingly that we can no longer see our racial imagination as a health crisis capable of being cured by individual changes of hearts and minds. Racism seeped into our institutions and culture so deeply that racism must be understood as an environmental crisis and racist ideas as a part of the very air we breathe. Running harder fails to cure a health epidemic caused by toxic air pollution. Rather than treating our racial epidemic one heart and one mind at a time, the time has come to address the ecosystem itself.

Nothing displays how deep our sickness runs than the very institution mandated to guard our nation against injustice—the judicial branch of government. In *The New Jim Crow,* Michelle Alexander maps how the myth of racial superiority integrated itself into our criminal-justice system to produce verdicts that continually denied African American's equality in the eyes of the law. From slavery to Jim Crow to today's prison system, racist verdicts flowed from our highest courts, forcing those in black and brown skin to pay for our justice system's racism with years stolen from their very lives and criminal records that never disappear.

Alexander's analysis begins in the colonial period. Following Bacon's Rebellion, which united poor whites and slaves in Virginia, white elites pushed the gospel of racial superiority to divide the potentially transformative partnership. The simple blueprint of this superiority possessed staying power: "If you can convince the lowest white man he's better than the best colored man, he won't notice you're picking his pocket," said President Lyndon B. Johnson centuries later. "Hell, give him somebody to look down on, and he'll empty his pockets for you."[30]

Alexander shows how the simplicity of white superiority provided flexibility for the mythology to adapt and evolve from slavery to Jim Crow to Nixon's age of law and order. Alexander details how following the civil rights movement, "tough on crime" and "War on Drugs" initiatives posed as colorblind policies when heralded by politicians behind podiums, but after politicians dropped the mic, the policies were enforced with a loathsome racial inequality. In truth, the policies in the last decades of the twentieth century flipped prison populations from two-thirds white to two-thirds black and brown,[31] damning black and brown Americans to a racialized justice system in a post-civil-rights world.

Like an evolving virus, time made racial rhetoric sophisticated and subtle, but no less depraved. Despite white youth making up the vast majority of drug users and dealers, black American arrests skyrocketed following the War on Drugs—increasing twenty-six-fold.[32] For the same crimes for which white parents of means send their children to resort-styled rehabs, our nation pays even more money to send black and brown children to prison. Alexander traces the racial sickness along every step of the criminal-justice process, from arrest to pathetic public defense to prosecutors who excessively charge people of color in order to induce plea bargains to juries rigged to produce racial verdicts and sentences.

By connecting the dots between our nation's founding racial-superiority ideologies and its evolving racialized public policies, *The New Jim Crow* reveals our justice system as a racially rigged game that produces overwhelmingly black and brown prisons, destroys black and brown families, and reduces a whole class of folks to second-class citizens for the rest of their lives.[33] "It is difficult to imagine," she writes, "a system better designed to ensure that racial biases and stereotypes are given free reign—while at the same time appearing on the surface to be colorblind—than the one devised by the U.S. Supreme Court."[34]

Alexander provides no religious dimension to her analysis, but in America racial inequalities always carry a religious edge. The racial work of our nation's court system was empowered not only by politicians but by her pulpits. White faith leaders like James Dobson issued clarion calls for "family values" to shape the political instincts of Christians across the nation. Yet "family values" failed to integrate the needs of black and brown families into its calculus and proved little different than the "protecting our way of life" rhetoric the Dixiecrats had employed to justify the violence of their racism during the days of segregation. While the effects of mass incarceration and mass deportation are the closest comparison to the damage slavery wrought on the family unit—creating parentless children and childless parents—the politicians who perpetuated this family wreckage received the full backing of "family values" voters. In the midst of an American nightmare, the dreamers dreamed on, and no one slept as soundly as white Christians.

And it is in the context, in a world where racist ideas formed not only individual's identities but society's most critical institutions and political and religious convictions, that Ta-Nehisi Coates pens *Between the World and Me* to provide a societal analysis of a more intimate nature, written as a letter for his coming-of-age son. "This is what I want you to know," Ta-Nehisi Coates writes, "it is traditional to destroy the black body—it is heritage." Coates writes with an intimacy impossible had his audience been anyone other than his son, but due to its intimacy a conversation occurs that deserves a hearing from sons and fathers and mothers and daughters who have yet to awaken to the realities the American dream performs on those trapped in America's nightmare. "Perhaps that was the hope of the movement," Coates writes to his son, "to awaken the dreamers, to rouse them to the facts of what their need to be white . . . has done to the world."[35]

~

Now that cell-phone cameras have removed the segregated safe space between mainstream America and the strange fruits of unarmed, bullet-riddled black bodies, America no longer enjoys the distance necessary to avoid the reality of our system's work on black life. If the racism that birthed slavery is our nation's original sin, the Obama years displayed the age of evolutionary racial progress, colorblindness, and illusionary inclusivity as the era of our greatest self-deception. But that self-deception is no longer secure. Somewhere between Trayvon Martin and Michael Brown, Sandra Bland and the Charleston 9, between smoking barrels and unarmed black bodies, the lie about America's post-racial innocence died. Like the open casket of Emmett Till, some things we will never un-see. The only question was how America would respond.

If the Black Lives Matter movement, Kendi, Alexander, and Coates hoped to awaken dreamers, they did; and the dreamers were angry and expressed their rage by supporting Donald Trump. The empire struck back. Convinced in the inevitability of progress, nothing seemed more inconceivable to progressive folks on either side of the aisle than a Trump Presidency. Yet the brilliance of Donald Trump rested on the biggest bet his campaign made. That bet was that a more transparent racism would garner the candidate more votes than it would cost him. Trump's explicitly racial appeals proved mouth-watering for some. For many, many others, Trump's tactic was troubling; but more troubling still were the truths revealed by cell phone that our nation was not ready to face. For Trump voters, our country was changing too fast, making the promise of restoring white normalcy by Making America Great Again too alluring to pass up, despite all the iniquities Trump clearly embodied.

If our self-perceived innocence died at the end of the barrel of the gun, it was in the voting booth where James Dobson and white Christians partnered with the vision of former Grand Dragon David Duke and the KKK that the age of illusionary inclusivity came to an end. The bipartisan politics of evolutionary racial progress evolved into the Presidency of Donald Trump. If Nixon brought us into the age of law and order and illusionary inclusivity, Trump brought us back to an age of a troubling transparency.

Under Trump, Dobson's ideological ties to David Duke and Roy Moore came into public view. Behind the scenes, the ties were already strong. Dobson's and Duke's circles overlapped for many years through collaboration with Tony Perkins, who purchased Duke's mailing list for over $80,000. Before Trump rose to power, Dobson compared Moore to Rosa Parks. Amidst multiple accusations of sexual indecency with children, Dobson's support was more emphatic: "God gave America another chance with the election of Donald J. Trump but he now needs the presence of Judge Roy Moore to make America great again."[36]

THE "TRINITY" MATTERS: THE ROOTS OF AMERICA'S RACIAL CRISIS

At the intersection of faith, race, and politics, American history teaches us that times of cultural crisis never naturally lead to the needed cultural revolution. Cultural revolution and the radical racial reformation King called for required a moral depth perception our nation refused to develop. Rather than heeding King's exhortation to restructure society by examining the "ideational roots of race hate," white Americans continued to idealize our nation, driving the ideational roots of race hate all the more deeply into white America's soul.

Yet, after the tragic human sacrifices of the Obama years and the white backlash that followed his Presidency, a new hunger arose for a more radical revolution that would free our future from the generational sins that continue to deform our life together. If the American crisis is ever to lead to a radical racial reformation, we must learn how American democracy and America's white Christianity were and are intricately and intentionally designed to perpetuate racist ways and inequalities. Until we see how our nation's founding, inspired by the conviction of humanity's equality, resulted in unique racial inequalities, ranging from—in the words of Martin Luther King— genocide to a cannibalistic poverty, we will be powerless to slow down the cycles of racial injustice.

Only by returning to the original crime scenes where America's ideologies were first crafted can we begin to understand our ongoing addiction to racist ideas, institutions, and ways of life. The crime scenes to which I seek to return to start the investigation are not in the 1960s but begin in the sixteenth century, and not on American soils, but on England's. It was in England, at the dawn of the Enlightenment, as the age of reason replaced an age of religion, where the metal of America's intellectual architecture regarding race, faith, and politics was forged.

The Enlightenment's philosophers were more than men of their times. They were revolutionaries that changed the way we play our racial, religious, and political games. The philosophers of the Enlightenment did not interpret the rulebook on race, faith, and politics—they rewrote the rulebook as they worked with an urgency to recreate an uncertain world. The "Wars of Religion" had devastated Europe to an extent that society itself needed a new structure. Awash in the blood of war, Christianity proved an uncertain cornerstone upon which to construct a stable society of peace and prosperity. The racist ideologies that the Enlightenment's philosophers crafted to replace the cornerstone of Christianity in Europe both became the cornerstone of the American project and formed the crucible of America's ongoing racial crisis.

Despite the failure of Christianity to bring God's kingdom to earth during the "dark" ages of religion, hope was on the horizon at the dawn of the Enlightenment. For the philosophers of the Enlightenment, hope came not from the church, but from the laboratory and factories, not from the theologically or religiously committed, but from the scientifically, economically, and rationally minded. During the Enlightenment, the quest began to harness the powers of science and rationality and implement them within the worlds of politics, economics, and religion in order to bring peace, stability, and opportunity out of the world's chaos.

A new world order emerged that brought peace, progress, and prosperity to particular people. The project reimagined democracy and a society of liberty, justice, and equality for "all." The light of reason dawned in a dark world, and the power of rationality was unleashed to bless the world. This is at least one way the Enlightenment's story is told. Much of this story is true. But it is a truth told on a slant, a half-truth that fails to describe how the age of prosperity also brought new justifications for the institutionalization of poverty via a new racial order; a half-truth that fails to reckon with how the rise of reason was simultaneous with the rise of racecraft.

As slaveholders chained the ankles and necks of Africans, sick ideas worked in the heads and hearts of white folks to justify the chains as necessary for the work of modernizing the world. From the beginning, the Enlightenment was as much about happenings in Africa as it was about those in Europe seeking greater peace, profit, and endless empires through the Americas. The Enlightenment's racecraft was the "rational" re-valuation of humanity based on the shapes of noses and lips and the color of skin. The racial ideologies were employed as tools to move the ambition for empire into reality by reducing whole communities of people into machines of sweat equity. Just beneath the surface of the Enlightenment's confidence in reason, science, and the quest for liberty and justice was a racial rationality that twisted every ideology it espoused into a noose for black lives by harmonizing freedom, liberty, and justice for white folks with the institution of slavery for black folks.

The ideologies of racecraft required squaring every block of American society with the cornerstone of slavery. To cut the ideologies to size, philosophers of the Enlightenment worked to sell inspiring ideologies and segregated their implications along lines of color. In this way, slavery acted as the organizational principle of the entire project. Racecraft sold us the slave master's myth that *people in certain communities and from certain countries are only irrational bodies to be exploited for the master race's pleasure, profit, and power*. The more skilled we became at this craft, the more interwoven the slave master's myth became in our way of life. Once addicted, white folks jonesed for power over black bodies, until they were unable to conceive of life without such dominion; until they believed that white superiority and power were woven into the very fabric of the universe's order.

The slave master's myth was as ancient as Pharaoh, but it was the Enlightenment's philosophers who sold us this myth in modern, race-based form and under the guise of rationality, property rights, and the nature of true religion. The project reached perfection quickly, allowing us to live out this myth with incredible efficiency while maintaining a clear conscience only shortly after it was conceived. The Enlightenment's rational politics, economics, and religion, saturated with the ideologies of democracy and liberty, freedom and justice, nonetheless rooted the slave master's myth into the soul of mainstream society.

Rather than our racial imagination existing in a silo that can be dealt with in a manner that leaves the rest of our moral ideologies and social order intact, race is intertwined with the way we imagine the character of politics, economics, and religion. The seeds that birthed slavery now provide for us the philosophical, religious, and political architecture of our lives. Racecraft was more than an error of the Enlightenment; it was interwoven into its DNA and passed on from those in white wigs who signed the Declaration of Independence to those in red baseball caps who sought to Make America Great Again.

To show how Enlightenment philosophy achieved all this, in subsequent chapters I focus on a "trinity" of thought shapers: the Father of Modern Political Philosophy, Thomas Hobbes (1588–1679); the Father of Liberalism, John Locke (1632–1704); and the Father of Modern Economics, Adam Smith (1723–1790). Together, these philosophers provided the West with ways of thinking that empowered the slave master's myth to thrive and evolve until the myth shaped our understanding of our world.

Most folks I know do not wake up eager to learn how three students from Oxford in the 1600s and 1700s changed the world. If, however, we wonder how we convinced ourselves of the humanity of our corporations while questioning the humanity of our poor, understanding the "trinity" matters. If we desire to understand how our democracy prioritized the interests of the wealthiest 1 percent at the expense of the 99 percent or how anxiety and the politics of fear—of Muslims, socialism, and black children in hoodies—gained greater power in the age of reason, the "trinity" matters. If it bothers us that education too often crucifies our children's spirits and curiosity rather than inspiring striving after a more perfect union and more truthful and meaningful ways of life, the "trinity" matters. If we are troubled by how Christian folks embraced great evils and stood indifferent to tragic injustices and inequalities, the "trinity" matters. The "trinity" matters for anyone desiring the depth perception necessary to pursue a more just way of life than the one we inherited.

With different giftings, convictions and styles, each member of the "trinity" plays an indispensable role in forming a society ready to embrace a world marred by injustices that are meted out along racialized lines. Hobbes provided a modern *imagination* formed by the slave master's myth. Locke provided a tangible way for government and religion to partner in *institutionalizing* that imagination in democratic and religiously "tolerant" societies. And Adam Smith articulated a morality of indifference to the gross inequalities our institutions fostered, *ingraining* the slave master's myth into society's soul.

As the slave master's myth matured from imagining, to institutionalizing, to ingraining, their work coalesced to shape the American mind around three political and three religious lies that become formative convictions and racialized our world. Political lie one: government is not about the common good. Lie two: economics is a moral-free math, and human equality need not entail racial equity. Lie three: justice is about retribution not restoration. The American experiment required writing these three political lies onto America's soul in order to justify the sadistic relationships that it sought to foster and the original sins of America's founding. In helping write these lies, the "trinity" served as the founding philosophical fathers who influenced Americans' understanding of the work and nature of politics from President Washington to Lincoln to Roosevelt to Trump.

Yet critical to the new work taking place—work that attempted to reduce Africans to animals and that justified the tearing of weeping baby boys and girls from the arms of their powerless parents—was a reformulation of the Christian imagination. In this, too, the "trinity" proved pivotal in its ability to subtly undermine critical ingredients in Christian life and discipleship. Later generations of believers often uncritically accepted the "trinity's" rhetoric on economics, politics, and racecraft even as they questioned the philosophical "trinity's" religious orthodoxy.

Nonetheless, the "trinity" successfully writes three lies into American Christianity that shape the course of the church formed in the colonies. The first lie was that Christians' need neither intimacy nor relationship with the broken and abused of our world to have intimacy and relationship with the biblical God who loves the broken and abused. The second lie was that "true religion" is soul salvation, despite both the Old and New Testament teaching otherwise. The final lie was that indifference to injustice is no threat to one's intimacy with God—despite such indifference being the very essence of the Bible's concept of hard-heartedness. Through these three lies that became rules, the "trinity" fundamentally reshaped the very character of Christianity on American soil, making the "trinity" nothing less than the forefathers of America's white churches.

In bringing together the "trinity's" wide array of writings, I am not only interested in the systems Hobbes, Locke, and Smith created, I am also interested in how the rhetoric and logic they employed complemented one another to form America's racialized faith and politics. It is, after all, rhetoric rather than philosophical argumentation that shape's folks paradigms and defines a people's priorities and principles. St. Augustine and Fredrick

Nietzsche leave their readers with unparalleled impressions because of the power of their prose rather than the consistency of their systems. Both the longing of "our hearts are restless until they rest in thee" and the defiance in "God is dead" are carried in words that continue to ring long after their authors are gone.

Hobbes's, Locke's, and Smith's rhetorical practices were more understated. But what made their prose powerful and their lies persuasive was a way of writing that appeared more revelatory than radical. The trinity wrote in a manner that made their sophisticated philosophy appear as common sense that rings true in the ears of good and decent people; they wrote in a way that persuaded good and decent people to accept a sadistic world order as if no alternatives existed. From the quills and inkwells of Hobbes, Locke and Smith, the political and religious lies sounded like a rationality honed to the perfection of mathematical truisms. The horse-sense-styled rhetoric of the West's philosophic "trinity" immortalized their words beyond mere lifeless relics of history.

The commonsense rhetoric and rationality they articulated sought to create common ground for the wealthy across religious divides, but it did not give rise to a unified society. Divisions did not disappear. As religion mattered less and less, race and wealth mattered more and more. Race and wealth, rather than religion, became the key organizing principles in a modern rational society. As these divisions dissected the American people, the rhetoric of equality provided a tranquilizing anesthetic to our nation's dismemberment. The "trinity's" rhetoric, logic, and lies live on, tightly interwoven in the worldview of modern Americans across religious, political, and economic divides. America's unholy ghosts are the ideologies that produced slavery and radical inequality, as our nation's ways of thinking about religion and politics led logically to placing the poor and the Black on American-made crosses.

We turn now to interrogating the cherished lies that created and perpetuated the cultural crisis in which we now live. If Nixon closed the door on King's call for a racial reformation, perhaps the election of President Donald Trump re-opens the door to the radical revolution our nation so desperately needs. Uprooting racism begins in understanding the "ideational roots of race hate."

2

Thomas Hobbes

Imagining a Rational —& Racist—World Order

FOR UNTO US TWINS ARE GIVEN

On Good Friday April 5th, 1588, Thomas Hobbes was born in Malmesbury, England, into a humble home headed by a clergyman, but neither humility nor piety characterized his life for long. War was in the air. The Eighty Years War raged into its third decade, and while young Thomas Hobbes was still in his mother's womb, an apocalyptic word reached Malmesbury concerning the Spanish Armada. "My mother was filled with such fear," Hobbes wrote in his autobiography, "that she bore twins, me and together with me fear."[37] Thomas remained intimate with his twin the rest of his life.

As we trace the racist roots that engrafted the slave master's myth into American society's soul, we begin with Thomas Hobbes and three of the political and religious lies he sowed into the modern imagination. It is with Hobbes that modern society is re-imagined by extending the scientific renaissance from astronomy, geometry, and chemistry into the arenas of politics, philosophy, and faith. Yet it is more than coincidence that the rise of racecraft coincided with the rise of reason for the slave master's myth required man's moral imagination to become less religious, less relational, and more rational, self-interested, scientific, and secular.

Critical to the rise of reason coinciding with the rise of racecraft was Hobbes's political lie that government is not about the common good and that economics is a moral-free math; critical to the rise of racecraft was Hobbes's religious lie that we can be in right relationship with a God who loves the poor without right relationships with the poor. Understanding how Hobbes persuasively sold these lies to the Christians in England helps us to wrestle with basic paradoxes that haunt the American experiment. Why do we think of ourselves as rational but never as racist? How did a land founded on convictions concerning humanity's equality harmonize her convictions with the genocide of Indians, the slavery of Africans, and the perpetuation of radical racial inequities? How did we raise CEOs to god-like status, transform corporations into people, and yet question the very humanity of our poor? How did the myth of scarcity justify massive accumulation rather than encouraging equity? How can anxiety and fear act as hallmarks of an age of reason and feelings of loneliness and isolation haunt an interconnected world? To understand how Hobbes impacted America's imagination on faith and politics—from colonization to Black Lives Matter—we begin with his story.

A BARE-KNUCKLED BRAWLER

To say Thomas Hobbes's father, from whom his name derives and who baptized him shortly after birth, was a clergyman could mislead. Despite Thomas Sr.'s holy ordination, he seemed more at home in a pub than a pew.[38] However, in a pew Thomas Sr. was quite comfortable. When not skipping church, he was known to nap during services over which he presided. When not sleeping or cutting church, Hobbes Sr. was often fighting on grounds made less holy by his presence. He waited for enemies on church steps and tracked them down in the streets. When words failed, he used fists. Excommunication was not the norm, but there was nothing normal about Thomas Sr., and excommunicated he was.[39]

The apple didn't fall far from the tree in the Hobbeses' orchard. Thomas Jr., the father of modern English philosophy, proved to be a bare-knuckled brawler as well. His weapon of war was his pen. And though he rivaled his father's obnoxious ways, unlike his father he allowed his words to do his work. His pen proved to pack more than enough punch.

Perhaps motivated to get out of Malmesbury as quickly as possible, Thomas Jr. matriculated to Oxford at the wee age of fourteen. Though he didn't think highly of the education he received, Oxford undoubtedly provided Hobbes with credentials that opened the door for a drastically different life than the one he left behind. Shortly after graduation, he received employment as a tutor to the immensely wealthy Cavendish family, and the Cavendish house came to be Hobbes's home for the next twenty years. His first student was William, and though the relationship began as tutor and pupil, many of their escapades had little to do with the life of the mind. Very few temptations or pleasures of wealth were left un-savored. The tutor in all things academic became the pupil in privilege.

But Cavendish privilege extended beyond hedonism and the playboy lifestyle Hobbes relished; Cavendish wealth created networks with society's movers and shakers throughout Europe. Hobbes met kings, corporate titans, scientists, and philosophers. In England, Hobbes received stock in the Virginia Company, providing him a vested interest in colonial expansion and every tool necessary for its success. During his travels, Hobbes came into the circles of Galileo, Bacon, and Descartes, intellectuals already empowering a more scientific worldview throughout Europe. In these social circles, Hobbes grew fascinated with the power, progress, and potential of modern science—not only for medicine or industry, but for reshaping the softer sciences—religion, philosophy, politics, and economics—into more modern disciplines capable of stabilizing a decaying world order.

During Hobbes's engraftment into England's aristocratic circles, the world was engulfed in war. The Thirty Years War (1618–1648) raged on claiming the lives of millions, and England's First Civil War (1642–1646) brought the flames of war ever nearer. Yet the threat of war failed to dim the imperialistic ambitions for the English as the slave ship *Jesus of Lübek* had paved the way for England to participate in the Atlantic slave trade decades earlier. In this context of a war-weary world and a nation seeking empire, this bare-knuckled-brawler from Malmesbury proved an unlikely prophet for how tyrannical power, if scientifically aligned, might not only provide for world peace but also provide the English nation with a new era of world domination.

On the pages of his magnum opus, *The Leviathan,*[40] Hobbes imagines a man made modern by jettisoning his religious inheritance and leaning into his rationality and self-interest. For Hobbes, humans tend towards the cruel and require a political system of totalitarian tyranny to survive their carnal cravings. In *Leviathan,* due to the very nature of man, humanity finds itself with two options—endless war or tyranny. As Hobbes writes, he instructs his readers on what is needed to empower the Leviathan to protect society from a dangerous world: the need to educate society to serve the Leviathan; the need to let the Leviathan cobble society together like a master mason for a unified strength; the need to employ a scientifically engineered fear; and the urgency of extending the Leviathan's empire by any means necessary. In a blood-soaked Europe, as England is torn asunder by civil war, and as successor vessels to the *Jesus of Lübeck* cram chained fathers, mothers, sons, and daughters just below their deck, and as the Colonies expanded and the demand for slaves double and triple in size, Hobbes argues for the creation of a Leviathan to bring rationality and peace out of the world's chaos. He begins by forcing his readers to reconsider their very nature.

REDEFINING MAN'S NATURE: & THE RISE OF A RATIONALITY COLORED WHITE

To think of humanity as rational is easier than it should be. With what we witness through our daily lives, the nightly news, and reality TV, it should be highly questionable whether humanity possesses any rationality at all. Yet we think of people as rational because the bare-knuckled brawler and the Enlightenment taught us that our rationality provides the essence of humanity.

"For what is the Heart, but a Spring," begins Hobbes as he introduces *The Leviathan* by comparing man to the working of a clock. "And the Nerves, but so many Strings; and the Joynts, but so many Wheeles?" Man is, for Hobbes, clockwork, nature's most "*Rationall* and excellent work."[41] Like a clock, man is intricate but thoroughly rational. Reason not only separates us from beasts but ties humanity to an even more rational craftsman. In a stark style soon to be labeled Hobbesian, love ties humanity to their own self-interest, not to God or to one another. For Hobbes, we must learn to think of man and God as primarily *rational* rather than *relational* or *religious*.

At the time Hobbes is writing, Galileo is hard at work perfecting the pendulum clock and providing Hobbes a timely and useful metaphor for his revolutionary work to change our understanding of human nature. During the times of Galileo and Hobbes, man was not understood primarily through the use of reason, but through the unique human capacities for religion and relationships. Humanity is crafted in the image of a God of self-sacrificial love who longs for intimacy. Humans are God's babies in need of their brothers and sisters and the redemption that only a loving Father can provide. Humanity, according to Western Christianity, is not refined or perfected by what we know, but by faith, hope, and love; by our relationship to God and one another.

Yet to say that before the Enlightenment the Western world understood religion and relationships to provide the core of human identity is not to say that reason and the life of the mind were humanity's undiscovered muscles. Plenty of brilliant, big-brained folk believed in the critical importance of reason and the life of the mind before the Enlightenment dawned. Aristotle, Augustine, Aquinas: these minds might not have intellectual equal since Aquinas's last breath in 1274.[42] Reason, the Western Christian tradition claimed, was a means of worship and a tool to align our lives into a deeper harmony with God's character and produce healthy relationships between one another. Through reason, we look at the world and learn more about its maker, increasing our understanding of the world and our shared awe of God. Not only should reason draw us closer to God through worship but closer to one another through, strangely enough, politics and the pursuit of the common good that embodied the community's shared hopes and convictions. In the Western Christian tradition, at least in theory, reason promoted intimacy by empowering believers to live out the two greatest commandments of loving God and loving neighbor. Reason was profoundly relational and only as healthy as the relationships it produced.

All this, for Hobbes, is hooey. Religion is not best known by the work it inspires in theoretical realms, but by the work it inspires in the world. For Hobbes, whose life was surrounded by religion-inspired war, we live in a world where "there Is Alwayes Warre Of Every One Against Every One,"[43] and any naïveté about man's nature only deepens the rivers of blood. Rather than love, man's propensity slants towards craving unceasing accumulations of worldly goods, and the craving of worldly goods leads to the cruelties of war. In time, the Enlightenment's view of rational European man takes on a more positive glow. But for Hobbes, man was haunted; for though he was a creature of reason, he was a creature never satisfied and always striving. The "inclination of all mankind," Hobbes wrote, is "a perpetuall and restlesse desire of Power after power, that ceaseth onely in Death."[44]

For Hobbes, we must realize that when we think of man, we are not dealing with safe and self-less saints but violent, selfish rationalists. And thus, for Hobbes, we must employ our reason to build society for a world of self-interested violent folks. Rather than reason aiming to promote intimacy, reason must aim to promote individual interests in general and self-preservation in particular. As Hobbes wrote earlier in *De Cive*: "All Society therefore is either for Gain, or for Glory; (i.e.) not so much for love of our Fellowes, as for love of our Selves."[45] Humanity might be as rational as a clock, but devious wheels spin inside their heads and hearts that lead to, "Contention, Enmity, and War."[46] The power of self-interest in society did not reach its poetic potential until Adam Smith took pen to paper and wrote of an invisible hand that harmonized the pursuits of self-interested butchers, brewers, and bakers through a free-market economy. Yet, nonetheless, Hobbes begins the process of organizing society around "love of our Selves" and of turning an ancient vice into a modern virtue.

Though religion claimed to redeem humanity's depravity, for Hobbes, religion too often enflamed man's violent vices. "That Feare of things invisible," he writes, "is the naturall Seed of that, which every one in himself calleth Religion."[47] This fear intrinsic to religion warred against man's reason and opened the door for leaders of false religion to manipulate man's primordial and powerful instincts for personal ambition: "If this superstitious fear of Spirits were taken away . . . by which, crafty ambitious persons abuse the simple people,"[48] peace might prosper. Yet peace failed to prosper in Western Christianity because the ambitiously religious mingled Christianity with Aristotle's pursuit of the common good leading to bloody quests for political power.[49] When Christianity and the pursuit of political power combined, rather than religion leading to lives shaped by faith, hope, and love, religion proved capable of justifying almost any evil in the pursuit of a higher and holier cause. Such justifications set Hobbes's world ablaze.

Those in holy robes not only fueled wars by masking personal ambitions with higher and holier rhetoric, they also warred against reason itself by sequestering reason's ability to align our lives to scientific truths. Instead of religion allowing reason to align our lives to sacred truths, "Authority Ecclesiaticall" desired to dominate the life of the mind in men and persecuted anyone who thought outside of the ecclesiastically sanctioned box, often persecuting those wiser and more pious than themselves.

So Hobbes employs his clockwork metaphor to tease man with the possibilities of taking the power of rationality out of the hands of small-minded ecclesial bureaucrats and employing it to rearrange the decaying world order. Through reason, man possessed the ability to create with precision and control. The world's madness could be managed if man matured and leaned more fully into his rational nature. For Hobbes, reason provided the only remedy for humanity's lethal vices, providing safer rules for his endless striving and an immune system against the manipulations of power hungry churchmen.

For Hobbes, the time had come to remove the chains from man's reason and to re-order the world through a rationality devoid of religious sentimentality. Since man is self-interested, we must not base reason in relationships or in religion; we must think for ourselves and aim towards our own good. In Hobbes, the idea arises that individualized and self-interested reason is sufficient for life in the modern world. After all, "all men by nature reason alike"[50] and "reason it selfe is always Right Reason, [like] Arithmetique is certain and infallible."[51] Rather than ordering the world based on the desire for intimacy with God or with one another, the new world order needed certain and infallible methods of pursuing self-love. The world needed reason without religious strings attached.

Thus what proved transformational in Hobbes's emphasis on reason was its independent and self-interested nature—his emphasis that reason no longer required religion in order to to aim for sanctified societies. The Enlightenment did not discover reason; the Enlightenment individualized it. By arguing the aim for reason is self-interest, that all men reason alike despite differences in background and experiences, and that reason's nature is akin to infallible arithmetic, Hobbes makes diverse intimacies and higher and holier hopes expendable parts in the clockwork of the thinking process.

Hobbes implores that we stop trusting books (other than his *Leviathan*) and authors (other than himself). We must instead do the hard work of the mind individually and follow reason's lead to truth. Rather than religion ruling our life together, individualized reason, reason sharpened to the certitude of geometry, needed to become the driving force for our shared lives. Humans must become rational, their thinking less dependent on relationships and certainly less dependent on religion and the hopes that it inspires.

In this radical shift of reason's fundamental aims, it fails to occur to Hobbes that the quest to establish a "rational" world order was likely to repeat all the failures of the quest to establish a religious world order. It fails to trouble Hobbes that soon priests of "reason" could employ rationality to justify the blood-thirsty pursuit of their own interests in the same way that priests of "religion" once employed Christianity. What was difficult to see at the time was that an individualized rationality, rationality without religion or relationships, opened the door for a new sort of superiority that would again set the world ablaze—a rational rather than a religious superiority.

What proved even more difficult to see was how this new rational superiority laid the groundwork for a racial superiority—a racial superiority colored white. Since the pursuit of "reason" was the quest of rich white men, what looked reasonable reflected the man in the mirror. A circle formed whereby what elite white men deemed rational became understood as the standard for unbiased, scientific rationality. This racist standard then confirmed the rational superiority of elite white men. White wealthy elites started to embody the "is-ness" of rational humanity. That which is not the embodiment of European excellence looks—not simply less reasonable—but less human and more savage. What proved difficult to see was how individualizing reason also racialized reason. And once reason is racialized, it becomes weaponized; it justifies rich white folks' self-interests over against the interests of others. As Hobbes begins crafting a new understanding of man around the metaphor of a clock, he begins sowing seeds for a rational and racial superiority.[52]

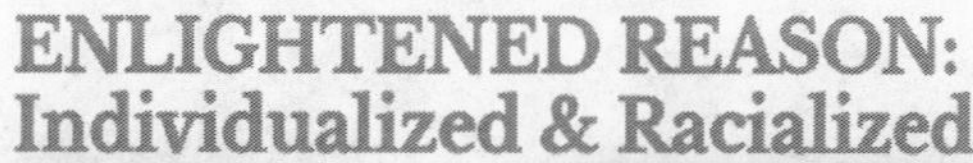

Perhaps the fingerprint of this racial superiority was best captured in an emerging style of ridiculous wigs powdered white. Such wigs were not fashion statements without social import; they communicated status and prestige. Individualized, self-interested rationality began equating whiteness[53] with rational and racial superiority. It is of no small moment that while Hobbes's hairline recedes on his brooding forehead without camouflage, complementing Locke's delicate features is one of these ridiculous wigs. It is also of no small moment that after Locke, the wigs that communicated status, like the ones that sit on the heads of Adam Smith and America's founding fathers, grew whiter still.[54] That, again, is no coincidence. Before long, white powdered wigs sat atop the heads of European and Colonial power-players and philosophers alike as a *universal* symbol of intelligence, power, and authority.

The Evolution of Hairlines

Hobbes *Locke* *Smith*

Yet the real problem of racializing reason was not the ridiculous style that it inspired but the monstrous savagery that the aristocratic style masked. Under such wigs, the Founding Fathers declared that God had created all *men* equal while refusing to treat those with Afros as men at all. When reason became racialized, a sadistic way of living in the world emerged that proved difficult to un-write.

American Christianity provided little antidote to this racial rationality. Church charters in the colonies solidified this racially sick rationality by theologically harmonizing the baptism of slaves with their shackles.[55] White churches promoted relationship with God but largely felt that they could know all they needed to know about God without intimacy with black folk who bore God's image. This illusion characterized the segregated church and her seminaries in America ever after.

But if Christianity failed to produce an antidote for the Enlightenment's racial sickness, science—which in time provides the alternative belief system for many—provided no better remedies. Though Darwin is two centuries away, the very title of his masterpiece displayed the racialized edge of scientific rationality. Though we know his masterpiece under the title *The Origins of Species*, Darwin originally did not; for he entitled the book *On the Origin of Species by Means of Natural Selection, or by Means of Preservation of Favoured Races in the Struggle for Life* (1859). The theory of evolution was part of the project of articulating the origins of white superiority.

By the time of Darwin, the white wigs are out of style. But the racist ideas the wigs embodied remained. Many of Darwin's contemporaries, men like the "Darwin Bulldog" Thomas Huxley—a father of sorts of modern agnosticism, Ernst Hackel, Friedrich Mueller, and Paul Broca rooted white superiority in the differences of hair between the races.[56] Nonetheless, Darwin, and the theories his work inspires, are eventually picked up in New York by Madison Grant, whose *The Passing of a Great Race* (1919) is praised by Hitler as "his Bible." In 1926 Hitler releases *Mein Kampf*, leading evolutionary theory itself to begin evolving from science to politics as Hitler seeks to address "the Jewish question."[57] When reason no longer aims to create right relationships or to realize holy hopes, it possesses the potential to act as violently as any religion it replaces.

When the Enlightenment's racialized reason combined with political power, sparks flew with religious ferocity. After colonization, slavery, a civil war, two World Wars and our own endless War on Terror, it is less than clear that European rationality made the world less violent than religion. What is clear, however, is that reason without relationships created an echo chamber in Europe and later in the Americas as white folks began thinking of themselves as intellectually, religiously, and intrinsically superior to the world's darker people. After *Leviathan*, the white intellectual and cultural superiority takes on the power of religious conviction. Yet the project is just beginning. For Hobbes, if the nature of man is different than what the church taught, we must re-think politics. We move from racializing rational humanity to racializing rational politics.

RETHINKING THE PURPOSE OF POLITICS IN A WORLD OF SCARCITY

For Hobbes, the world was at war due to Christianity's misunderstanding of man's nature and society's failure to build the proper political institutions to protect humanity from itself. If humanity's nature is defined by a violent and self-interested rationality, then it behooves society to form a political order capable of keeping the peace in light of true human nature. Even if we do not need our neighbors to reason rightly, we nonetheless need neighbors to survive in a world of wolves.

Thus Hobbes steers this revolutionary rationality towards the creation of his political masterpiece—the Leviathan. The greatest instinct of man's rationality is survival, and for this reason he erects the Leviathan: "For by

Art is created that great LEVIATHAN called a COMMON-WEALTH, or STATE." In crafting a common-wealth, man mimics God's creative act, "that . . . Let Us Make Man, pronounced by God in the Creation."[58] Unlike the God of creation, however, Hobbes envisions a politics far east of Eden, a politics where Pharaoh, Nebuchadnezzar, and Nero take center stage and demand obedience as earthly gods of the modern world.[59] In a world fighting for survival and scarce resources, only an all-powerful Leviathan could force peace onto the world's chaos.

This is the drama that played out in Hobbes's mind: at the feet of the Leviathan, men lay down their right to govern themselves and join together in a community pact that brings an end to war and a beginning to society. But this community is not the byproduct of man's need for intimacy, a reflection of Genesis's "it is not good for man to be alone," but of man's need for protection. In return for laying their collective all on the altar of Leviathan, Leviathan harmonizes the people's collective strength to provide a safe haven from the threats of the world, a haven for the preservation of life and "all other Contentments."[60] To preserve life and happiness, man sacrifices liberty and enters society and thus "is the Generation of that great LEVIATHAN . . . of that Mortall God, to which wee owe under the Immortall God, our peace and defence."[61]

As the need for protection supersedes the need for intimacy in the modern mind, a society formed from fear emerges with no higher or holier design than protection—protection from threats from afar and from each other. Though it will take time, such a society acts as the incubator for the new ideologies of self-sufficiency and individualism that aim to form safely isolated individuals rather than intimate communities. A modern political perversion begins as the Leviathan's politics follows reason's lead from the love of neighbor and the pursuit of the common good to a politics focused exclusively on the love, interest, and preservation of self-centered citizens.

What becomes obvious in reading *The Leviathan* is that the move to self-preservation was not aimed to limit the Leviathan's power or make his politics more humble, restrained, or contented. Instead, self-preservation ironically provided the first step to justifying the lust for an unending empire, as the Leviathan begins taking on the bloody, insatiable ambitions of the citizens it was instituted to protect. The second step in justifying the Leviathan's pursuit of empire is the logic of *scarcity*. Hobbes plants the seeds of the logic of scarcity by translating a world incapable of satisfying everyone's endless desires into a world defined by want of resources. Here is the irony: if the goal of politics is self-preservation, if the world's resources are scarce, and if all the power-players on the world stage are ruthless and self-centered, with unquenchable thirsts for the world's resources, then the Leviathan becomes duty bound to accumulate as much of the world's resources as her power allows. According to the logic Hobbes engrafts into the Enlightenment, scarcity demands accumulation—not equity.

And thus, in order to glean the world's resources, the nation sends out her "children" in the form of colonies who "inhabit a Forraign Country, either formerly voyd of Inhabitants, or made voyd then, by warre."[62] And just like that, Hobbes writes genocide into the Enlightenment's colonial project as if it were a political necessity. Hobbes's clock metaphor was about a new world order that functions with mathematical precision. Through the colonies, Africa and the Americas are engrafted into the project and become fuel for England's empire. What Hobbes helped provide was a logic whereby Europeans justified their desire to either exterminate or employ those of other lands for personal profit.

In a land that desired to justify injustice, any logic sufficed. Since Africans and Native American "savages" were deemed less rational than their European counterparts, they were said to exist in a state of nature, a state of untamed barbarity, and such a state is a state of war, "this warre of every man against every man. . . nothing can be Unjust. The notions of Right and Wrong, Justice and Injustice have no place."[63] In this war, man's reason rightly and justly rages with vicious intentions: "every one is governed by his own Reason; and there is nothing he can make use of, that may not be a help unto him, in preserving his life against his enemyes; It followeth, that in such a condition, every man has a Right to every thing; *even to one anothers body*."[64] In a world with no right and no wrong, neither justice nor injustice, the value of Africans and Native Americans in European eyes is neither their God-given gifts nor their brilliance but their bodies. Brown and black bodies are seen as fuel that empowers the colonial project to go. And, in America, the "freedom" to use black bodies as fuel inspires both a Revolutionary and a Civil War.

In a world in which Hobbesian rationality combined with political power, to be deemed less rational according to rich white folks' standards was lethal; it was to be viewed as less than human, less imprinted with God's European image. Previously, folks got burned at the stake for heresies, but soon after the Enlightenment caricatures of non-Europeans as "un-civilized" or "savage" would justify any atrocity, whether genocide via colonialism or slavery via plantation life. It is this rationality that rationalized slavery as the Enlightenment worked to mask racism as reason. However, the racial implications of Enlightenment rationality, its simplicity and sickness, was easy for Europeans to ignore and underestimate; for throughout history, only the oppressed understand the diseased nature of a society's common sense.

Perhaps no one brought together racialized logics with racialized religion to produce racialized politics any more poignantly than Cotton Mather. Born in 1663, Mather became both the most influential minister and intellectual in America, with deep roots both within Harvard College and the Puritan Church. In *Magnalia Christi Americana,* Mather's pious rationality frames how those nurtured on the Enlightenment's philosophies navigated the New World and life with their neighbors:

> The Nation of Narragansetts was one of the most populous among the Indians, and once filled this mighty wilderness. Unto that woeful nation the gospel of our Lord Jesus Christ was freely rendered, but they with much affront and contempt, rejected it . . . the glorious Lord Jesus Christ, whom they had slighted, was with our army . . . Their city was laid to ashes. Above twenty of their chief captains were killed; a proportionable desolation cut off the inferior savages, mortal sickness and horrid famine pursued the remainders of them, so that we can hardly tell if any of them are left alive on the face of the earth.[65]

If forming man around European rationality marked Hobbes's anthropological revolution, moving politics from the pursuit of the common good to self-preservation and from self-preservation to world domination marked Hobbes's political revolution. From Hobbes's time onward, self-preservation and scarcity justified ruthless political and economic orders with religious zeal. In the coming generations, modern man will not sacrifice animals to appease the gods above, yet man will sacrifice intimacy, find security in segregation, and believe that the quest for self-sufficiency through the unending quest for power and wealth is inherent, natural, and rational.

With the simple metaphor of a clock, Hobbes begins perfecting the various gears of the new world order. He persuasively crafts a rational man whose reason requires neither relationships nor religion, forms a society around man's need for security rather than intimacy, and imagines a world perpetually at war for insufficient resources. Such a world order was the enlightened alternative to the dark ages dominated by religion.

Each of these moves plants a modern neurosis on American soil. In the age of reason, rationality becomes increasingly individualized and segregated, and the ability to communicate across differences dwindles with each passing generation. In the age of reason, the role of government reduces to protecting rather than providing for the citizenry. The death of the common good was articulated succinctly, if un-poetically, by Grover Cleveland, the first Democratic President following the Civil War: "Though the people support the government, the government should not support the people."[66]

In 1903, President Cleveland employed a states' rights logic to protect Prisoner Leasing schemes that re-enslaved blacks throughout the South following the Civil War. "The South—the white and the black South—should be let alone to settle their problems in their own way." In the twentieth century, states' rights once again nullified human rights.[67]

Inspired by a society designed to promote protection and individuality rather than intimacy, society's long aim to create self-sufficient people protected from needing one another eventually succeeded, culminating in a society where, despite densely populated cities, we now "bowl alone."[68] However, as influential as any American neurosis of which Hobbes is a founding father is the vision of a world endlessly at war for limited resources. This vision roots what President Eisenhower referred to as America's Military Industrial Complex ever more deeply into America's social fabric until endless war and military buildup is a natural and logical way of life, even as 13,000,000 of our children go hungry.[69]

The seeds of unholy ghosts are being sown. The critical lies that government is not about the common good and that one can be in right relationship with God without being in right relationship with those society seeks to break and abuse are beginning to take shape. Yet Hobbes's work is just beginning. Solidifying the world order is not accomplished by erecting the Leviathan, but by empowering the Leviathan to manage all threats to the world order. Ironically enough, the greatest threat to such a world order turns out to be *equality*.

A MODERN PARADOX: HOW EQUALITY EMPOWERED THE SLAVE MASTER'S MYTH

A strange tension pervades Hobbes's writing in the *Leviathan* between the common folks and society's elite. Hobbes never genuflects before the elite as if the elite were the common folks' gifted superiors. He was from the common folk, and he thought himself more gifted than the bourgeois. Yet, by the time that Hobbes crafts the *Leviathan*, he is entrenched within elites circles and enjoys the elites' inequalities. Hobbes's origins in the common folk and his rise into the aristocracy set the stage for him to pursue a paradoxical commitment to personal equality amidst socioeconomic inequality, a pursuit Hobbes makes so persuasively that it becomes a distinguishing feature of Western society ever after. Hobbes's work begins with contracts and ends with slave whips, but by laboring to make economics a virtueless enterprise, a worldview emerges in which the riches of the few and the poverty of the masses look like the rational and unavoidable results of a righteously ordered economic system.

The equality of man bleeds throughout the pages of *Leviathan*. Though some people posses unique strength of mind or body, what Hobbes finds remarkable are not differences but the equality of humans. "Nature hath made men so equall, in the faculties of body, and mind," wrote Hobbes, that "when all is reckoned together"[70] differences nearly disappear.

In the future, the concept of equality will spark celebration in man's mind, but equality causes celebration only in a world convinced of humanity's intrinsic goodness. In the mind of one assuming that folks are greedy and resources scarce, equality assumes more sinister implications. For Hobbes, equality is nothing short of terrifying. The equality of people in a world at war for rare resources provides the world with a nightmarish quality. For Hobbes, equality is not something to celebrate, but rather a reality demanding diligent, even ruthless, management.[71] For "if any two men desire the same thing, which neverthelesse they cannot both enjoy, they become enemies; and in the way to their end, which is principally their own conservation, and sometimes their delectation only, endeavour to destroy, or subdue one another."[72] And it is these twin assumptions concerning the violence of man's greed and the scarcity of the world's goods that make management of equality so critical in the Hobbesian project.

The Leviathan acts as the project manager to ensure that people play their proper role and hold their assigned place in society. In Hobbes's ideal community, every man needs to "strive to accommodate himselfe to the rest." The image employed is that of stones cut for a building. The architect need not adjust the building to the needs of stones. Stones adjust themselves for the needs of the building. Folks who fail to know their place, are like "that stone which . . . for irregularity . . . and . . . hardnesse, cannot be easily made plain, and thereby hindereth the building." Patience cures not unfit stones; such stones are "by the builders cast away as unprofitable, and troublesome: so also, a man . . . for the stubbornness of his Passions, cannot be corrected, is to be left, or cast out of Society."[73] Medgar Evers, Martin Luther King Jr., Malcolm X, those on Black Wall Street,[74] and anyone who refuses to fit in and leave a society's injustices unchecked and unchallenged become sparks the Leviathan must extinguish.

What becomes necessary, in order for Hobbes to justify radical inequalities among equals, is the eradication of moral depth perception by the promotion of thinner notions of justice than notions of equity and the protection of human dignity. Rather than notions of justice that protect the dignity of the most vulnerable, society must learn to settle for a justice that is paper thin; society must be based on contracts not virtues. Hobbes writes: "Justice, consisteth in keeping of valid Covenants."[75] For Hobbes, the proper way for folks to cut out their place in their commonwealth is by cutting contracts—or what Hobbes refers to as covenants or compacts. The ties that bind are the papers we sign. And these papers build a framework that justly fits together butchers, brewers, and bakers into a community constructed for a unified strength.

The paperwork of contracts provide for Hobbes the appearance of fairness and through fairness, the appearance of justice. As Hobbes ruminated previously, "justice is a certain equality, *consisting in this only* . . . one should not arrogate more right to himself, than he grants to another, unless he have *fairly* gotten it by compact."[76] In the modern world, rather than designing contracts to ensure equity between equals, contracts can be engineered to generate inequities without violating the dictates of justice and in so doing provide inequities an appearance of fairness. By intentional design, paperwork becomes yet another weapon for predators to prey upon the poor. The foundations for the modern injustices of payday lenders, plea-bargains, subprime mortgages, and the endless list of predatory practices against vulnerable people were laid in the Enlightenment's contract theories. On these foundations, generations of financiers, tycoons, and everyday swindlers received protection from the cry for justice by the hidden power of fine print within the contracts written to be misunderstood.[77]

In our modern world, a world framed by contracts engineered through legalese, the virtue of equity vanishes from our basic understanding of justice. When Hobbes reduces the question of justice to "consisting in this only," justice is reduced to playing by the rules of the game while the game itself, who writes the rules, or who pockets the proceeds, goes unquestioned. When injustices occur through contracts written to be misunderstood, the authors of the predatory paperwork walk away unscathed while the lives of their victims are thrown into the flames. Through contracts, a vision of prophetic economic justice shaped by grace, mercy, and equality begins losing ground to a legalistic and pharisaical understanding of economic justice shaped by the thinnest notions of fairness. And like bullies on a playground who make up rules as they go along, the powerful control the game by creating an illusion of fair participation.

Alexander Hamilton, Founding Father and first Secretary of the Treasury, studied Hobbes throughout his life—including during winter encampments in the Revolutionary War. In the 1790 *Report on the Public Credit,* Hamilton etches Hobbesian contract theory into the American experiment. Here's how: unable to pay soldiers their wages following the Revolutionary War, the Veterans received securities that nosedived in value. Veterans, desperate to survive, sold their securities to speculators at deep discounts. Rather than providing any reward to veterans, Hamilton convinced Congress to side solely with speculators whose profits ranged from 700 to 800 percent. This set a precedent for speculators with no ceilings on unjust profits.[78]

Yet Hobbes understood that the world's inequalities run deeper than what contracts justify. Another explanation is required so that inequality does not lead to revolution. For Hobbes, whatever inequalities contracts cannot explain away, the favor of God through the favor of the king can. In this world, "a man may be Worthy of Riches, Office, and Employment, that neverthelesse, can plead no right to have it."[79] The Leviathan must embed his right to favor certain folks in the minds of a people who would know their proper place and not be angry at the inequality.[80] As Hobbes later says curtly: "and no man but the sovereign receiveth his power *Dei gratia* . . . , from the favour of . . . God: all other, receive theirs from the favour and providence of God *and their sovereigns*."[81] At the end of Hobbes's pen, a pen that knew little need for piety, the ancient lie that the way things are reflects God's design and desires continued to form the modernizing world.

But piety has a short life span in Hobbes's writing. The Christian tradition that understands the world order through the lens of Christ, expressed through the beatitudes that honor the poor, the hungry, and the mourning, turns nothing upside down for Hobbes. "Good fortune (if lasting,) Honourable; as a signe of the favour of God. Ill fortune, and losses, Dishonourable. Riches, are Honourable; for they are Power. Poverty, Dishonourable."[82] By rationally tying fortune to honor and poverty to dishonor, inequality is no longer an evil of society's structures but a reflection of the virtues and vices of particular individuals. For Hobbes, the first are not last and the last are not first. In a rational world, the world's order need not be reversed but set in stone, as if God's own finger etched the poverty of the masses and the wealth of the few into the ways of the world.

After nimbly moving man's nature from a religious being created in God's image to a rational being in the image of a clock, to communities carved together for protection rather than intimacy, and on to contracts that swap justice for a legalistic understanding of fairness, Hobbes takes the next step and moves into a creative space to "rationally"—and revolutionarily—reconsider the *value* of man. It is when Hobbes begins considering the value of men and their place within society's economic life that the tensions with immensely wealthy folk like his Cavendish employers arise. He describes money as the "blood of a commonwealth" that "circulating nourisheth every member of the body."[83] Yet, as critical as "those who have beene versed more in the acquisition of Wealth than of Knowledge" are for circulation, they threaten to act as blood clots, and money "gathered together in too much abundance, in one, or a few private men, by Monopolies"[84] threatens the life and health of the commonwealth.

Yet, despite their threat to society, the Cavendishes' knowledge in matters of money is needed for establishing the economy on sure footing, and the economically elite are endowed with a peculiar power in the life of the commonwealth; a power that rivals the Leviathan itself. Hobbes writes: "The Value, or Worth of a man, as of all things [is] his Price . . . And as in other things, so in men, not the seller, but the *buyer* determines the Price."[85] Hobbes's definition—which paints a modern ideology as a logical truism—bases man's value on his relationship *not* to God but to the *economy.* In this relationship, valuation takes place through the omniscient eyes of folks like the Cavendishes, the buyers, whose interest it is to devalue those upon whom they gaze as buyers, especially those whose skills in industry are easily replaceable. In the Hobbesian system, reducing humanity to economic entities provides the scientific value for modern man.

Reducing justice to fairness and workers to economic entities provides Hobbes a path to begin treating economics as a moral-free math. Learning to value humanity as a cog in an economic machine proved transformational. In the industrializing world, workers were treated as exchangeable pieces of an engine while the economically powerful, the robber barons, investment bankers, and CEOs that followed rose to god-like status. Hobbes's alluring logic simplified questions that occur at the intersection of ethics and economics, morality and the marketplace. With the definition of humanity's value chained to the realities of the economic grind, what justifies the treatment of other humans is simply calculated by economic efficiencies rather than considerations of human dignity.

Moving Economics to a Moral Free Math

A perversion takes place. As Hobbes moves economics to the arena of mathematics, times are a-changin' and buyers need paradigms of thought with the strength to face the realities of the day. Training in economics must become tough and brutally "realistic" in this brave new world. Since the buyer is endowed with godlike powers, and the economic game is strictly mathematical, no longer does economic man need training in the virtues of grace and generosity—the world must be reduced to grids and graphs. What were once considered economic virtues—compassion and mercy—morph when graphed and plotted into the modern vice of "inefficiency"; meanwhile, economic vices—self-interest and greed—are well on their way to being viewed as virtues. In the future, students of economics learn to write the suffering of poor folks out of the economic calculus through training that encourages a focus on gross domestic production, without an equal attention to gross domestic poverty.

By relying on reason alone and by reducing economics to a moral-free math, an ideological foundation is laid to place the buyer in a self-justifying economy that need not worry about opinions from the God above or the oppressed below. A virtue-less productivity alone justifies the new world order. As Coates reminds his son, "You must always remember that the sociology, the history, the economics, the graphs, the charts, the regressions all land, with great violence, upon the body."[86]

~

For Hobbes, the work of this self-justifying order is just beginning as he moves from employees and employers to slaves and slave masters: "The master of the servant, is master also of all he hath." Hobbes continues: "And may exact the use . . . of his goods, labour, and of his *children*, as often as he shall think fit. And in case the master, if he refuse, kill him or cast him into bonds, or otherwise punish him for his disobedience, [the slave] is himself the author of the same; and cannot accuse [the master] of injury."[87] What must be remembered in Hobbes's ghastly work on the slave's body, and similar words soon to be uttered by John Locke, is that Hobbes is not simply *describing* the existing reality of slavery but *prophesying* on the new form slavery should take in the modern world. At the risk of repetition, Hobbes and Locke are writing a rulebook on modern slavery, not reading it.[88]

When reading the *Leviathan* through the lens of the work taking place on the bodies of the poor and the slave, the reader comes away with the eerie realization that the slaveholder's whips, guns, and trading blocks were not a stumbling block for Hobbes's vision for modern society. Whips and gunpowder were instruments of industry, and the slave block was a cornerstone on which his enterprise was constructed. Hobbes's logic is that of the slavemaster of the seventeenth and eighteenth centuries, the robber barons of the late-nineteenth century, the corrupt financiers of the twentieth century, and all who profit from the suffering of the working poor. In time, *the ethics of the slavemaster* becomes a *paradigm* for the economically powerful. At the slave block, we fully experience the collective impact of Hobbes's philosophy.[89]

And thus Hobbes manages equality, one logical step at a time, until equality is reshaped to harmonize with the slavemaster's myth. In the European and American mind, humans in chains devolved into carnal bodies exchangeable with other economic goods, while the white economic elite evolved into earthly gods. Equality in a world of greed and scarcity demanded management. Management demanded contracts. Contracts justified inequalities. Justified inequalities expressed God's ordained favor. God's favor placed the powerful in control of the poor and of slaves' lives and limbs. A cycle develops as the tradition of Pharaoh resurrects a new and peculiar rationality in the modern mind.

Hobbesian equality haunts America. As the industrialized nation with the greatest wealth disparities, in the land with an uncanny ability to produce a few billionaires and masses of poor folk, we sought to incarnate the lie that the equality of man's nature need not translate to economic and political realities. The lie led to slavery, civil war, segregation, and mass incarceration. As time passed, the buyer and his corporations became more powerful while the 99 percent became more expendable and their dignity more in question. We learned to trust in and depend on corporations, while corporations learned to thrive without us.

Soon the economic train ran in both directions, not simply turning the poor into economic entities but economic entities into people. American courts continually endowed economic entities the status of personhood,[90] while denying and questioning the humanity and rights of black folks. The project reached its logical destination in 2010 in the Supreme Court's landmark decision, *Citizens United*, which granted corporations the power to shape elections through unlimited donations. As society elevated corporations to the embodiment of man's potential and ingenuity—worthy of government protections and consideration—the poor were reduced to economic drains, the embodiment of just how low humanity can go. As Mitt Romney reminded us in his 2012 Presidential campaign: "Corporations are people, my friend" and "47 percent [of Americans] are dependent upon government, believe that they are victims. . . .[and] pay no income tax. . . . *My job is not to worry about those people*." In time, society grew certain that rich corporations are people but less certain that poor people are people. If people are poor, perhaps something is awry in their humanity.

Hobbes knew loyalty to the Leviathan and managing the equality of man was not something to leave to chance. The Leviathan needed to write its purpose on the hearts, souls, and minds of a people. For only those trained to serve and christen the Leviathan can be managed. What was needed was education to root tyranny into the minds, hearts, and ways of men.

CRAFTING AN OBEDIENT PEOPLE: EDUCATING IN INNOCENCE AND EXCEPTIONALISM

Not until I moved into Houston's Fifth Ward did I encounter the passion for education that possessed my grandfather, who dropped out in middle school to provide for his family during the Great Depression. No one confused Roy Chandler with a feminist, but he organized his life to position his daughters to go to college. When my mom moved for college, so did my grandfather. He wanted to ensure that cupid did not hinder graduation.[91] Unsurprisingly, the most passionate educational advocates are often the "un-" and "under"-educated. Unsurprisingly as well, the one who envisioned "rational" man also foresaw the centrality of education and its role in the emerging modern world. Before there was America's educational philosopher John Dewey (1859–1952), there was Thomas Hobbes influencing instincts that thoroughly shaped America's educational systems and practices.

For Hobbes, through education the righteousness and justice of a nation is solidified in the minds and hearts of the people to inspire obedience and maintain unity.[92] In Hobbes's imagination, two mediums for education existed: the schoolhouse and the church house. And though two different houses provide the citizenry educational instruction, there was one sermon: obedience. "Take away in any kind of State, the Obedience . . . and they shall not onely not flourish, but in short time be dissolved."[93] Education's aim is not to inspire creativity, feed curiosity, or seek truth. Education inspires devotion and empowers people to play their part in strict obedience.

The unity necessary for the self-preservation of a people is not inevitable. It is wrought. If unity is not prized, it perishes. According to Hobbes, ensuring the unity of the people necessary to preserve society means teaching obedience through well-honed educational practices: "Reason is the Pace; Encrease of Science, the Way; and the benefit of all man-kind, the end."[94] Universities provide "the Fountains of Civill, and Morall Doctrine."[95] and have the responsibility to act as society's refineries for unity. Yet rather than building unity, universities, like Oxford, too often functioned as breeding grounds for ideologies of discontent.[96] According to Hobbes, just like religion, almost everything wrong with education traced back to Aristotle's errors. Aristotle's writings on *Metaphysics*, "absurd"; his *Politics*, "repungent"; his *Ethics*, "ignorance." In Hobbes's mind, when the universities aligned themselves with Aristotle's errors, they produced educational failures that filled the world with blood that needed not have been spilled.

Hobbes writes to transform the refinery by un-writing Aristotle's absurdities. Rather than envisioning a system for societies' elite, he envisions a public system for the common people who lacked the sentimentality the elite inherited: "The Common-peoples minds . . . are like clean paper, fit to receive whatsoever by Publique Authority shall be imprinted in them."[97] But education for the common people was not, in Hobbes's mind, intended as a rung to climb the social ladder. Education acted as a glue to keep citizens united and in their proper place by fostering blind obedience and love of country. Hobbes argues that in the same way God rightly expected obedience and not curiosity from Adam in Genesis, so too rulers "are not by their Subjects to be censured, nor disputed."[98] Education, in this modern and rational world, is refining the mind to *not* ask the critical questions.

"The People are to be taught," Hobbes writes a few pages later, "First, that they ought not to be in love with any forme of Government they see in their neighbour Nations, more than with their own, nor . . . to desire change."[99] To devastate the potential for change and solidify the Leviathan's power, Hobbesian education must disempower the common folk from pursuing change while empowering them to play their role. Hobbes rightly understood that education, when it is reduced to obedience, possesses the potential to crucify the curiosity required for meaningful change.

Despite the power of man's rationality, there was at least one thing for Hobbes to which man must not aim. "They that go . . . to reforme the Common-wealth, shall find they do thereby destroy it," Hobbes writes. "Like the foolish daughters of Peleus . . . which desiring to renew the youth of their decrepit Father, did by the Counsell of Medea, cut him in pieces, and boyle him, together with strange herbs, but made not of him a new man."[100] If citizens are unable to improve their society, if poor folk need be poor, underperforming schools must underperform and prisons overpopulate for our safety; if the way things are is the only way that they can be, the hope to participate in change must be cut out of the hearts and minds of children lest they believe otherwise and dare to dream against the grain of the status quo.

Hearts and heads must be hardened by an educational system designed for obedience. For people to play their part, the common people need the harder sciences that offer the types of surety produced by geometry and that lead to greater industriousness. Hobbes sees little value in the softer, more social sciences that stoke curiosity's flames. The "how" of productivity—math, chemistry, physics—must grow more central to education in the modern world. The "whys" of our life together—literature, philosophy, and political science—must become more and more marginalized in the classroom. In the modern world, that which fails to standardize the students is no longer necessary.

Yet for Hobbes, history, the "history of facts," plays a central role in inspiring the obedience education is designed to induce.[101] In some of his last remarks on education, Hobbes warns future rulers of the significance in how history's story is told. History cannot be told from just any perspective, but from the perspective that inspires loyalty to Leviathan. History is to produce reverence for one's nation and forefathers. Realities of history that throw into question the morality of a nation's inception must be whitewashed before entering history's books, for "there is scarce a Commonwealth in the world, whose beginnings can in conscience be justified."[102]

For education aimed at obedience, history must travel through a filter that distills the unsavory truths of our forefathers' character and our nation's inception in order to produce purer stories to feed to the citizenry. If education fails to purify stories of the nation's creation, such a failure is "one of the most effectuall seeds of the Death of any State." How a nation's history is told is how their ongoing project is sold. Thus, for Hobbes, history needs to travel through the filter of innocence to inspire loyalty by remembering the forefathers' virtues but not their vices.[103] A quaint memorial in Virginia captures the Hobbesian spirit in its musing: "The virtues of our fathers we write on tablets of stone, and their shortcomings on the sands of the sea."[104] The sentimentality that Hobbes lacks in almost every other area of the commonwealth seems reserved for the annals of history.

Whether by intent or instinct, the American educational system found uncanny harmony with Hobbes's educational principles. In U.S. classrooms, the importance of standardized tests—tests originally aimed to promote a racial hierarchy and that continue to perform racial work—and the "hard sciences" continue to replace creativity and critical thought. By empowering citizens to productively play their part while reducing their ability to critically question the society in which they live, the American education system increasingly embodies a Hobbesian trajectory.[105]

The aforementioned John Dewey, one of America's most influential educational reformers, was quite familiar with Hobbes, as seen in his 1918 essay *The Motivation of Hobbes's Political Philosophy*. Dewey was no Hobbesian, but his work follows Hobbes's path by aiming education at social efficiency.[106]

The Hobbesian character of our educational practices is nowhere better seen than in America's relationship to the telling of her own history. We regulate the stories of our forefathers to heroic mythologies. Pilgrims bravely conquering a new world in pursuit of a society of freedom and justice override the realities of the genocide of pillaged Indians and the slavery of African Americans. George Washington and Thomas Jefferson receive memorials from the perspective of their admirers and not the slaves they chained, beat, and raped. Students receive training in the rhetoric of "No taxation without representation!" and the demand for liberty, freedom, and equality in a way that rationalizes the American Revolution. Of course the irony is that the American colonies were one of the least-taxed colonies in the world, and that America's founders desired to protect the institution of slavery as England moved towards abolition, a fact that proved as integral to the revolution as any ideology of liberty.[107] When men like Washington, Jefferson, Adams, and Hancock—men whose lives focused on perfecting, perpetuating, and profiting from slavery—give birth to a nation, it is unsurprising that their baby proves addicted to racist ideas, institutions, and instincts. Yet such ironies and realities rarely make it out of a Hobbesian refinery in America.[108]

Mt. Vernon was home to a number of Mulatto servants, and the slave Venus identified George Washington as the father of her son West Ford. Pulitzer Prize–winning biographer Ron Chernow claims Washington's parentage is "highly unlikely," yet to believe Washington *was not* the father requires believing Venus *was* a liar and places trust in the slavemaster's nobility over the slave's integrity.[109]

The slaying of curiosity through American education baked two interrelated Hobbesian convictions into the American experiment and her citizenry: American exceptionalism and historical innocence. The myths of American exceptionalism and innocence produced more than a benign ignorance of information; they produced a sick imagination that fostered and fosters racial divisions. As the American project moved forward and our racial sickness evolved in every passing generation, the myths of American exceptionalism and innocence produced segregation, cynicism, and a nation where races within the same city lived in different worlds. Throughout American history, exceptionalism and innocence performed the work they were designed to do—that is, to inhibit social change by weaving the vices of our forefathers into our national fabric so seamlessly that we no longer recognize the sins that hold our lives together.

The whitewashing of America's past and present makes Frederick Douglass's declaration that "there is not a nation on the earth guilty of practices more shocking and bloody than are the people of the United States" and movements such as Black Lives Matters nonsensical for those trained to be blind to the systems' injustices. When American exceptionalism and innocence become part of one's mental and moral makeup, the voices of protest are viewed as ungrateful, ignorant, and insufficiently patriotic. In "the divided states of America," we must remember that the projects of exceptionalism and innocence were—from the days of slavery and segregation to Black Lives Matter—designed to elicit our embrace of the Leviathan's sickness, not one another.

"The schools were not concerned with curiosity," Coates writes to his son. "They were concerned with compliance. I sense the schools were hiding something, drugging us with a false morality so that we would not see, so that we did not ask."[110] Even those without intimacy with Hobbes's philosophy nevertheless experience intimacy with his ghosts.

~

We move now from the schoolhouse to the church house. Hobbes understood that securing obedience in the mind and not the heart doomed to failure efforts to restructure society. Religion provided a critical component for his clock to operate with the needed precision. Hobbes's relationship to religion was both simple and revolutionary. If Hobbes was heretical, it was not that he operated outside of the Christian tradition. Hobbes's heresy was in reducing and domesticating Christianity into a religion that fostered "enlightened" obedience and harmony with modern political impulses; Hobbes's heresy was in writing out of Christian calculus the Bible's prophetic tradition and its commitment to socio-economic equality, justice and the poor.[111]

For Hobbes, religion is not rooted in faith, hope, or love, but in fear,[112] and expressed not primarily through the care of the widow and orphan, but through obedience to rulers.[113] Centering religion in love of neighbor or in the needs of the least of these would open the door to desire for change. "All that is NECESSARY to Salvation," writes Hobbes, "is contained in two Vertues, Faith in Christ, and Obedience to Laws."[114] Folks who can simultaneously confess Jesus as their Lord and yet unquestioningly follow the dictates and oracles of their rulers were perfect cogs for tyranny's wheel to operate unchecked and unchallenged. "The Designes Of The Authors Of The Religion," Hobbes reminded his readers, "[for] the first Founders, and Legislators of Common-wealths . . . were only to keep the people in obedience."[115]

Hobbes's formula was nothing less than prophetic for an American Christianity that eventually trimmed Scripture's vision of salvation down to John 3:16 ("that anyone who believed in him shalt be saved") and Christian political responsibility down to Romans 13 ("Let everyone be subject to the governing authorities"). Scriptures providing moral depth to faith through love of neighbor, care for widows, orphans, immigrants, and the poor never enjoyed the same authoritative status on American soils. Following the Hobbesian formula, Christianity became a superficial thing in the face of injustice. Reducing Christianity to "what is necessary for salvation" produced a religion capable of experiencing two Great Awakenings and countless Graham crusades without awakening true believers to the reality of our nation's racial sickness. In America, cultural Christianity committed itself to the transformative power of personal piety but labored to ensure that no Christ-centered transformation trickled into areas of social justice, racial solidarity, or the demand for political change. From slavery to segregation to immigrant oppression, the military, and the prison-industrial complexes and every war—just or unjust—the American church consistently found herself on the wrong side of social issues concerning people without white skin.[116]

Reflecting society at large, those gathered in the cathedrals and sanctuaries did not simply ignore the cries of the slaves and prophets; White Christians received training in indifference to the cause of the oppressed till they no longer heard their pleas. The church felt that it could ignore prophets contemporary—like Martin Luther King—and live faithfully to prophets ancient. Christianity often became strictly about the spiritual, the eternal, the stuff of heaven, not the dirt and dust of earthy living, not economics and certainly not progressive politics that sought intimacy and solidarity with darker hues of skin.

As much as any pastor embodying the call to obey rulers and ignore prophets was Virginia's Rev. Jerry Falwell, the founder of the Moral Majority. "Christians, like slaves and soldiers," declared Falwell to his church, "ask no questions."[117] Falwell railed against the ministers who engaged in the civil rights movement[118] and its political vision, and worked to ensure—in subtle and not so subtle ways—that black preachers never transformed America's racial ways. Under Falwell and the leaders who rose with him and in his wake, white religion worked to reinforce rather than to re-imagine America's racial order.

"It is a terrible violation of human and private property rights," writes Falwell in his autbiography. "It should be considered civil wrongs rather than civil rights." Long after Falwell lost his fight against the civil rights movement, he clung to his conviction that the nation was wrong in failing to allow those who designed the Jim Crow South to end it.[119]

~

Diverse avenues of education—secular and religious, whether in the lecture hall, library, laboratory, or sanctuary—complemented one another to silence good folks and to get them comfortable with the "unavoidable" injustices that are as American as apple pie. In *the Leviathan*, the perfecting of the commonwealth is nearing completion by man leaning into his rationality, society managing its members' equality, and providing an education that inspires obedience. Yet, was a well-managed, rationalistic man educated in obedience enough to empower the tyranny necessary to control the vices of the masses? For Hobbes, the answer is no. When reason and education fail, fear prevails.

A FEAR THAT PASSES ALL UNDERSTANDING

In a world seemingly spinning out of control, Hobbes approaches his project of restructuring the architecture of society with the confidence of a brilliant savant undaunted by the task that lies before him. With a surety in his own grandeur, Hobbes muses within the *Leviathan* of his hopes that a future tyrant will diligently study his words and that universities will exchange their curriculum for his magnum opus in order "to convert this Truth of Speculation, into the Utility of Practice."[120]

But in reading the chapter "On Religion," another side of Hobbes comes to the surface for a brief but illuminating moment. "For being assured that there be causes of all things that have arrived hitherto, or shall arrive hereafter," writes Hobbes, "it is impossible for a man, who continually endeavoureth to secure himself against the evil he fears . . . not to be in a perpetual solicitude . . . his heart all the day long, gnawed on by fear of death, poverty, or other calamity, and has no repose, nor pause of his anxiety but in sleep."[121] Modern man is an enigma. Despite the confidence his writings exude, Hobbes's intimacy with fear lurks just behind the veil of confidence. He famously confesses that in a world of war "the life of man, [is] solitary, poore, nasty, brutish, and short."[122]

Yet Hobbes's intimacy with fear only deepens his commitment to his project. The Leviathan shall not be thwarted. Since fear is a human reality, like equality, it must be managed and manipulated in order to hold society together. Fear requires scientific analysis and engineering so that, rather than producing chaos, it produces unity and fosters obedience in the people.

"The Passion to be reckoned upon," Hobbes tutors, "is fear."[123] As he works to reckon with fear, Hobbes divides fear into two categories: fear of things visible and fear of things invisible. In the use of visible fear, Hobbes offers nothing remarkable. Fear "is the only thing" that empowers men to overcome the temptation to "profit and pleasure" by breaking the law.[124] The greatest failure of leaders is not in grabbing too much power, but not enough. The Leviathan must seek all power in order to act as the nucleus of man's visible fear "to keep them in awe, and tye them by feare of punishment."[125] It is a powerful, if unremarkable, analysis of fear in the political world.

Hobbes's remarkable work with fear, a work arguably perfected in the American democratic experiment, emerges in his manipulation of invisible fears. This invisible fear becomes an arrow in Hobbes's quiver that can be aimed with the precision of an Elvan archer. "This perpetual fear, always accompanying mankind in the ignorance of causes, as it were in the dark, must have needs of something."[126] Rather than defining fear, so as too alleviate it, Hobbes increases political precision by stoking fear and keeping it vague; for it is *precisely vague fears* that free political powers to manipulate fear with *precision.* Anxiety produces the need for security, and the need for security inspires the embrace of tyranny. It is a powerful formula.

Hobbes's manipulation of fear is frighteningly brilliant. In Hobbesian politics, the naming of fears becomes hauntingly similar to the provision of random coordinates for the armed forces' artillery. On American soils his brilliance would be embodied by politicians who coined phrases such as "taxation without representation," "the domino theory," and the ever-ambiguous "war on terror"—phrases that focus politics on abstract fears abroad rather than concrete political malpractices against society's most vulnerable on the home-front.

However, that is not to suggest that vague fears were only aimed abroad, for often the crosshairs of the politically ambitious were trained on neighbors from the other side of the track. Once the other is feared, there is nothing such fear can fail to justify—from lynching, to race-based incarceration, to walls to divide "us" from "them." From McCarthy and Nixon to

Cheney and Rumsfeld to Trump and Bannon, American politicians have perfected the Hobbesian formula: find the fear, stoke it into a frenzy, be the solution.

And though it was the political power players who found themselves in front of the camera, the true puppet master, the true maestro of Hobbesian fear was the man behind the camera: Roger Ailes. It was Ailes who helped Nixon and Reagan secure their presidencies.[127] When the Fairness Doctrine[128] was eliminated, it was Ailes who turned Fox News into the megaphone for the conservative cause. For the era bookended by Nixon and Trump, the Hobbesian genius of Ailes proved transformative for American life. In politics, propaganda matters. Too often, when it came to politics, Christians who drank from the Fox News fountain found a deeper political harmony with the fears and hatreds of Ailes than the self-sacrificial love of the politics of Jesus. And Jesus wept.

We see in Ailes and the success of Fox News the long tail of Thomas Hobbes, who labored philosophically to etch anxiety onto the soul of modern humanity by writing war onto his nature and scarcity onto his world, and by stoking vague fears to de-prioritize concrete political malpractices while increasing political control. Though modern folks no longer believe in ghosts or goblins, it is less than clear that the age of anxiety is any less haunted by demons than the so-called dark ages. As President Trump proved nearly four hundred years after Hobbes, if we train a society to fear black folks, immigrants, Muslims, and refugees, a foundation can be laid to support tyranny and the zealous persecution of our neighbors as our enemies. We live in Hobbesian times.

PREPARING FOR TYRANNY'S PERFECTION

In writing the *Leviathan*, Hobbes battled for man's mind, heart, and loyalty; he battled to make man more rational and to reject any form of religion that would make the world bloodier. Hobbes fought against the Western Christian tradition and against the church and her power-players, who had picked up the sword Christ rejected to make the world fall in line with their reading of the gospel. Hobbes dares to pose a radical alternative to power masquerading as piety; he proposes to unmask and reconfigure power through a rationally empowered Leviathan that citizens could see, fear, and obey. In a rational world, the common citizen's responsibility would no longer be to honor God with all their heart, soul, and mind. The citizen's responsibility would be limited to what they could handle: loyalty to the system while praying for salvation from above.

It is ironic that Hobbes's response to corrupted ecclesial bureaucrats is an autocrat endowed by God with every vice the ecclesiastically corrupted had embodied—but that is essentially what happened. With rational man, no longer can the dictates of religion justify power-players' evil deeds. Yet after the *Leviathan*, rather than employing theological language to justify violence, violence was rationalized through secular, rational, and scientific ideals. The nature of man as rational, violent, and self-interested; the nature of politics as ceaseless striving to accumulate resources in a world of scarcity; and the nature of citizens as obedient and fearful people: these are the ideologies Thomas Hobbes midwifed into the modern world.

And by imagining these ideologies, Hobbes shaped the emerging modern world order around the slavemaster's myth. He successfully plants the seeds for the political lies that government need not pursue the good of the people and that economics can be approached as a moral-free math. He plants the religious lie that our relationship to God is not affected by our relationship to the poor and marginalized, but by our obedience to those in power. In so doing, Hobbes contributes to the modern limitation of religion to soul salvation.

All of these seeds needed nurturing to receive acceptance. As formative as Hobbes proved to be on the modern imagination, he failed to figure out how to convince society's movers and shakers to embrace tyranny in the political form he championed, and thus he failed to institutionalize the imagination he fostered. His rhetoric was too barbaric, his tyranny was too transparent, and his demand for unmitigated obedience proved more than society was ready to embrace. In Hobbes's arrogance, he even coined the phrase "Tyrannophobia"[129] to mock the fear he believed his rationality sufficiently slayed.

Yet, despite his shortcomings, Hobbes prophetically carved out a theoretical possibility that he could quite convince himself of—that is, a *democratic* Leviathan. He placed such a possibility within the definition of the Leviathan itself, within the terminology of a "sovereign assembly." But as his comparison between assemblies and monarchies moved forward, he sensed that democracies only increased the problems of governing. Hobbes foresaw that the politics of assemblies were likely to only serve the interests of the wealthy, that partisanship within assemblies stalled practical progress, and that, ultimately, democracy would produce the "same condition, as if the Government were in a child."[130] Despite Hobbes's refusal to acknowledge the depravity of tyranny, few understood the perils of democracy better.

Thus, Hobbes's impact on the slavemaster's myth was imagining a rationality that justified exploiting the poor, the vulnerable, and other people's land for the empire's greater good. Perfecting the institutionalization of the slavemaster's myth passed to the next generation. And the next step in the perfection of tyranny would come from the mind of an ironic Hobbesian disciple—a disciple with more crafty wordplays that were not so immediately troubling; a disciple who would envision a similar economic/political/religious trajectory and yet present the package in more acceptable wrappings. We turn now to John Locke, for it was Locke who provided the political and religious systems to institutionalize the Hobbesian imagination within a "democratic" and "Christian" people.

3

John Locke

Institutionalizing an Aristocratic— & Racist—Revolution

BORN IN A STORM

Nearly forty-give years after the birth of Thomas Hobbes and twenty years before Hobbes's *Leviathan*—on August 29, 1632—the Puritan parish rector Rev. Samuel Crook took the church's Holy Waters and baptized the newly born John Locke.[131] That John Locke was baptized on the day of his birth testified to the intimate, if un-orthodox, place the Christian faith held in Locke's life, from his infancy until friends gathered around his bedside for prayer and to read him the Psalms through his final hours.[132]

Despite being born during Hobbes's middle years, the world changed little. Like Hobbes, Locke's life was wrapped in the birthing pangs of the Western world coming into the modern age, as Christianity and the world's secular powers grappled with one another like Jacob and Esau for their place in the emerging new world order. The Thirty Years War raged on even as internal tensions brought England closer to civil war. Locke later wrote: "I no sooner perceived myself in the world, but I found myself in a storm which has lasted almost hitherto."[133] But if the world changed little from the times of Hobbes to Locke's "hitherto," it would soon—in part through his influence—begin changing drastically.

Locke nurtures and perfects the lies that Hobbes planted into the modern imagination concerning the nature of government, economics, and religion through innovations that replaced the tyrannical Hobbesian edge with smoother aristocratic ways of reasoning. For black, brown, red and poor white folks, the aristocratic alternatives proved no less lethal as Locke's liberalism began recreating the world in harmony with the interests of the economic elite. Through the work of Locke a new style of common sense arises that seems nothing less than "self-evident"—especially among the aristocracy of the New World. From the pen of Locke flows a style of reasoning that harmonizes liberal ideologies of freedom, liberty, democracy and soul salvation with the institution and perpetuation of slavery.

As we continue to trace how the slavemaster's myth ingrained itself into America's faith and politics, we move to the second step of the process from *imagining* to *institutionalizing* a world order shaped by the slave master's myth. If we wonder about the curious state of our institutions—how democracy serves the best interest of the wealthy rather than the best interest of the people; how racial inequalities led society to question the virtues of black folk rather than the failures of our educational, criminal-justice, and economic systems; how we learned to fear the entitlement of the poor rather than the entitlement of the wealthy; or how churches continue to save souls without changing the ways, hearts and minds of a racist nation, no philosopher is more important to understand than John Locke, the philosophical father of liberalism.

THE MAKING OF AN ARISTOCRAT

To look at the portraits of Hobbes and Locke side by side is to see men seemingly possessed by two different natures. Hobbes looks robust and fierce, as if the artist's portrait captured not simply the man but the philosopher who wrote with a brutally stark style. The artist who portrayed Locke, on the other hand, depicts a man who appears sickly but nonetheless sophisticated, subtle and perhaps even a touch sentimental. That sophisticated subtlety was more than his slender stature. Sophisticated subtlety was the signature of Locke's philosophical style.

Locke attempted to separate himself as far as possible from Hobbes. He claimed to learn nothing from the man and posited a Hobbesian as a Christian's opposite. It was a Puritan burn that left much to be desired. Now, 300 years after Locke's death and as the death toll continues to rise from centuries rife with racial strife and inequality, the stunning similarities between the two philosophers who posed as opposites are hard to deny. Both received almost identical educations at Oxford,[134] both wrestled with the same problems through remarkably similar methods,[135] both incubated their ideas in nearly identical social circles among the socially elite, both enthusiastically embraced slavery, empire, inequality and the brutal management of the masses.[136] Yet, unlike Hobbes, Locke made the interests of the elite the nucleus of his project, and for a philosophy looking to birth a movement, the aristocratic accent made all the difference.

Like Hobbes who went before him, much of Locke's style was inherited. Both philosophers' fathers were men closer to the common folks than the aristocracy. Unlike Thomas Sr., however, John Sr. was not a bare-knuckled brawler but a modest puritan lawyer who curried favor from those for whom he labored. The name "John" possessed deep roots in the Locke family, tracing back at least to sea captain John Lok who bartered in slaves and gold by means of his three ships—*the Trinity*, *Bartholomew,* and *John the Evangelist.* It seems the family's fascination with slaves and gold proved every bit as poignant as their Puritan piety—and they were quite pious.

Two events changed the course of John Jr.'s life. The first event that transformed Locke's life was a parliamentary endorsement inspired by the excellent service from his father during England's civil war. The endorsement provides Locke the opportunity to enter into the Westminster School at the age of fifteen, leading Locke forever out of the circle of common folk. From Westminster it was to Oxford. Locke thrived at Oxford and a few years after graduation he returned to the university as a tutor at Christ Church where he developed a fateful friendship with the great Robert Boyle. Boyle was a deeply committed Christian who integrated theology, philosophy, and science and earned himself the title "the father of modern chemistry." The relationship with Boyle was later mirrored by Locke's intimate friendship with Isaac Newton. Boyle, Newton, and Locke were united not only by passions for faith and science; they shared a sick racial imagination as well.[137] It is during Locke's time tutoring at Oxford that he makes his first purchase of stock in *The Company of Royal Adventurers in England Trading into Africa.* Through Locke's investment, the family's slave-trading ways continue in modern form. The transaction proved to be an investment that would only deepen throughout the rest of his life.[138]

The second event that changed Locke's life was when, following an encounter to assist Anthony Ashley Cooper, Locke received an invitation to join Cooper at his Exeter estate as a personal physician. Cooper changes Locke's life and its trajectory by becoming an unlikely mentor for the Puritan-raised Locke. Cooper becomes for Locke what the Cavendishes were for Hobbes—an entranceway into society's elitist echelons. Cooper was a leading man of the times, well connected and a thoroughgoing deviant—"the greatest whoremaster in England" according to the King.[139] Cooper was also, in the words of Locke's premier biographer Maurice Cranston, a "progressive capitalist in politics"[140] who embraced religious toleration out of the conviction that *religious* tolerance provides the best soil for *economic* flourishing. Cooper's passions were directed towards empire and the almost unlimited potential to garner wealth from resources on other shores through stockholdings in colonial and slave-trading companies. At Cooper's Exeter House, Locke's potential is immersed in the upper echelons of the aristocratic world, and his genius is unlocked and unleashed.

A year after entering Exeter House, Locke is elected as a Fellow of the Royal Society. In these new surroundings, Locke learns to see the world's predicaments and potentials through the lens of economic opportunity. The interconnectedness of religion, politics, and economics begins percolating in Locke's mind. The brew proves powerful, and he begins to write. On both politics and religion, Locke's writings are so neat, clean, and well argued that they prove more than persuasive—they prove prophetic. Locke possessed a rare ability to present a novel way of viewing the world that seemingly uncovered the failed logic and practices of Christendom, while simultaneously revealing pious ways out of Christendom's current quagmire in terms Christians readily accepted. Locke accomplishes this all the while writing as though the worldview he presented was neither novel nor original genius. Locke wrote as though the work he was doing was merely uncovering the basic essence God himself had written on the heart of religion and politics. Locke wrote in a style that seemed humbly revelatory rather than radical or revolutionary.

Through his writings beginning at Exeter, Locke begins imagining a flourishing society shaped by a politically empowered and religiously pious aristocracy—a captivating vision that has shaped both American democracy and Christianity in ways difficult to overstate. What our founders deemed self-evident, and what generations of Americans have considered common sense and "orthodox" concerning the very natures of faith and politics, find their primordial beginnings neither in Jerusalem nor in Judea, neither in Greece nor in Rome, but in the inkwell of John Locke's pen.[141] Locke begins his work by cleaning the slate of what men think they know.

TABULA RASA

Nullius in verba or "Take nobody's word for it" acts as the guiding motto for the Royal Society. No work better embodied the society's motto than Locke's first philosophical masterpiece, *An Essay Concerning Human Understanding*, which he began only a few years after joining the society. In his "Epistle to the Reader," Locke reports that the *Essay* is a product of conversations at Exeter that he planned on fitting onto a sheet of paper, but "grew insensibly to the bulk" of four books. "To confess the truth," he writes sheepishly, "I am now . . . too lazy to shorten it."[142] Locke introduces his *Essay* as an investigation into the "original, certainty, and extent of human knowledge." As Locke investigates the limits and potential of the mind, he works with a double-edge razor whereby he shaves from man's minds what they thought they naturally knew, and in so doing etches into white people's minds a question that further racialized our world.

Locke begins his project out of the conviction that the life of the mind is in need of total and complete re-organization. As in our own day, the greatest symptom of the incoherence of the popular mind was society's inability to produce meaningful conversations between people with different perspectives. For Locke, making meaningful conversation impossible were the bipolar tendencies of perfect skepticism and pious slothfulness. The perfect skeptic questioned everything enthusiastically only to despair at our intellect's inability to produce certain responses to every question our world poses. According to Locke, perfect skeptics make no progress, produce no principles, and only deepen the doubts of men. And for the practically minded, that is a problem. The slothfully pious, on the other hand, question nothing yet hold ideas they inherit with a religious fervor that prohibits intellectual progress and societal flourishing. Conversations with the skeptical and slothful are like talking to folks who live inside their dreams, and "where all is but dream, reasoning and arguments are of no use."[143]

In Book I of the *Essay*, Locke attempts to bring both the humility and responsibility necessary for the mind to practically fulfill its powerful potential. Locke writes the introduction of Book I largely to the skeptic. He reassures his skeptical readers that, "The candle that is set up in us, shines bright enough" and "'tis great use to the sailor to know the length of his line, though he cannot fathom with it the depths of the ocean."[144] Locke then moves in the final three chapters of Book I to the slothful "philosophers" who insult God by hiding the candle of the mind under a bushel by accepting certain ideas they inherited as innate without thorough investigation. The concept of innate ideas argued that folks are born with certain ideas imprinted in their mind. Christians claimed that such innate ideas evidenced the image of God within us and established a baseline through which God holds humanity accountable for their actions. As the Apostle Paul wrote: "Since the creation of the world God's invisible qualities—his eternal power and divine nature—have been clearly seen. . . so that people are without excuse."[145]

Locke, who was as intimate with Paul as any, thought that establishing any idea without interrogation placed the cart before the horse in the reasoning process to excuse the lazy from the needed tugging that progress in the life of the mind always entails. Rather than God providing innate ideas, Locke argues, God provides man *capacities* to reason, question, and search for the truths that God ingrained into the universe. Man learns through *experience*, by receiving from the world simple ideas through his senses and reflecting on what is received through the genius of his mind.[146] "The capacity, they say is innate, the knowledge acquired."[147] And this, for Locke, is not simply for man's most exalted knowledge, but for his most basic. Man's mind is a sheet of "white paper" and it is experience and reflection that place pen to paper producing ideas. Nothing is innate. The work of writing is necessary.

Yet, what of this curious thing humanity calls a conscience? Locke attacks man's holiest faculty. More than any philosopher of his age, Locke immersed himself in ethnography and studied the habits, mores, and customs of foreign lands and people.[148] The more Locke learns of other people, the more he witnesses the flexibility of what people believe to be moral. He notes that areas in Asia place the desperately sick out to pasture to allow nature's elements to finish death's work, that the Mingrelians bury children alive, in other places folks practice cannibalism and atheism. If innate principles ordered the world and formed men's consciences, how could foreign lands practice such depravity?

But Locke knows that one need not look to foreign lands to understand humanity's questionable moral make up. All one needs is neighbors. By the action of men we know that consciences are too corruptible to assume people are born with the knowledge of right and wrong.[149] Life, family, and society form consciences. "Education, company, customs of their country" set the "conscience to work," and these forces prove capable of producing both light and darkness. He closes with confidence: "From what has been said, I think it past doubt, that there are no practical principles wherein all men agree; and therefore none innate."[150]

When Locke philosophizes in Book I of the *Essay*, he is playing a very practical game of chess.[151] Without innate ideas, the "*white* paper" of man's minds is erased of their traditioned ideas and a new work can begin. In Book I, Locke works to wipe out what folks think they know so that he can begin dictating the game on his own terms. Like a chess master, it is only after it is too late that the significance of his first moves are understood. When Locke moves his readers to question the trustworthiness of their own conscience, of that still and quite voice within their chest, he begins positioning for one final move before checkmating and wiping clean from men's minds everything that men thought they knew.

THE GOLD STANDARD

What becomes clear with hindsight is that as the *Essay* moves from Books I and II to Books III and IV, Locke's moves become increasingly practical as he looks to solidify and perpetuate a "rational" racializing of the world. Locke works to racialize the world by raising a question that those who went before him took for granted, and that question is: "What is a man?" Before Locke, we believed we recognized our shared humanity despite the diversity of skin colors within our world. But for Locke, someone's essential humanity is anything but obvious. For too long, he writes, we "do suppose of certain . . . essences of substances, which each individual . . . partakes of," we supposed that when we looked at an individual that they possessed essential ingredients that placed them within the family of humanity. Yet, what is the "real essence" of man Locke asks. The truth is, we do not know—and the "archetypes" that dictate our assumptions are "far from being adequate."[152]

Locke argues that we mentally order our world through our senses and outward appearances.[153] Yet outward appearances tell us nothing of "real essence." Locke repeatedly brings up this issue and repeatedly takes gold as his example of choice. You cannot tell gold by outward appearance alone; it must be examined, investigated, and purified. To accept as gold what merely looks like gold is to run the risk of treating fool's gold as precious. For Locke, we are fools *not* to question the humanity of those with darker tones of skin who may merely look human.

After raising doubt concerning the humanity of those with the outward marks of humanity, he requests that his readers take the author's word for it, *sit fides penes authorem,* a curious request coming from one in the Royal Society, but there are creatures in the world that look human but have "hairy tails" and women in West Africa who conceived the children of baboons. To protect himself from sounding absurd, Locke reminds his readers "we have reason to think this not impossible, since mules . . . from the mixture of an ass and a mare . . . are so frequent in the world."[154]

In the spring of 1783, General George Washington purchased *An Essay on Human Understanding.* In 1785, Washington started breeding mules and thus becoming "in addition to the Father of His Country . . . also revered in certain circles as the Father of the American Mule." His passion for slaves and mules makes it difficult to assume Locke's argument never came to his attention.[155]

Locke's racist lie promoted the central racist question: Should those with black skin, who look human but who might be fathered by baboons, be considered as human as those wearing white powered wigs? For Locke, it is a new question that is impossible to answer, for it is impossible to know the "real essence" of a man. But Locke need not answer *that* question for the "new question" to do the work on man's minds that it is designed to do. Locke simply needs to place in the minds' of men the question of whether or not Africans in general—and individual Africans in particular—who look human actually embody *the gold standard* of full humanity.[156]

In erasing man's minds of what they thought they knew, displaying the corruption of the conscience, and placing a question mark over those in non-white skin, we would anticipate that Locke desires to prepare the ground for moral relativity. But he was traveling in the opposite direction towards certainty. "I am bold to think," Locke proclaims, "that morality is capable of demonstration, as . . . mathematics."[157] Later, in the context of questioning the humanity of the mentally impaired and those born from intimacy with beasts, he insists on his surety in "the idea of whiteness," "mathematics," and "that moral knowledge is capable of real certainty."[158]

Locke was not tilling the ground to receive moral relativism. He tilled the ground to receive a racist imagination claiming certainty and superiority.

Nowhere does Locke's racial analysis touch ground more effectively than in Thomas Jefferson's analysis of slavery in *Notes on Virginia*. Jefferson's work plagiarizes Locke's logic. Jefferson uniquely roots white supremacy in white beauty, arguing that black sexual desire is for white flesh; but then he turns the Lockean corner by arguing that the sexual desire of "orangutans [is] for the black woman." Jefferson continues: "I advance it therefore as a suspicion only, that the blacks, whether originally a distinct race, or made distinct by time and circumstances, are inferior to the whites in the endowments both of body and mind. . . .Will not a lover of natural history then, one who views the gradations in all the races of animals with the eye of philosophy, excuse an effort to keep those in the department of man as distinct as nature has formed them?"[159] After reviewing Jefferson's writing on slavery, John Adams declares it "worth diamonds."[160]

As seen in Jefferson's plagiarism, Locke's racist lie and question that attempted to philosophically justify Exeter's aristocrats growing addiction to slavery proved successful. But despite Locke's genius, it is unlikely he imagined how important the gold standard would prove in solidifying inequity on *both* sides of the racial divide. On American soils, *the gold standard* provides the basic logic whereby the wealthy divide the cause of poor white folks from the cause of impoverished and enslaved brown and black folks. From Bacon's Rebellion to Make America Great Again, the question mark Locke places over the humanity of black lives proved powerful enough to separate the cause of poor folks along racial lines. In so doing, Locke's "new question" haunts all lives that are un-aristocratic.

The impact of the "new question" not only haunted religion, economics, and politics; Locke's question proved to be fuel for the fire of scientific inquiry. *Stamped from the Beginning* traces how *the* new question haunts the scientific community for centuries. In 1735, only sixty years after the *Essay*, Carl Linneus wrote *System Naturae*, and "took the lead classifying humanity into a racial hierarchy for the new intellectual and commercial age,"[161] plagiarizing Locke's philosophy in a scientific vernacular. Fast-forward another hundred plus years to 1859 and it was Darwin's *On the Origin of Species by Means of Natural Selection, or by Means of Preservation of Favoured Races in the Struggle for Life*. Only four years after Darwin's racist masterpiece, in 1863, Herbert Spencer improvises off of Darwin in *Principles of Biology* to coin the term "survival of the fittest." In 1869, the racist scientific baton passes to Sir Francis Galton, who moves the conversation one step forward in *Hereditary Genius* to pose *the* new question as "nature vs. nurture." Galton answers his own question, "nature is undefeated,"[162] and proposes a new practice—eugenics —for the annihilation of any humanity failing to reach the golden standard.[163] Yet, in 1871, Darwin again takes to answering *the new* question in a new way through the *Descent of Man*. Darwin writes in as simple of terms as possible: "The American aborigines, Negroes and Europeans differ as much from each other in mind as any three races that can be named." Kendi ends his analysis of the intersection of race and science with the human genome project where, when tested across racial lines, DNA results were 99.9 percent identical, only for the question of what exactly is the .1 percent to arise in racist minds.

In Locke's time, questioning the *essential essence* of Africans' humanity worked to justify the tool of slavery through which Exeter's elite looked to make their dominion more profitable. In our time, Locke's "new question" justifies our indifference to racial inequities. If black folk are more likely to go to jail, the "new question" becomes, Are they more criminal? If black folk are more likely to be un-employed, the "new question" becomes, Are they more lazy? If black schools underperform, the "new question" becomes, Are their children not as intelligent? Without even knowing black folks caught in the cycle of poverty, a racist imagination finds it all too easy to raise racist questions while never thinking of such questions as racist. This is the point: *when racial inequalities arise rather than question our racialized systems, it becomes common sense to question and interrogate the virtues of those our systems victimize.*

By the time Dred Scott stands before the U.S. Supreme Court in 1856, the white wigs no longer sit atop the heads of those in power on America's Supreme Court. Such style was deemed too English. But the sick question that Locke wrote on men's minds roams within the heads of the Justices—Do black lives meet the gold standard of full humanity and deserve basic human rights? Do black lives matter? Though by the time of Mr. Scott, the Supreme Court already conferred human rights to corporations, when it came to Mr. Scott the court answers that property cannot expect to be treated as human. Three-fifths human is just not human enough. From the Declaration of Independence and throughout the American experiment, white superiority acted as an unmentioned "self-evident" truth at the heart of too many of the Supreme Court's decisions.[164]

By making man's mind a blank piece of "white paper," by getting men to question their own conscience and the humanity of those without white skin, Locke has reached Tabula Rasa. Locke's philosophical game of chess reached checkmate. By philosophically making the quality of black humanity a question rather than an assumption, Locke is now positioned to begin writing new rules to institutionalize the slavemaster's myth into society's systems.

PROPERTY POLITICS

After declaring checkmate in the *Essay,* Locke's works move from *playing* chess to *rewriting* the rules of the game. The two pieces of the board that need the most refining are what I will refer to as society's king and queen—politics and religion. In Locke's world, as in ours, politics and religion provide the two most critical ingredients in a culture's worldview. By re-writing the way we understand the aims of politics and religion, Locke re-wrote how we interpret the daily grind for how our world works.

Before attending to Locke's re-writes, however, it is important to understand the rules of the game Locke inherited. In Locke's time, the historically rooted understanding of *religio* formed the imagination of the masses. In that imagination no sacred and secular dividing line existed. The idea of "religion" understood as private, universal, inward convictions and the idea of "politics" as a public and secular enterprise were not ideas in the heads of the common man. In Christendom, the job of kings and priests were interconnected and interdependent enterprises as both sought to shape and mold the character of a community within and without the churches' walls. Politics needed religion for direction and discipline—in order to pursue true and worthy ends of society. Religion, on the other hand, needed politics for meaningful and earthly expressions of its truths. Politics and *religio* were lovers needing one another for self-understanding and self-expression. Yet after Luther—in the times from which both Hobbes and Locke write—religious and political power players warred as only lovers can, and the paradigm that once held the Christian world together blew it asunder.

After the *Essay*, Locke is positioned to lawyer a divorce between the king and queen and to set the lovers free to seek self-fulfillment without the need for one another. The challenge to lawyering the divorce between religion and politics was two-fold. First, Locke needed to lay a "secular " foundation for politics that theological disputes could not upend *but* which a Christianized world could embrace. The second challenge was particular to those philosophers desiring to solidify the interests of the wealthy. This challenge was to envision a world order where the work of politics and religion harmonized with the interests of society's economically elite. It was by carefully crafting this harmony that the privileges of the aristocratic were institutionalized, rather than upended, in an otherwise decaying world order. Thus when Locke re-writes the rules of politics and religion, despite the liberal sentiments he engineers, he provides no voice for the slaves or the poor, for Locke and the powerbrokers thirsted for a thoroughly *aristocratic revolution*.

The idea Locke crafts to guide the divorce of politics and religion, and thus initiate the aristocratic revolution, is the creation of the ideology later named "the separation of church and state." Locke's writings lacked the drama of Luther hammering his ninety-five theses to the church door in Wittenberg, but through Locke's writings another and more formative reformation is born. Locke's writings erect a dividing wall between religion and politics, the sacred and the secular, by redefining the very nature of each so that never again shall the two meet. And, as it turns out, never again shall either reign.

We begin with the rules Locke writes for politics. After Hobbes persuaded the modern mind regarding what government *is not* about—namely the pursuit of the common good—it fell to Locke to take the next step and provide a very precise and limited definition for what government *is* about. Locke articulates his ideas concerning a new nature for government and the pursuit of politics in a *Second Treatise* and a *Letter Concerning Toleration*. These works are so well crafted and so formative to the modern political imagination that when we read Locke, we read what we already "know." Locke articulates the intentions of his *Second Treatise* as a work "of *necessity* [to] find out another rise of government, another original of political power, and *another way* of designing and knowing the persons."[165]

Despite Locke's explicit desire to move political philosophy in a different direction, Locke wisely begins by harmonizing his project with the piety of the people he seeks to persuade by readily accepting the cornerstone he inherited—a theological man. Humanity's origins are divine, "the workmanship of one omnipotent and infinitely wise maker."[166] And from the theologically orthodox cornerstone, Locke begins designing a new political orthodoxy by refocusing man's *aims* and energies. Like Hobbes, rather than looking to the heavens and setting political aims to harmonize with God's character as in the days of *religio*, Locke forces man to focus on things of earth, for "we are not born in heaven but in this world, where our being is to be preserved with meat, drink, and clothing, and other necessaries that are not born with us." Our necessities, he writes, "must be got and kept with forecast, care and labour, and therefore we cannot be all devotion, praises and hallelujahs."[167] And with this earthy practicality, *religio*'s subtle migration to the sideline of the modern political calculus continues in a way that makes sense even to a pious imagination.

But with God and the things of heaven no longer acting as the nucleus for man's political ambitions, a vacuum is created and a new nucleus and creed must be designed to organize man's efforts and ambitions. And in articulating this new nucleus and creed for political philosophy, Locke's philosophy becomes poetry for the practically minded, poetry later to inform the Declaration of Independence's introduction of "life, liberty and the pursuit of happiness." This is how Locke wordsmithed it: "Society of men [exists] *only* for the procuring, preserving, and advancing of their *own* civil interests," and then Locke's poetics that form the Declaration, "life, liberty . . . and the possession of outward things, such as *money, lands, houses*."[168] Locke could not say enough about the centrality of possession to politics. He continues: not only is property why we begin society, but "the chief *end*" of "civil society . . . is the preservation of property."[169]

Religio judged good politics by its harmony with God's character and society's care of the poor, orphan, and widow. Under *religio*, providing for the poor and pursuing some semblance of equity acted as key features of politics, but soon such pursuits for the sake of justice will be considered the greatest political sin of all. After Locke, the new measuring line for politics is humanity's ability to store up treasures on earth—"money, lands, houses." Once God was understood to be the beginning and the end of life together, but in a radical swap, property replaces such piety as the new nucleus of society. The aristocratic revolution begins, and society becomes possessed with the possession of "outward things." Property—rather than God—is politics' new nucleus, and preserving and accumulating property—rather than the pursuit of the common good—is society's new creed.

Organizing society around the goals of preserving and accumulating property rings as common-sense simplicity to those nurtured on the logic of capitalism, but in Locke's day such simplicity sounded a revolutionary ring. What made Locke's preservation of property a persuasive goal from the Christian tradition's alternative is that now one thing that government is no longer about is the salvation of souls. Caesar's job is simplified to protecting the sheep and their property from wolves and lions and tigers and bears.[170] In centering politics on property, government now provides the tolerance that peace and increased economic prosperity require, for "it is not the diversity of opinions, but the refusal of toleration to those that are of different opinions, that has produced all the bustles of wars that have been in the Christian world upon the religion."[171] By centering government on property, Locke works to lay a foundation for politics that theological arguments will not upend, creating a world with less potential for conflict and greater potential for peace—at least for those with sufficient property to meet life's necessities.[172]

But there was a much simpler appeal that made a government limited to protecting property much more alluring than Hobbes's Leviathan. The aristocratic possess no desire to serve a Leviathan; they desire a Leviathan that serves them. They desire a small government that preserves their property and protects them as they labor to accumulate more. These simplistic political goals translate to the desire for a small government with a big military. And that is just what Locke gives them.[173]

Since Locke's vision became common sense to many Americans, we are tempted to lose its revolutionary nature and how it upended almost all political logic that preceded it. In mathematical terms, making the preservation of property the nucleus reverses the order of operations. No longer are aristocrats subservient to kings nor are they allies in providing for the needs of the masses. Henceforth, kings and the masses serve the aristocrats. In changing the order of political math, the fundamental aim of politics is radically reduced. The good of those with property becomes the only good the government ensures, while the best interest of the people as a whole no longer possesses even a theoretical preference in the political process.

Locke's aristocratic revolution leads directly to the American Revolution. It was Locke's conviction concerning the sacredness of property that led him to declare: "If any one shall claim a *power to lay* and levy *taxes* on the people . . . without such consent of the people, he thereby invades the *fundamental law of property,* and subverts the end of government: for what property have I in that, which another may by right take, when he pleases, to himself?"[174] Inspired, our forefathers sloganeered Locke's philosophies to the quip of "No taxation without representation" in order to get the common folk to join them in their revolt from England. The solution our forefathers sold to the tyranny of taxation without representation was, in Lincoln's Gettysburg words, a "government of the people, by the people, and for the people." Yet in true Lockean fashion, our democracy was crafted for the propertied not for the people. It was no accident that voting rights were restricted to white male landowners, that the first president of the United States was one of the nation's wealthiest slaveholders, and only 1.6 percent of the population cast a vote. America embodied the aristocratic nature of the revolution Locke envisioned.

As time passed, Locke's nucleus only grew stronger and property more holy in the minds of those committed to a politics designed to harmonize with the interests of society's wealthiest. Perhaps no one proved a better prophet of Locke's vision of politics for the propertied than the beloved President Ronald Reagan. Reagan radicalized the Republican conviction that the role of government was to move out of the way of those attempting to make a buck and to carry a big stick to keep everyone else in line. Reagan radicalized the conviction that the government could do no good for the poor—he even invented a mythical welfare queen to display the dangers of the government intervening on behalf of the poor.[175] "The nine most terrifying words in the English language are: I'm from the government and I'm here to help,"[176] Reagan declared with his trademark refined rhetoric.

Under Reagan's watch, the top tax rates plummeted from 70 percent when he entered office to 28 percent when he exited.[177] Simultaneously to taxes on the wealthy nose-diving, spending on the military exploded—embodying Eisenhower's worst fears concerning the military industrial complex—and the War on Drugs drastically expanded the prison population and expenses. Despite Reagan's war on welfare, the national debt increased an incredible 128%. Unsurprisingly, as national debt dramatically increased so too did the wealth filling the nation's deepest pockets. The rich got richer as the nation grew poorer. A new era of economic and racial inequality was inaugurated. By and large, the next four Presidents (two Republicans and two Democrats) harmonized their policies with Reagan's revolution.

By 2010, the top 1 percent accumulated more than twice as much wealth as the bottom 90 percent of the nation combined.[178] That type of accumulation and dispossession never happens on accident. That type of accumulation required the political will, focus, and intentionality of a rhetorically brilliant politician.

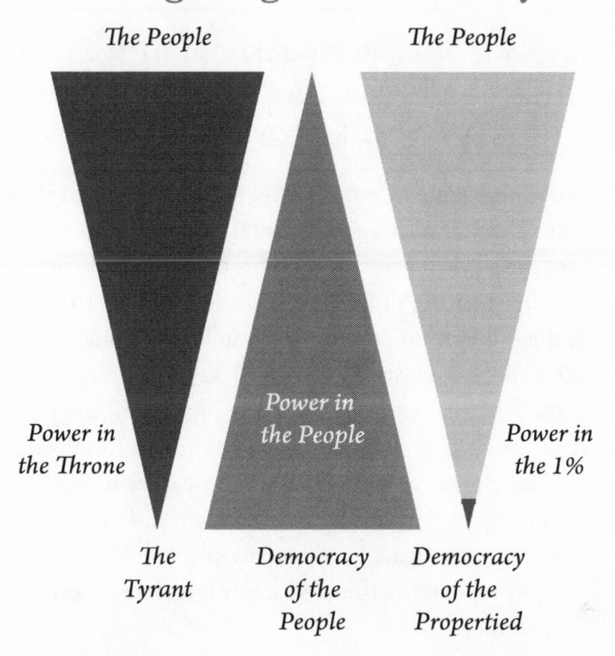

Now, four decades into Reagan's promise of trickle-down economics, as millionaires became billionaires, as too many black folk sat in for-profit prisons for nonviolent offenses, the trickle down has yet to rain down wealth on the poor as Reagan promised. Unsurprisingly still, the dissonance between his promises of wealth and the predicament of the poor has proved to trouble Reagan's followers not at all.

But before there was Reagan's Republican revolution there was John Locke's aristocratic revolution. We started this section discussing the great divorce between society's political king and religious queen. Perhaps we should be unsurprised that the terms of such a divorce revolved around property. After the dust settles, neither politicians nor priests rule the world in the same way again. The game became even more about property and power passed from political and religious institutions to corporations. By politicians pretending to be powerless to help, we learned to expect nothing, embrace inequity, and believe that accumulation and dispossession were random and unrelated realities. For Locke, the work of the aristocratic revolution is just beginning. The next step is making the accumulation he aspires to appear to be in harmony with the dictates of justice; he must make the aristocracy look like a meritocracy.

THE CREATION OF THE ONE PERCENT: HOW THE MODERN ARISTOCRACY LEARNED TO POSE AS A MERITOCRACY

Locke understood the value of inheritance. His father passed shortly after his Oxford years and left him a small rental property that provided him protection from the poverty that plagued his close Puritan companion Sir Isaac Newton. After making property the nucleus of government, Locke's intimacy with the difference between plenty and not enough inspired him to further protect the aristocratic from the threats of poverty by working to justify unmitigated accumulation. It is one thing to posit the preservation of property as the nucleus of politics; it is quite another to valorize the citizen who accumulates great wealth in a land of great want. But Locke valorizes just such citizens. Since Locke sells his system through the rhetoric of *equality*,[179] justifying unmitigated accumulation required nifty philosophical footwork, requiring making the aristocracy look like a meritocracy, and so Locke starts to dance.

In keeping with an aristocratic revolution, Locke seeks to justify accumulation by harmonizing it with piety. Locke builds his argument from Paul's writing in 1 Timothy: "God has given us all richly." Why, Locke asks, did God give to us richly? The answer is obvious: "To enjoy." We should feel free to enjoy "as much as any one can make use of to any advantage of life before it spoils: whatever is beyond this, is more than his share, and belongs to others. Nothing was made by God for man to spoil or destroy."[180] Before society is organized, man must be satisfied with moderate portions—for that was the only way to ensure that the resources of God's good earth are not left to rot. Articulating a vision that finds easy harmony with the heralded Protestant work ethic, Locke places a high value on work and argues that the rise of wealth is directly related to the sweat of one's brow and the stewardship of God's good creation. Want not waste not. This is how Locke begins to provide the illusion that aristocratic wealth traces back to a merit-based system.[181]

But since the work that is needed is an explanation of wealth, of accumulation, and why such accumulation is just in a world whose poor live on the brink, Locke cannot stay pious for long. His argument is essentially this: since currency does not spoil, the accumulation of it, even in a society with the hungry, naked, and homeless, is not incongruent with the goodness of God's designs for a flourishing creation. "It is plain," writes Locke, "that men have agreed to a disproportionate and *unequal possession of the earth*, they having, by a tacit and voluntary consent, found out, a way how a man may fairly possess more land than he himself can use the product of, by receiving in exchange for the overplus gold and silver, which *may be hoarded up without injury to any one*; these metals not spoiling or decaying in the hands of the possessor."[182] In Locke's mind, the advent of currency brings an end to the era of unjust overindulgence, after currency hoarding of the wealthy hurts not the hungry. It is a terrible argument that requires great ignorance regarding the plight of the poor. Yet it is an argument that is just beginning and gets worse.

As Locke continues to write, hoarding for a lifetime becomes insufficient and a system emerges intentionally designed to allow hoarding for generations. In the Lockean imagination, the passing on of wealth from one generation to the next through inheritance provides the glue that binds together the passing generations. To keep an aristocratic world running required converting aristocratic children to the aristocratic way. Rather than muscling his aristocratic philosophies on future generations, Locke incentivizes: "if they will enjoy the *inheritance* of their ancestors, they must take it on the same terms their ancestors had it."[183] Where a parent's persuasion failed, inheritance provided leverage to coerce the child to accept ways of their forefathers' world that their conscience desired to reject. After making preservation of property society's beginning and ending, inheritance provided the means for the aristocrats to perpetuate their power within society.

Yet, the centrality of inheritance and the unmitigated passing of wealth from one generation to the next set in motion a system of generational wealth whereby wealth becomes more removed from labor with each and every passing generation.[184] Thus, with the passing of each generation in Locke's land of equality, freedom, and liberty, genealogy becomes a more precise indicator of wealth and potential for wealth than one's labor. The logical result of a system that protects, accumulates, and passes forward wealth unmitigated by a sense of justice is the institutionalization of both privilege and poverty.

Despite the veneer of the Protestant work ethic, Locke's scheme places labor and wealth on disparate train tracks. As Locke's philosophy continues to increase its strength, the rich create a rhetoric that demonizes the entitlement of the poor without realizing the irony that it is not the poor that are haunted by issues of entitlement but the wealthy.[185] Through inheritance, Locke engineers a system clearly designed to make wealth hereditary rather than wrought from one's labor. Through inheritance, wealth that begins in labor stays in the meritocracy even when the ones holding it are generations removed from the labor that generated it. That is how aristocracy poses as meritocracy.

On American soils, it was James Madison—whose wealth derived from his father and from his slaves—who championed equating wealth with merit in the transformative *Federalist Papers*. Madison argued that inequality of property originates with "the diversity in the faculties of men." For Madison, "an abolition of debt [and] an equal division of property" was "a wicked project" that threatened a merit-based nation. The perpetuation of slavery and radical generational inequality was no problem for Madison.[186]

Currency, in the powerful imagination of Locke, acts as a just and judicious symphony conductor able to harmonize the realities of accumulation and poverty into melodious performance. Locke is not well remembered for the argument that after currency the rich hoard "without injury to any one," for it is an argument that takes a remarkable amount of ignorance to ring true.

Nonetheless, Locke's a brilliant theoretician. In centering political society on the preservation and accumulation of property, he provided a place at the table for everyone in society with wealth and a self-justifying calculus to make decisions in the best interest of those with seats. By making the wealthy look like society's worthy and the poor look like society's problem—more of that in a moment—a worldview arises where the prosperous are imagined as society's saints and the poor as society's sinners. Even to good-hearted folks, it makes sense to design a politics that rewards society's worthy and punishes people deemed society's problem. It proves a difficult myth to demythologize, especially among good-hearted folks who love saints and hate sin.

At every turn that Locke re-writes the rules of politics, he labors to harmonize his system with the interest of the wealthy and the interest of the wealthy with one another. In so doing, Locke protects his political system from *internal* strife. But to protect his proposed politics from *external* strife required rewriting the rules for society's queen, the *religious institutions*. Like Hobbes who went before him, Locke needed to write his system on the hearts of the masses at large and convince the populace that centering political energies on property and allowing for unmitigated accumulation was in harmony, not simply with the ways of the world, but with the gospel itself.

A TAILOR MADE FAITH: HARMONIZING RACISM WITH CHRISTIAN RELIGION

Locke receives his fair share of credit for forming American political ideologies, but like the other members of the philosophical "trinity," it is too often overlooked how his ideas about the nature of "true religion" crafted a uniquely American Christianity. Just as Locke marked a new trajectory for political theory by making property the nucleus of political life, so too did he mark a new trajectory for Christianity by re-writing the rules of religion, rules that crafted a filter to provide the faithful with a purer and truer religion. The first lie of American Christianity was written by Hobbes, which said that we need no relationship with the broken and abused to relate to Christianity's God who himself was broken and abused. It falls to Locke to perfect the second lie, reducing true religion to salvation. Locke's lie proved critical in crafting a religion in America that could harmonize with the nation's original and ongoing racial injustices. Locke begins writing a new rulebook for society's religious queen.

Locke sought a seductive style when writing on Christianity, a style that placed the mask of simplicity on the face of sophistication. In Locke's words that introduce *The Reasonableness of Christianity*: "The little satisfaction and consistency . . . in most of the systems of divinity . . . made me betake myself *to the sole reading of the scriptures . . . for the understanding the Christian Religion*."[187] Locke's implied superior simplicity unleashes a revolutionary understanding of the Christian faith precisely by ignoring Christian tradition and her "systems of divinity" that made theology a complicated thing overly intermingled with political power. Via this supposed simplicity, Locke's writings work to provide his readers an "unbiased" understanding of religion and a reading of Scripture that points Christianity in a direction more in keeping with its "true" nature.

However, in a cunning way Locke's "simplistic" reading performs political work precisely by making faith an *a-political* notion. The general foundation for his theological project was already well laid in the aforementioned *A Letter Concerning Toleration.*[188] In this writing, Locke's piety bleeds through page after page, and his unorthodox sincerity begins molding what in many ways became the paradigmatic way of understanding religion in modernity. Since the marriage between church and state brought out the demons rather than the better angels of both partners, Locke writes as clearly as possible: "The *only* business of the Church is the salvation of souls; and *it no way* concerns the commonwealth, or any member of it."[189] For Locke, the best way forward for the church was to focus her investments on personal piety and to remove itself from politics; it was to address things celestial and ignore things civil. Since Christianity was unskilled in bringing the things of heaven to earth through politics, Christian thinkers and practitioners should focus exclusively on their forte—getting people's souls from earth to heaven through the proclamation of an a-political Christianity.

Making salvation not simply central but definitive concerning the "isness" of Christianity was another brilliant move for Locke. It is an insufficient interpretation both historically and exegetically, but it proves ridiculously persuasive.[190] In many ways, what property was for politics, salvation becomes for religion. However, rather than salvation acting as a nucleus, it acts as a filter. By making eternal salvation the filter through which "true religion" passes, Locke strains out both Christendom's vices as well as anything that challenges his political vision or the aristocratic way of life.

With a filter in place, Locke works with efficiency and precision in testing what *true* Christianity *is* or *is not* by that which *is* or *is not* integral to salvation. For Locke, the heartbeat of Christianity is the original impulse that leads individuals into the church's communion. As Locke says in *A Letter:* "The hopes of salvation, as it was the only cause of his entrance into that communion, so it can be the only reason of his stay there."[191] Man, according to Locke, enters into Christian communion not for the beloved community on earth—with no longer Jew or Gentile, slave nor free, male nor female and none in need—but for the salvation of the soul and a heavenly home.

"All the life and power of true religion," Locke continues, "consists in the inward and full persuasion of the mind; and faith is not faith without believing."[192] The power of Christianity resides in the believers' innards, in the truths of the gospel resonating with their intellectual capacities in a manner where the truths of the faith harmonize with man's rationality producing sincere belief. Religion without inward persuasion of the mind and faith without belief reduces the Christian message into a military drill whose drum major is not God but the expectations of man. And no one whose aim is simply to please man can please God. "Faith only, and inward sincerity, are the things that procure acceptance with God."[193]

Locke got many things right concerning the nature of Christianity, and not simply by naming faith's legitimate ingredients but even more so by identifying what in Christendom is not Christian. Christianity "is not instituted in order to the exercising of external pomp," wrote Locke, "nor to the exercising of compulsive force."[194] Jesus rode an ass in Jerusalem, and faith inspired by such a savior rejects the pomp of Pilate and the haughtiness of Herod and instead embraces the meekness of Mary and the gentility of John. The Apostles lived as sheep in a slaughterhouse. The Savior held onto his wounds and took on the likeness of a slain lamb.[195] The disciple that attempted to use force to bring God's kingdom was not John or Peter; it was Judas. Christ's style was self-sacrifice, his weapon was nothing more or less than gospel truth, and his power to persuade had everything to do with the truths his life incarnated and nothing to do with violence. What we learn through the cross is that the sword of Caesar may have the power to slay God's Son, but it does not possess the power to establish God's kingdom. If Christians "sincerely desired the good of souls, they would . . . follow the perfect example of that prince of peace who sent out his soldiers . . . not armed with the sword, or other instruments of force, but prepared with the gospel of peace."[196]

And on these points Locke's critique of Christendom is thoroughly Christian and finds an easy harmony with both Christianity's greatest critics and greatest prophets. He critiques the logics of Christendom simply by pointing to Christ. To this point Locke is perhaps moving a modern understanding of Christianity closer to its ancient origins. But since Locke's aim was creating an a-political Christianity for modern man, he moves his argument forward from humility, sincerity, and peace to the relationship of Christianity and property. For Locke, if the gospel is about salvation then it is not about property and does not "either advantage or prejudice the life, liberty, or estate of any man." For Locke, property acts as the great dividing line between the political and the religious. These were the terms of the divorce: everything involving property is politics and runs by a worldly-wise logic that ensures property is preserved for the propertied; everything other than property is religious and runs by a logic that ensures salvation for the earnest seeker.

By making property a dividing line, Locke runs not simply against the corrupted ways of Christendom, but against the entire prophetic tradition of Scripture. In the mind of the prophet, property, at least in some measure, acted as a medium for participating with God in the redemption of the world by providing a balm for the poor through the acts of self-sacrifice, justice, and compassion. For the prophets, the heart of politics and true religion resided in the needs of the most vulnerable. In the prophetic tradition, to refuse to speak of religion in terms of property, to refuse to speak of religion in terms of widows, orphans, and the poor, was to refuse to seriously discuss religion at all; it was to trade "true religion" for its opposite—*sentimentality*. "True Religion," according to the prophets, involved protecting God's children from a world with no respect for the human dignity of the dispossessed.

The Prophetic vs. The Modern Imagination

The Prophetic Imagination	The Modern Imagination
True Religion: ...to look after ***orphans*** and ***widows*** in their distress and to keep oneself from being polluted by the world	**True Religion:** Things of ***Salvation*** and ***Heaven***
Property: ***A Meeting Point***	**Property:** ***The Great Dividing Line***
Government: He will judge...your ***afflicted*** ones with justice...He will defend the afflicted among the people and save the ***children*** of the ***needy***; he will crush the oppressor....	**Government:** The ***Preservation*** of ***Property***

Attacking cultural Christianity is easy—just point to Scripture and Christ. Attacking the prophets requires work. The only way to overcome the force of the prophets' commandment "to do justly and to love mercy" or the gospel's teaching that "when you have done it to the least of these you have done it me," is to convince readers they "know" that Christianity is an "a-political" thing *before* the Bible is investigated. This is precisely what Locke seeks to do—to train Christians *not to see* the political ramifications of Scripture by training them to know Christianity is a-political *before* they investigate the Bible.

An example of this training occurs in his tract *The Reasonableness of Christianity*. One of the most significant passages in *Reasonableness* concerns the relationship between Paul, Moses, and the law. Locke writes: "When St. Paul says, that the gospel establishes the law, he means the *moral* part of the law of Moses; for that *he could not mean* the . . . political part of it."[197] By determining what Paul can and cannot mean, Locke takes the wheel to steer the religious imagination away from the very writers of the biblical text and creates a paradigm of interpretation that spiritualizes away political implications. In short order, Christians begin to approach

How Locke Reduced the Spectrum of Christian Virtues

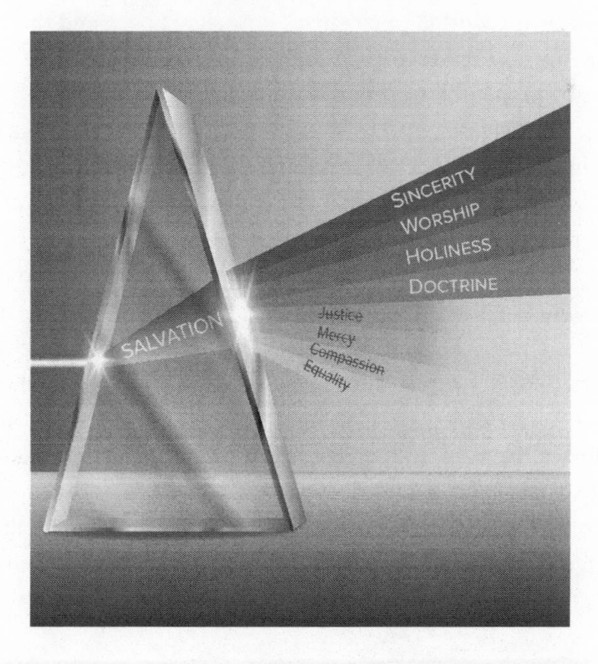

Scripture already convinced of its apolitical nature and in so doing read Holy Writ through the a-political spectacles Locke placed on their noses.

And with Locke's spectacles on their noses, the virtues of Christianity quickly reduce to virtues that harmonize with the aristocratic way of life. Locke writes that the church was instituted, at least in part, "to the regulating of men's lives according to the rules of virtue and piety." The Christian must "make war on his own lusts and vices [and pursue] holiness of life, purity of manners, and benignity and meekness of spirit."[198] Holiness, purity and meekness spirit, this is where Christianity's accent falls. And though such virtues need not be tainted and are integral to Christianity from its inception, the spectrum of virtues has been limited.

A conversion in what Christ-likeness consists of occurs, and no longer does the fear of God, poverty, brokenness, and suffering display a likeness with a crucified messiah. Christlikeness now is limited to those virtues of piety and purity that harmonize with the moral calculus of the aristocratic elite. No room for social justice is left. And just as the virtues of the prophetic tradition—justice, equity, compassion—are written out of Locke's Christianity, so too are such virtues written out of the cultural Christianity that follows in his wake. When one reads James's declaration that the "religion that God our Father accepts as pure and faultless is this: to look after orphans and widows in their distress *and* to keep oneself from being polluted by the world," one realizes how slyly Locke and the American Christianity he inspired retain the ancient desire for piety while distancing themselves from the prophet's desire for justice.

Reducing "true religion" to soul salvation brought an end to the prophetic tradition in America's white churches. Locke's understanding of true religion is foreign to the Bible, but it was central to separation of church and state that Locke needed to get his aristocratic revolution going.[199] In Locke's rendering, the separation of church and state flow from the two natures of each. The state is about preservation of property. The church is about soul salvation.

In time, Locke proves more persuasive than the prophetic tradition he replaced. White American Christians learned to read Scripture without learning to see the poor and persecuted through the eyes of Isaiah, Jesus, or the early church. It is a tragic irony that when it comes to de-prioritizing the pursuit of justice for the poor and minorities, today's godfathers of conservative Christianity—Jerry Falwell Jr., James Dobson, and Franklin

Graham—find an easier harmony with John Locke, the father of liberalism, than the prophets, Christ, or the biblical texts.

Though conservative Christians learned to question Locke's separation of church and state after the fall of segregation, the re-politicization of white Christianity proved anything but a revival of the prophetic tradition. Conservative Christian politics reduced their thinking to "single issue" voting and in so doing produced a voting block incapable of three-dimensional thinking that incoporates the suffering of black and brown humanity into its political calculus. Instead of learning from King and the Prophetic Black Church, white Christians began their own political operation that ran in the opposite direction and wondered why black folks refused to jump on board.

HARMONIZING RACISM WITH THE GOSPELS

JERRY FALWELL JR. FRANKLIN GRAHAM JAMES DOBSON

Just as the courthouse proved capable of ignoring the very humanity of Dred Scott, so too did the church influenced by Locke consistently find itself on the wrong side of history regarding the rights, dignity, and value of those possessing non-white skin. From Jonathan Edwards to Dwight Moody[200] to today's conservative Christian godfathers, few racial injustices existed with which the majority of white Christian leaders could not find contentment.[201] "Of all forms of negro hate in this world," said Frederick Douglass after a visit from Dwight Moody, "save me from that one which clothes itself with the name of loving Jesus."[202]

Around the age of 14, Edwards absorbed Locke's work at Yale with "more satisfaction and pleasure in studying it, than the most greedy miser in gathering up handsful of silver and gold from some new discovered treasure." At 27, Edwards used 40 percent of his early salary to purchase a young girl named Venus. On the back of his receipt of purchase, he penned a sermon.[203]

After Locke, prophets just weren't what they used to be. As in the parable of the Good Samaritan so long ago, when black folks found themselves in the ditch of white repression, more often than not white preachers passed by on the far side of the street. Yet, for those under the influence of white Christian leaders, seeing how reducing religion to loving on Jesus and private and inward dispositions was designed to harmonize with racist instincts were not easy dots to connect. Locke's success in laying the groundwork for the separation of church and state came from forming a theological-philosophical system that worked as smooth as clockwork, with multiple movements happening simultaneously and so seamlessly that the smoothness of the system made Locke's system seem innocuous. In fact, centering politics on property and religion on salvation seemed humanitarian in comparison to the terror Christendom had unleashed upon Europe.

Yet underneath the humanitarian face of liberalism's secular and spiritual clocks, the gears grinded out the humanity of children, poor folks, and slaves. Our failure to see the dehumanizing work of Locke's project was not the result of Locke not making such work transparent. Indeed, the suffering of children, the poor, and slaves was as explicit as it was integral to Locke's project and the rules he wrote.

SMILING FACES TELL LIES: ON SENTIMENTALISM AND SLAVERY

In one of Hobbes's more famous passages, he describes the relationship of parent to child as "absolute subjection." Parents are freed to "alienate" their children "by selling, giving them up in adoption or servitude to others . . . kill them for rebellion, or sacrifice them for peace."[204] Thank God Hobbes died a bachelor. Locke's relationship to the poor, their children, and the slave followed Hobbes's footsteps. Yet, what made Locke's work more influential was that he disguised the ruthless management of the poor and the enslaved as a rational response to the vice of the impoverished and as a means for their redemption. For Locke, the powerful's ruthlessness was but humanitarianism and justice at work.

To place the work on the poor and the slave in proper perspective, we will get our bearings on Locke's convictions concerning the children of the wealthy. In *Some Thoughts on Education,* Locke distills for his readers "a just treatise of education, suited to our English gentry."[205] Locke writes not simply from his experiences of tutoring at Oxford, but from his responsibilities over the children at Exeter House. It becomes clear that Locke's role as a tutor made him a keen observer of the ways of children and the proper methods for how to mold them for "a gentleman's calling." Rather than a public education for all, Locke envisioned an education for the wealthy that centered in the household and was aided by the helpful hands of tutors. He offers comprehensive guidance that encompasses exercise, sleep, diet, and clothing. Locke believes that education needs to aim at fostering adolescents' habits of industry and self-control while also protecting the spunk so critical in the life of children.

In classical style, Locke says the tutor is "to fashion the carriage, and form the mind; to settle in his pupil good habits and the principles of virtue and wisdom; to give him by little and little a view of mankind, and work him into a love and imitation of what is excellent and praise-worthy."[206] But if his classical goal is not remarkable, his rejection of corporeal punishment is. Locke continually sides against harsh discipline and chiding: "Lavish and corporal punishments, are not the discipline fit to be used in the education of those we would have wise, good, and ingenuous men."[207] Locke's abhorrence of violence is poignantly registered in his remarks concerning children who "torment and treat roughly young birds, butterflies and such poor animals [which will] by degrees harden their minds even towards men . . . Children should from the beginning be bred up in an abhorrence of killing or tormenting any living creature."[208] *Some Thoughts on Education* provides a gentle hand to foster the wealthy folks' children into well-formed adults and offers a vision in harmony with progressive educational methods still in use today.

But if Locke proved prophetic in educational methodologies, it is clear that education is not to provide mingling between social classes. In *Some Thoughts Concerning Education,* Locke protects class delineations within the household of the well-off as he seeks to ensure that children are kept from bad company and from the pernicious influence of servants who might corrupt their bourgeois upbringing by drink, language, and the display of *too much* compassion and affection for children after they receive discipline.

If *Some Thoughts Concerning Education* provides Locke's vision for the aristocratic and their children, his *Essay on the Poor Law*[209] provides the definitive vision for those of all ages outside the aristocratic circle. Locke diagnoses the problem of the growing poverty and the burden that the impoverished placed on the wider public. The problem was neither scarcity nor opportunity, for God had provided plenty; "the growth of the poor must therefore have some other cause, and it can be nothing else but the relaxation of discipline and corruption of manners." Rather than leavening his work to consider any vices of the aristocratic, whose hoarding he elsewhere labored to justify, Locke equates earthly poverty to moral poverty and argues that the singular problem of the poor is the poverty of their character. It is a socially thin understanding of the times, but for those without social depth perception it becomes the paradigmatic interpretation of the predicament of poverty in modern society. Again, it is a difficult myth to demythologize.

Alexander Hamilton not only brings contract theory to America, but introduces child labor to American manufacturing with a sentimentality remarkably similar to John Locke's. Hamilton's *Report on Manufactures*: "In general, women and Children are rendered more useful and the latter more early useful by manufacturing establishments, than they would otherwise be . . . [In] Cotton Manufactories of Great Britain, it is computed that 4/7 nearly are women and children; . . . many of them of a very tender age."[210]

Locke writes that poor vagabonds are to be "seized" and shipped to workhouses or indentured servitude on "his majesty's ships." The work on the poor began early. Children of the poor above the "age of three" were to be gathered into workhouses and, like their parents, they were to be "soundly whipped" if their enthusiasm for work failed to meet the expectations of their overseers. "By this means," the father of liberalism wrote, "the mother will be eased of a great part of her trouble in looking after and providing for them at home, and so be at the more liberty to work; the children will be kept in much better order, be better provided for, and from infancy be inured to work." And, of course, forced church attendance of the workhouses was of no small benefit to Locke. Through workhouses and churches, the children of the poor were to be purified from their paganism and fitted for their proper place in society. "Whereas ordinarily now," Locke feared, "in their idle and loose way of breeding up, they are as utter strangers both to religion and morality as they are to industry."[211]

In Hobbes, the ruthless management of the masses ensured society's security. In Locke, ruthless management of the poor promoted an industrious society and soul salvation. The Protestant work ethic and Christian charity combined and began taking a dubious course. Yet, as incompatible as seizing the poor and their children were in a land declaring liberty and freedom, such realities were not the most discordant ones produced by centering politics on property and reducing religion to soul salvation. The most discordant reality Locke's sentimentalism produced resided in the relationship between slave and slave master.

Locke's liberal ideologies failed to end slavery simply because slavery was the very institution all liberal institutions were designed to protect. Slavery was, after all, a profitable institution for much of liberalism's brain trust, and in slavery resided the hopes of unlocking the potential fortunes of the colonies.[212] Rather than liberal ideologies challenging the chains and shackles of slavery, Locke's liberalism labored to make such chains and shackles all the firmer by making them look like the very evidence of the power of justice in modern society.

Locke employed currency to justify accumulation, but when it came to slavery he required a more austere tool to harmonize the claims of equality with accepting the reality of slavery. The tool Locke chooses is the tool humanity turns to when no arguments work and no reasoning proves persuasive. What Locke turns to is war. "This is the perfect condition of *slavery,*" writes Locke, "which is nothing else, but *the state of war continued, between a lawful conqueror and a captive.*" Locke places the slave on the block for examination and begins philosophizing: "*slaves,* who being captives taken in a just war, are by the right of nature subjected to the absolute dominion and arbitrary power of their masters." Here is the tragic irony: real wars between European power failed to justify the slavery of Europeans, while a mythical war justified the slavery of Africans. Over time, such tragic ironies become constitutive of liberal sentimentality.

Rather than seeking the details of slavery's origins, Locke seeks to justify its perpetuation. He continues: "These men having, as I say, forfeited their lives, and with it their liberties, and lost their estates; and being in the *state of slavery,* not capable of any property, cannot in that state be considered as any part of *civil society*; the chief end whereof is the preservation of property."[213] Before the Lockean lady of justice, a slave's place in society is defined by the possessions he lacks rather than the humanity that the Lockean mind learned to question. Slaves, for Locke, are not to be pitied nor viewed as victims, but as the provocateurs of their predicament. "Indeed," writes Locke to buttress his argument, "having by his fault forfeited his own life, by some act that deserves death; he, to whom he has forfeited it, may (when he has him in his power) delay to take it, and make use of him to his own service, and he does him no injury by it."

For Locke, slavery is the consequence of an unjust war waged against too strong of a people; it is the lived reality of war's aftermath where the just reign over the unjust, the righteous warriors over the unrighteous perpetrators. Slavery is not a stumbling block for a just and liberal society, but an embodied and living testimony to both the power and justice of the slavemaster's society. Locke is no moral relativist; the humanitarian who wouldn't hurt a fly still needed the readiness to crucify slaves, for such readiness was critical to the industriousness of the aristocratic way of life.

And just as slaves are complicit in the origins of their slavery, so too are slaves complicit in the perpetuation of their slavery, for a slave can end slavery at any point they desire: "For whenever he finds the hardship of his slavery outweigh the value of his life, it is in his power, by resisting the will of his master, to draw on himself the death he desires."[214] In *A Second Treatise* Locke's realism lacks even an airbrushed sentimentality. Slaves find their freedom shackled between two options, either perfect submission to the slavemaster's "perfectly despotical"[215] reign or *suicide*. Reducing freedom to surrender or suicide is the demented endpoint of the work property rights performed on the dispossessed.

Nonetheless, over this brutality comes the mask of humanitarianism through Christian inclusivity. Before it was trendy, Locke foresaw the necessity of a multicultural church and writes the need of such a church into *The Constitution of South Carolina*. "Since charity obliges us to wish well to the souls of all men," Locke writes in the *Constitution* "and *religion ought to alter nothing in any man's civil estate* or right, it shall be lawful for slaves, as well as others, to enter themselves, and be of what church or profession any of them shall think best, and, therefore, be as fully members as any freeman." As if his point was not clear enough, Locke clarifies: "But yet no slave shall hereby be exempted from that civil dominion his master hath over him, but be in all things in the same state and condition he was in before. Every freeman of Carolina shall have absolute power and authority over his Negro slaves, of what opinion and religion soever."[216] In Locke's calculus, after a Christian slavemaster led their slaves' souls to salvation, they are once again free to place them on the cross of slavery.

In the American experiment, as in Locke, sentimental and superficial approaches to society's deepest problems empower a fundamentally sadistic worldview. Slavery displayed the perversion made possible through a sentimental society so thoroughly preoccupied with its property that it failed to see the humanity of those whose suffering paved the way for their wealth. The church became so infatuated with soul salvation that it was uninterested in the humanity of those it evangelized.

Though Locke's influence looked different after the fall of the slave trade, society's linking together of a person's value with their wealth, and religious institutions' readiness to overlook the predicaments of the oppressed they seek to convert, still haunts the American imagination at a deeply subconscious level. Just as the logic of sentimental sadism was written not only on the lived lives of Exeter's elites but into the institutions they inspired, so too is such logic and sentimentalism deeply interwoven in the very lives we live and in the institutions in which we participate. Too often American sentimentalism makes it impossible to cultivate the political will, intelligence, and imagination required to face the realities our institutions fostered. Thus, in a land committed to justice and equality, injustices roll on like rivers and inequities like never-failing streams.

Jefferson's sentimentalism expressed itself in his desire to eradicate slavery either after his lifetime or beyond Virginia's borders. On March 1, 1784, when Congress fell one vote short of banning slavery in territory northwest of the Ohio River, Jefferson lamented: "Thus we see the fate of millions unborn hanging on the tongue of one man, and heaven was silent in that awful moment," without shedding a tear for the slaves at his Monticello plantation.

WILLIE LYNCH & VIRGINIAN LUXURIES

If the purchase of slave-trading stock provided Locke's first *economic* investment into slavery, *The Fundamental Constitution of the Carolinas* provided Locke's first *political* investment into the colonies. It would not, however, be the last. Beginning in 1696, Locke was elected to the Board of Trade, and his focus centered on Virginia over the next four years. His fingerprint would be felt as Virginia harmonized his sentimentality and sadism as much as any colony in the world.

In 1712, on Christmas Day eight years after the passing of John Locke, Willie Lynch came to Virginia with a Christmas message. Lynch was highly educated, almost erudite. He spoke of the necessity of psychology and a long-range economic plan to make slavery as profitable as possible. The letter Lynch shares on the banks of the James River proves a difficult read, for it possesses Lynch's insights concerning a "scientific" process for breaking slaves and ensuring their servitude for generations. It will be like "breaking a horse," he promises. But Lynch's method is more barbaric than anything horses ever endured.

Step one: the male slave. "Take the meanest and most restless nigger, strip him of his clothes in front of the remaining male niggers, the female, and the nigger infant, tar and feather him, tie each leg to a different horse faced in opposite directions, set him a fire and beat both horses to pull him apart in front of the remaining nigger."

James Madison's neighbor Thomas Chew improvised off of Lynch's methods by burning a slave named Eve alive. After relating how Chew burnt Eve alive, Madison's preeminent biographer Ralph Ketcham relates "another bloody deed [of Madison's community]. . . a court order to exhibit the head of an executed slave on a pole, and [named] a brook Niggerhead Run."[217]

Step two: the female slave. "Take the female and run a series of tests on her to see if she will submit to your desires willingly. Test her in every way, because she is the most important factor for good economics. If she shows any sign of resistance in submitting completely to your will, do not hesitate to use the bullwhip on her to extract that last bit of resistance out of her." In case Lynch's audience didn't realize that men's will included sexual desire and that this was a call for white men to rape black women, Lynch clarifies the need for "many drops of good white blood and putting them into as many nigger women as possible, varying the drops by the various tone that you want, and then letting them breed with each other until another cycle of color appears as you desire."

Step 3: Repeat. "Continually through the breaking of uncivilized savage nigger, by throwing the nigger female savage into a frozen psychological state of independence, by killing of the protective male image, and by creating a submissive dependent mind of the nigger male slave, *we have created an orbiting cycle that turns on its own axis forever.*"

The only problem with Lynch's sermon was that since he was talking to one of John Locke's colonies, he was preaching to the choir. Lynch's sermon was too late to be prophetic for his Virginian audience as they already wrote his method into the laws of their land. In 1662, the Virginia legislature passed a law that specified "Children got by any Englishman upon a Negro woman shall be bound or free according to the condition of the mother" in order that white men who rape black women do so without paternal responsibilities.[218] In 1705, Virginia's *An Act Concerning Servants and Slaves* read: "If any slave, that hath run a-way . . . it shall and may be lawful for the county court, to order such punishment to the said slave . . . by dismembring . . . for the reclaiming any such incorrigible slave, and terrifying others from the like practices."[219]

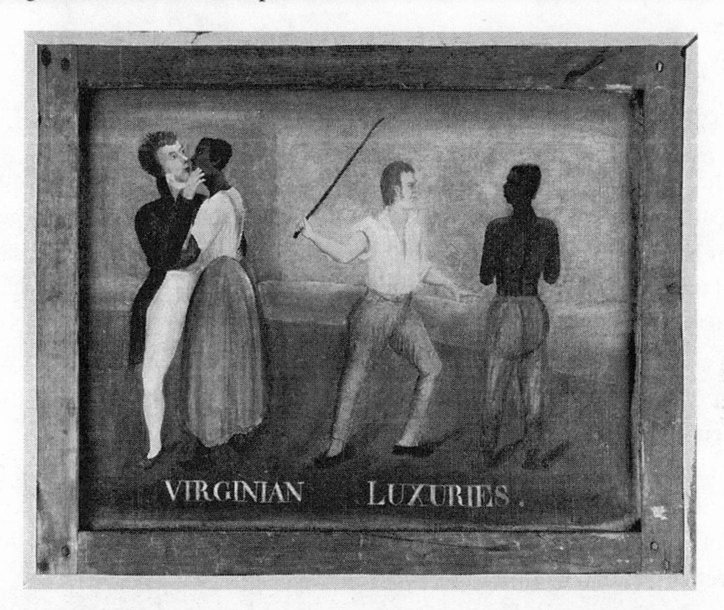

In Willie Lynch and the laws of the Virginian lands, the ghost of Locke's philosophies are embodied and the power of the rulebook he penned is etched both onto a slave-holding society's soul and the slaves' broken, beaten, burned, and raped bodies. In time, Virginia proved to be the most critical colony of the revolutionary era, providing the cultural cradle for the Virginian dynasty of America's first President and Father of the Nation, George Washington; the author of the Declaration of Independence and third President, Thomas Jefferson; the architect of the Constitution, Bill of Rights, and fourth President, James Madison; and the last Founding Father and fifth President, James Monroe. Rather than un-writing Lynch-like laws, these statesmen wrote Virginia's character onto the national project.[220]

Neither Willie Lynch's letter nor American slavery were created ex-nihilo—their shared roots are the very roots that birthed and nurtured America's political and religious institutions. In the American experiment, the ideologies of freedom, liberty, and justice were all forced to harmonize with Willie Lynch's methods as America's institutions twisted together liberal ideologies and Jesus's teachings to violently secure a depraved racial order. Throughout American history, America has found herself in the crucible of racial crisis; for despite our humanitarian rhetoric, racial inequalities are the result that our institutions were and are designed to foster and perpetuate—like "an orbiting cycle that turns on its own axis forever."

ON ENTHUSIASM: THE SLAYING OF THE PROPHETS AND THEIR FORGOTTEN PEOPLE

In the *Essay*, Locke writes on the threat of religious enthusiasm as a compassionate observer within the circle of faith. Enthusiasts may in fact be good men but "good men are men still" and "liable to mistake."[221] Enthusiasts find themselves captured by the circular logics that their passion produces: "It is a revelation, because they firmly believe and they believe it, because it is a revelation." The fire of their passion is mistaken as the light of revelation. Locke was not a religious enthusiast, but his philosophies produced an enthusiasm in America that produced circular styles of reasoning that led to his ideas becoming institutionalized in our most sacred political and religious institutions. By institutionalizing Locke's ideas, the world became tailor-made for aristocratic flourishing and fertile grounds for the myths of slavemasters to take root.

The lies that Hobbes planted germinated under Locke's nurturing. After Locke, the lies about the very natures of government, economics, and religion rang as "self-evident" truths. The lies that government was about the preservation of property rather than the common good, that economics is a moral-free math, and that the essence of religion is soul salvation formed America's most vital political and religious leaders and institutions.

By cleaning the slates of men's minds and making *the* question central to men's curiosity, Locke places himself in a position to re-write the rules of the game along racial lines. The rules of the game produced a democracy of the propertied that was able to pose as a democracy of the people and empowered the aristocracy to pose as a meritocracy. By learning to view the wealthy as the worthy and the poor as the problem, we learned to fear the entitlement of the poor but not the entitlement of the wealthy. In a Lockean world where aristocrats become the Leviathan, the notion of property rights would be embraced with religious fervor. The world experienced times of greater prosperity, but too often without upending institutionalized poverty and racial inequality. Locke's rules of the game protected those with wealth not only from the greedy overreach of political powers but also from the cries of the poor and the slave. Despite the humanitarian rhetoric of equality, making property rights the central political principle was never intended to produce equity.

The rules of religion made our problems worse. In making salvation the filter for "true religion," a religion friendly to the bourgeoisie is born. And the new religion Locke crafts is a more "tolerant faith." That Christians no longer killed in the name of Christianity was one end that Locke pursued successfully, but that in less than a generation the American Revolution began in which self-professed Christians killed other Christians in the name of the very virtues Locke sought to provide peace—"life, liberty and the pursuit of happiness"—provided an ironic historical twist. Locke's liberalism successfully stemmed Christian violence but not the violence of Christians. In future generations, Christians killed Christians and non-Christians alike under supposedly secular banners; killing for market ideologies, killing to spread democratic principles, killing to promote liberty and human rights. Following the advent of liberalism, violence in the name of religion begins to make less and less sense to the modern moral imagination. Religious violence contradicted the heart of religious essence. But the fact that violence in the name of liberal ideologies proved time and time again persuasive displayed just how much liberalism's power players had in common with the religious zealotry of their medieval forbearers.

Sentimentality made American Christians confuse their faith with prophetic Christianity, as white Christians failed to even realize the racial, political, and economic implications of their convictions. Modern Christians feared the implications of secular rationality on the church's confidence in the creeds. Though such fears proved legitimate, they often overlooked how secular rationality was not only at war with the creeds but seeking to crucify Christ himself by placing black folks on crosses.

Throughout American history, in the face of slavery, segregation, and the New Jim Crow, good-hearted and pious white churches warred against Christ himself by refusing solidarity with the broken and abused in general and their black and brown brothers and sisters in particular.

As Locke's rules took root, the rich got richer and too often the poor stayed poor as the modern institutions performed exactly the work they were designed to produce. Yet, as the inequalities increased, the pressure to justify the growing inequities intensified. A sense of the pressure is felt in a letter Locke wrote to a friend advising "in earnest" that "you should feel nothing at all of others' misfortunes."[222] Some scholars believe that "others'" was written with slaves in mind, but one way or the other, the letter reveals the pressures on conscience that the emerging inequitable world order produced.

For as persuasive as Locke was at initiating an aristocratic revolution, he needed help in developing a new morality—a new understanding of justice in a world with great inequalities—in order to keep the inequalities going and growing. After imagining and institutionalizing the slavemaster's myth, there was a need to ingrain this morality into the people to allow good folk to sleep with themselves in wealthy cities scarred by poverty and racial inequalities. For that new morality, we now turn to Adam Smith.

4

Adam Smith

Ingraining Hardhearted—& Racist—Instincts and Ideologies

MAINTENANCE MAN

Adam Smith came kicking and screaming into Kirkcaldy, Scotland, on July 17th, 1723, nearly twenty years after the death of John Locke. Smith was born to the recently widowed Margaret Smith, named after his late father, and was baptized on the day of his birth in keeping with the custom for children whose health and viability are in question.[223] If the modern world was in utero during the life of Thomas Hobbes and moving from the womb into its infancy during the life of John Locke, in the times of Adam Smith the modern world was a toddler and attempting to learn to walk and talk on her own terms.

Smith faced different pressures than either Hobbes or Locke faced. The ink that effectively ended the wars of religion through the Treaty of Westphalia dried seventy-five years earlier, and the tentacles of England's empire reached throughout the world and were entrenched in America. Thus, unlike the days of Hobbes and Locke, neither ending religiously inspired violence nor justifying the colonies and the institution of slavery acted as primary concerns for the politically and economically minded philosophers of Smith's day.

Rather than a radical reformation of the modern project, the perceived need of the moment was perfecting the work that the generations of Hobbes and Locke began, as the empire had failed to work with the clock-like precision after which modernity strove. The colonies proved simultaneously incredibly profitable *and* incredibly costly. The colonies were so profitable that it was hard for England to imagine life without them. And they were so costly that it was not clear England could survive their attempt to hold the empire together. "The terror of a rupture with the colonies," Adam Smith confided in *The Wealth of Nations*, "has struck the people of Great Britain with more terror than they ever felt for a Spanish armada, or a French invasion."[224] Navigating these perilous tensions fell to Smith, who worked to steer Hobbes and Locke's enlightened project away from the path of self-destruction and onto more sure political and religious foundations.

Smith saw through the lies of Hobbes and Locke more clearly than his contemporaries. He believed government was for the common good and that economics carried with it profound moral implications. He believed religion was about discipleship and that many modern believers were self-centered sentimentalists who threatened the moral makeup of society. He advocated for protecting the dignity of the poor and the slave. Yet, despite all the flaws he saw in the philosophies underwriting the modern age, Smith believed his era neared the precipice of a new world order with the potential to provide abundantly for all—even those of the humblest stations. He believed an "invisible hand" led society along a fragile but benevolent path towards an *equitable* opulence. And it was this *equitable* opulence for which Smith labored.

However, rather than remedying our thinking on government or religion, the deepest impact of Smith's works ended up making the injustices at the heart modernity's politics and religion even worse. It was Smith's poetry that crafted the final political lie (that justice is retributive rather than restorative) and the final religious lie (that indifference to injustice is no threat to one's intimacy with God). In crafting these lies, Smith becomes the preeminent wordsmith for modern morality as his wordplays forged a deep indifference to the rights and dignity of the destitute.

We move from how Hobbes *imagined* and Locke *institutionalized* the slavemaster's myth, to how Smith *ingrained* a morality of hardheartedness into society that made citizens comfortable with the radical inequities modernity ushered in. If we wonder why the modern era, with the new-found ability to eradicate need and want, refused to do so; how a new era of inequality failed to usher in a new era of conscious regard for the poor; how self-interest replaced self-sacrifice as society's premier virtue; how individualized acts of benevolence replaced communal pursuits of justice; or how the religion of white folk remained Christian in name while becoming increasingly Stoic in nature, there is no philosopher of greater importance than Adam Smith.

MOMMA'S BOY

As Adam Smith's final days approached, he worked meticulously to protect his legacy. Rather than publish his sequestered genius, he desired to burn all his notes and many of his unpublished manuscripts. Smith asked two of his closest friends to place a match to his unperfected works after his passing. They promised they would, and their promise eased Smith's mind—at least until it didn't. Seventeen days before his death, Smith called his friends, and together they began the bonfire for the words and works that failed to meet Smith's standards. Smith's health failed before the fire finished its work, but true to their word, his friends fed the remainder of Smith's work to the flames shortly after his death. "He died on 17 July 1790, having done," in the words of one biographer, "as much as was humanely possible to preserve his intellectual privacy."[225] In the end, history remembers Smith the way he wished to be remembered—by the two masterpieces he authored: *The Theory of Moral Sentiments* and *The Wealth of Nations.*

On the surface of things, there exists significant overlap between Smith's life and the lives of Hobbes and Locke. Like Hobbes and Locke, Smith took the name of his father and was born to a household of little notoriety but of significant Christian commitment. Like Hobbes, he began college at the wee age of fourteen, initially at the University of Glasgow before matriculating to Oxford. Smith believed as deeply as Hobbes and Locke that the university provided a nearly useless education.[226] Also like Hobbes and Locke, tutoring the children of the elite led to an opportunity to tour Europe and meet some of the world's foremost intellectuals, including Voltaire.[227] Like Locke, Smith was inducted into the Royal Society, and his companions were counted among England's leading intelligentsia, with Smith's closest friend being none other than the infamous skeptic David Hume.[228]

Yet despite these biographical incidentals, there existed both a rootedness at the heart of Smith and his work that differentiated him from his modern forerunners. The rootedness of Smith came from the one relationship that defined his life more than any other. Whereas Hobbes and Locke lived their adult lives under the spell of Cavendish wealth and Exeter's elite, Adam Smith had Momma Margaret, and Momma Margaret made all the difference. She took up residence with her boy as soon as he established one and remained with him the rest of her life. Adam outlived her by only six years. He confessed to a friend shortly after her passing that she "certainly loved me more than any other person ever did or ever will . . . and whom I loved and respected more than I ever shall love or respect any other person."[229]

Momma Margaret kept Adam and his work rooted in the world in which he was reared. Hobbes and Locke, on the other hand, shrank their worlds to the inner circle of society's elite while the needs of the common folk—who made up the vast majority of humanity—disappeared right underneath their noses.[230] By keeping a foot in the world beyond society's elites, Adam's world was infinitely larger and included its butchers and brewers and bakers and pen makers. The minute details of this larger world, as-it-was and as-it-is, fascinated Smith and provided his poetics the dust and dirt of daily living, giving his writings a poetic but simple realism.

Smith fit the caricature of an academic recluse. He locked himself away in his library for long stretches of time and often walked the streets of his village talking to himself and laughing as if he told himself a new joke. And yet he was socially beloved. Smith's hospitality and seemingly small need for the approval of others made him great company to people ranging from his students to his pious Scottish Presbyterian mother to folks like Hume and Voltaire.

Adam devoured the writings of poets, playwrights, philosophers, and historians. In great writers, it is said, "the style is the man."[231] And it was a truth that was apparent in Adam's masterpieces. Smith devoured the details of history with the same voracious appetite that he consumed the details of the marketplace and he used these details to bring to life images capable of capturing the nature of society's systems within single sentences. He did not simply absorb the writings of Homer, Shakespeare, Cicero, Marcus Aurelius, and Epictetus with an academic interest that ended in knowledge alone. He read their writings like a student of swordsmanship readying for war. He analyzed how it was that they moved the reader to feel what they felt, to see what they saw and believe what they believed. He gleaned from the ancients, poets, and playwrights the power of beautiful writing and worked to translate their work into various languages so that their power would become his power.[232] He proved a worthy student. As Edmund Burke proclaimed: "His language is easy and spirited . . . it is painting rather than writing."

By rooting his arguments in the dust and the grind of the workaday world, by providing a detailed historical analysis with a poetic punch, this momma's boy became a man whose writings transformed the world and its ways. Smith would be remembered as an economist, but that was only because Momma Margaret's child was selectively and poorly read by those who claimed his name to justify small thoughts and narrow thinking. He was who his university position at Glasgow indicated him to be—a professor of morality. No professor shaped modern morality more and no professor has been more misunderstood and misrepresented.

But there is a reason for that. The wheels spinning in Smith's head spun in different directions. As a historian, Smith placed himself within the tradition of the prophets. No philosopher understood the brokenness of modern morality and how that brokenness expressed itself in our world and the life of common people better than Adam Smith. The prophetic historian in Smith made him an advocate for the rights and dignity of the oppressed. Yet, as a philosopher, he looked at his world through the lens of a Stoic disciple. If no historian understood the brokenness of modernity's moral compass better, no philosopher made the problems worse. In Stoic fashion, Smith provided accurate and in-depth diagnoses of cultural sicknesses, but he wrote prescriptions that only inflamed the sicknesses he perceived.

Due to these competing traditions between the prophetic and the Stoic within Smith's writings, we will move through his works differently. Before addressing how Smith made matters worse, we will look to understand the problems within the modern project through Smith's penetrating analysis, for it is only in understanding the problems Smith desired to address that we can understand his eventual impact on the American soul. After getting oriented to Smith's prophetic perspective, we will look at the Stoic solutions Smith articulates for his readers and how his persuasive powers made the problems he perceived all the worse. We begin with Smith-the-advocate and his convictions regarding the modern project with its merchant class, unjust wages, colonies, and desperate need for equity.

ADVOCATE SMITH: CLEAR EYES & NO LIES

In his *Lectures on Rhetoric,* Adam Smith provides a scathing critique of Exeter House's "pompous"[233] Lord Shaftesbury. Shaftesbury was too "delicate"[234] for serious thinking. He was "no great reasoner" and attempted to "set off by the ornament of language what was deficient in matter."[235] The superficial writing was a byproduct of the impact of superficial philosophical influencers in his life. Smith identifies two: Shaftesbury's tutor John Locke, who was "too lightly religious"; and Thomas Hobbes, whose system was too self-interested. Both critiques are highly ironic for those lightly literate in Smith's work.

Nonetheless, Smith wrote that Hobbes and Locke were married more to ideological fantasies than knowledge of man and society formed by historical facts and social realities. Smith believed the philosophical fantasies of Hobbes and Locke threatened to bring back the dark ages by recreating the broken political and economic systems that worked for the wealthiest folk and stuck it to the rest of us. Modernity's domestic political and economic failures produced chaos in the colonies, produced the atrocities of slavery and genocide, and fostered dire poverty for nearly everyone else. These depraved inequities are what Smith desired to upend.

Rather than sanctifying the economy's powerbrokers, Smith referred to *The Wealth of Nations* as "the very violent attack . . . upon the whole commercial system."[236] His aggressive onslaught in *The Wealth of Nations* provided for the world but a taste of the lectures he provided his students year after year at the University of Glasgow, where he labored to disabuse them of their naïveté concerning our world and its ways. In reading both his lectures and *Wealth*, it is hard to tell where the prizefighter is at his finest, but what is clear is that Smith knew how to turn his words into spears wherever he went.

For his students and readers, Smith traced the philosophies of Hobbes and Locke back to their foundations to show that their enlightened project rested on the quicksand of an ideologically rooted misunderstanding of man and community. Society began "not as some writers imagine from any consent or agreement of a number of persons to submit themselves to such or such regulations, but from the natural progress which men make in society."[237] Hobbes and Locke were ridiculous. It was not man's need for self-preservation or the preservation of property that brought us together. Humanity was made for each other. Man, argued Smith, "can subsist only in society . . . bound together by the agreeable bands of love and affection, and are, as it were, drawn to one common centre of mutual good offices."[238] Man is not an angel and community is not utopia, but the foundation of society is to empower community and intimacy, not isolation and self-sufficiency.[239]

Smith saw that the ideologically rooted misnaming of man's nature and society's ends were not innocent mistakes. The misnaming was precisely aimed to justify fundamentally sadistic forms of government. "Civil government," wrote Smith in *Wealth of Nations*, "so far as it is instituted for the security of property, is in reality instituted for the defense of the rich against the poor, or of those who have some property against those who have none at all."[240] For Smith, rooting government in preservation of property wars against the very nature of a flourishing society. As a historian with a prophetic bent, Smith reads history as the story of the rich's struggle against the poor for power and their place in the world. "All for ourselves and nothing for other people," noted Smith "seems, in every age of the world, to have been the vile maxim of the masters of mankind."[241]

At the Constitutional Convention and later at the Virginia Convention, James Madison demanded the protection of property rights as a way of protecting "minorities" from the "majority." Madison employed the suffering of slaves—he owned hundreds—as an example of how society's majorities abused minorities. The minority Madison desired to protect was, however, the wealthy and often slaveholding minority and it is that minority protection that became a foundational principle of the founding fathers.[242]

He was even more blunt with his students. "Laws and government may be considered in this and indeed in every case as a combination of the rich to oppress the poor, and preserve to themselves . . . inequality."[243] If the rich can twist the knife and drain a few more nickels out of the poor's pockets, they will. It wasn't just an ideological claim of a power-to-the-people ideologue, but a historian who detailed for his students laws regulating the poor from even simple pleasures due "to the great inclination they have to screw all they can out of their hands."[244]

With meticulous details, Smith lays out how the nobility of the middle ages laid waste to the greater part of Europe through their addictions to the "arts, commerce and luxury," passions that warred against a "hospitable way of living."[245] To place hope in the wisdom of the aristocracy, the job creators, business executives, the titans of corporations and Wall Street, would be to resurrect the desolate wisdom that prolonged the dark ages.[246]

Despite the advancement of modern man that provided the opportunity to defeat poverty for the first time in history, Smith feared that the ideologies of the merchants threatened to concentrate the new sources of wealth in the hands of the few and continue to leave the masses living in squalor. Thus, one of the main targets of Smith's critiques is the merchant class and their war against economic equity.

—The Merchant Class Matters—

One of the more famous Smithian prophets on American soils was the atheistic philosopher Ayn Rand (1905–1982). In *Atlas Shrugged*, Rand gave birth to a new political hero, the "job creator." For Republican Speakers of the House, from Newt Gingrich, to Dennis Hassert, to John Boehner, to Paul Ryan, Rand became the philosophic novelist who best captured Smith's economic vision. Rand linked virtue and the well-being of society itself to the well-being of the wealthy—the class designated as the "job creators." Unfortunately, Rand was a false prophet for Adam actually saw no such interconnections. Instead, Adam believed significant wealth often carried with it significant conflicts of interest with virtue, society's good, and political wisdom.

Part of the allure of Rand to American politicians was also her devotion to American Exceptionalism. As an immigrant to America, Rand writes: "I can say—not as a patriotic bromide, but with full knowledge of the necessary metaphysical, epistemological, ethical, political and esthetic roots—that the United States of America is the greatest, the noblest and, in its original founding principles, the *only* moral country in the history of the world."[247]

For Smith, the wealthy were not "job creators." Most wealthy folks were dependent on momma and daddy, or in the words of Smith: "A family which had been once raised to dignity and wealth could hardly ever be deprived of it."[248] But within the ranks of the wealthy a new class was emerging and that was the class of merchants and master manufacturers. Rather than holding this new class of wealthy folks up as beacons of light for moral and political wisdom, however, Smith argued that they were the primary threat to—not the hope of—an opulent nation. Whether through inheritance or industry, an opulent nation needed to be wary of the wisdom of the wealthy.

Smith begins by revealing the great secret that the rich needed the poor much more than the poor needed the rich.[249] "The labour and time of the poor is in civilized countries sacrificed to the maintaining the rich in ease and luxury,"[250] The poor do the dirty work. The poor wash the clothes, wait the tables, clean the houses, mow the yards, make and clean the clothes, and keep the carriages rolling. The poor have no dependence on the rich "for in general the poor are independent, and support themselves by their labour."[251]

For Adam, instead of the rich acting as paragons of virtue and wisdom, the rich primarily excel at staying rich. To stay rich, the rich needed three skills. First, the rich needed "superior knowledge of their own interest."[252] Even for the rich, great wealth, with great foolishness, over a great period of time is a path to poverty.

Second, rich folks needed the sincere conviction that the protection of their inequality benefitted all; that their interest harmonizes with and promotes the interest of everyone. This sincerity, more often than not, was rooted in self-deception but when rich folks are surrounded by want and need, self-deception is a necessary component in the economic and political systems that support their lifestyle.

Smith highlights this self-deception in how the rich talk about the prices of their products. Rather than confessing to the role of their profits in their product's price increases, the rich blame their prices to their workers wages.[253] "Our merchants and master-manufacturers complain much of the bad effects of high wages in raising the price," Smith notes in *Wealth*. But "they say nothing concerning the bad effects of high profits. They are silent with regard to the pernicious effects of their own gains. They complain only of those of other people. . ."[254] Smith, however, refused to silence himself. "Profit is. . .always highest in the countries which are going fastest to ruin,"[255] he wrote.

Milton Friedman (1912–2006) was the leading free market theorist in U.S. history. His social analysis was brilliant, sometimes helpful, and often depraved. In his masterpiece *Capitalism and Freedom,* Friedman writes: "The Hitler Nuremberg laws and the [Jim Crow] laws in the Southern States. . .are both examples of laws similar in principle to FEPC [Fair Employment Practice Committee]." That Friedman sees fair employment as exchangeable with the atrocities of Nazism and Jim Crow Segregation displays not only his distance from the suffering of society's oppressed people, but also the distance between his economic theories and any semblance of moral sanity.[256]

For Smith, there is no law of gravity where profits trickle down, profits are a bottom up process where the potential wealth of the people are *syphoned* into the real wealth of the merchants and manufactures through the combination of low wages and high prices. "There is one more fatal, perhaps, than all these put together." That fatal flaw of profits and the ensuing inequality was not numerical, but moral, "sober virtue seems to be superfluous" and is exchanged for "expensive luxury."[257] And once addicted to luxury, the self-destructive cycle of the nobility of old resurrects in modern form as what is vital for the viability of the many is sacrificed for the vanities of the few and a cycle is put in motion that brings a nation to ruin.

For the rich, expertise in self-interest drives sincerity, sincerity produces self-deception, and nothing says politics like self-interested, sincere, self-deceived rich folks. Navigating the world of politics is the third critical—and perhaps most important—skill for the rich to secure their wealth. To secure inequality requires rich folks to persuade politicians "to give up both his own interest and that of the public, from *a very simple but honest* conviction that their interest, and not his, was the interest of the public."[258] Good-hearted rich folks, especially in a democracy, make incredibly effective political advisors. This is why Smith feared the impact of good-hearted rich folks on the overall opulence of a nation for "the interest of the dealers. . . is always in some respects different from, and even opposite to, that of the public."[259] Good-hearted rich folks are experts at making themselves wealthier, not other people's lives better.

For Smith, merchants tend to reduce the citizenry to their role as consumers and mistake consumption as the greatest political good. "To found a great empire for the sole purpose of raising up a people of customers" wrote Smith, "is extremely fit for a nation whose government is influenced by shopkeepers. Such statesmen, and such statesmen only, are capable of fancying that they will find some advantage in employing the blood and treasure of their fellow-citizens to found and maintain such an empire."[260] There is an inhumane ruthlessness in the political calculus of merchants that is unfit for navigating the challenges that face nations and their leaders. How would an empire overly influenced by shopkeepers respond to 9/11? In the words of President George W. Bush: "I encourage you to shop more."

Like a preacher exhausted from his pulpit, Smith brings Book I of *The Wealth of Nations* to a close. "The proposal of any new law. . . which comes from this order ought always to be listened to with great precaution," Smith warned, "and ought never to be adopted till after having been long and carefully examined. . . with the most suspicious attention. It comes from an order of men. . .who have generally an interest to deceive and even to oppress the public, and who accordingly have, upon many occasions, both deceived and oppressed it."[261] Smith feared that the richer a politician's advisors became, the poorer the people would grow. Merchants were masters of public deception, masters of turning the public's loss into their private gain. This is how Margaret's boy viewed the precarious intersection of politics and "job creators." He was ready to say what he saw. And he was just beginning.

—The War Over Wages Matters—

The history that Smith is attempting to write to disabuse modernity of its self-destructive direction paints the struggle between the rich and the poor as blood sport. Nowhere is the blood sport more present than in the ongoing battle over wages. In the arena of wages, the rich girded themselves for war to increase their wealth, influence, and luxuries. For the poor the battle was for life itself, for basic shelter for one's family and food for the children. But in this battle the purity of one's cause never translates to the power for achieving one's purpose.

Leverage was on the side of those pursuing vanities rather than the side of those seeking viability. "The contract [is] made between those two parties, whose interests are by no means the same," remarked Smith. "The workmen desire to get as much, the masters to give as little as possible. . . It is not, however, difficult to foresee which of the two parties [has] the advantage in the dispute, and force the other into a compliance with their terms."[262] The battle over wages never takes place on an even playing field or within a free market. For Smith, a free market for wages is a figment of naïve imagination either unfamiliar with or intentionally blind to how the world actually works. The battle tilts towards the rich for three reasons: they easily partner to suppress wages with other employers; time itself is less urgent for the employer than the employed; and the rules of the political game are written for the rich to win.

The first advantage: When Smith describes how the battle for wages transpires, the images he employs are not the morally neutral grids and graphs of supply and demand that his economic progeny employ to justify the dictates of the market. The war of wages occurs in smoke-filled rooms unseen to the public eye: "The masters, being fewer in number, can combine much more easily" than laborers. The collaborations are cloaked in secrecy thicker than the London fog so that only those within the room know that they took place, but "whoever, imagines, upon this account, that masters rarely combine, is as ignorant of the world as of the subject . . . these are always conducted with the utmost silence and secrecy till the moment of execution."[263]

The second advantage: Time. "A master manufacturer, a merchant, though they did not employ a single workman, could generally live a year or two upon the stocks which they have already acquired." While workers strike and employers wait, the real leverage is on the home front, as the laborers' cupboards grow bare, their children's stomachs growl, and the landlords threaten evictions. So while employers wait a year without a lifestyle compromise "many workmen could not subsist a week, few could subsist a month, and scarce any a year without employment." Smith continues to paint the battle scene: "In the long run, the workman may be as necessary to his master as his master is to him; but the necessity is not so immediate."[264] Through collaboration with one another and with time on their side, the rich fight the battle over wages secured within well-supplied fortresses entrenched in the mountaintops. The poor charge uphill armed with sticks and stones.

War Over Wages

But the leverage in the battle is not only about the terrain and the supply lines. *The third advantage*: The rules of the battle are written for the rich to win. "We have no acts of parliament against combining to lower the price of work," writes Smith, "but many against combining to raise it."[265] The battle plays out with eerie predictability as the rich break the will of the poor through teamwork, hunger, and political power. Despite the worker's zeal and purity of purpose, the striking poor "submit for the sake of present subsistence, generally end in nothing, but the punishment or ruin of ring leaders."[266]

Smith paints a grim picture concerning the battle over wages but the battle is not over. Once the strike is over and the work renews, the battle to survive on unjust wages rages on. Whose bodies litter that battlefield? Smith forces his readers to grapple with the real victims of the war over wages: "In some places one half the children born die before they are four years of age; in many places before they are seven; and in almost all places before they are nine or ten. This great mortality, however, will every where be found chiefly among the children of the common people who cannot afford to tend them."[267] Smith attempts to open the eyes of his students and readers to the very realities we desire to ignore—that the children of our cities are hungry for we are starving them. Starving children is sad enough, but the fact that it could and should be otherwise compounds our tragedies with complicity—and it is the reality of this complicity that Smith attempted to sear on our soul.

Two hundred and four years after Smith, another historian published a book that tells the history of a different nation but through a remarkably similar lens. In *A People's History of the United States,* Howard Zinn tells U.S. history through the eyes of workers—often through labor strikes. Time after time, the war over wages replayed the Smithian equation with ominous predictability. The wealthy united, the poor went hungry, and the laws too often empowered the Rockefellers and Carnegies against their workers. Like long ago, it was the children that lay dead on the battlefield. Though infant mortality rates improved over time, the children of the poor still die at rates three times as high as as their wealthy counterparts. In current-day Mississippi, infant mortality stands "somewhere between Botswana and Bahrain,"[268] while Houston, city that sent a men to the moon, sends thousands of children of the working poor to bed hungry.[269] The cruelty of the war over wages simply has not changed and neither has the reality of our complicity.

Yet, as heinous as it is for the wealthy to kill the children of the poor through unjust wages, the sickness of the commercial system ran deeper still.

—Columbus and Colonial Matters—

For Smith, in failing to address wages, the project of Hobbes, Locke, and the Enlightenment's brain trust failed to address the core domestic issue that shaped the lives of working people. But what of international affairs, what of England's empire and the future world that modernity was shaping through the colonies? Smith had something to say to that as well. In fact, he dedicated almost one hundred pages of *The Wealth of Nations* to it and released the work in the critical year of 1776.

For Smith, the first step in analyzing the colonies was getting the facts of history straight. Like the Romans of old, the covetousness of domestic land in the hands of the few and the lust for luxuries—particularly gold—inspired the colonies.[270] Columbus went looking for the riches of the Indies once witnessed by Marco Polo but found instead St. Dominic's "naked and miserable savages."[271] Whatever skill Columbus lacked in navigating the seas, he made up for in political salesmanship. "In consequence of the representations of Columbus," Smith writes, wearing his historian's hat, "the council of Castile determined to take possession of the countries . . . incapable of defending themselves." What justified taking land from a people, what Smith referred to as "the cruel destruction of the natives"?[272] It was "the pious purpose of converting them to Christianity [that] sanctified the injustice of the project." But the money trail revealed that "the hope of finding treasures of gold there, was the *sole* motive."[273]

And though the lust for gold failed to lead to gold, the lust did uncover other savory sweets in a land ripe for the harvesting. In Smith's words on the colonies: "To the undiscerning eye of giddy ambition it presents itself amidst the confused scramble of politics and war as a very dazzling object to fight for."[274] For the "undiscerning"—from Hobbes and the Cavendish clan to Locke and Exeter's elite—the colonies harmonized an array of aristocratic lusts for power and wealth. The lust for empire harmonized with the lust for gold, the lust for gold led to the lust for a host of resources the colonies held; and once these lusts harmonized, they quickened one another to unleash the most pernicious vice of the modern project—the lust for slaves.

By the time Smith writes, the attack on the institution of slavery is well underway. Rather than rehashing what his students already know, Smith attacks slavery from the "flanks"—that is, from the perspective of female slaves and dying children; from the devastation slavery brings to the families of the working class, and from how slavery wars against freedom itself. Smith warmed his engines for his first lecture dedicated to the topic,[275] arguing that over the passing of time the institution of slavery only grew more cruel, until "masters had no restraint put on their cruelty, and the hardest usage was commonly practised on them; their lives were taken away on the slightest occasion."[276]

And then Smith's flanking maneuvers: "Besides these hardships which are commonly taken notice of by writers," he writes, "they laboured under severall others which are not so generally attended to. They were, in the 1st place, reckoned incapable of marriage . . . for this reason we see that *the corrupting* a female slave . . . was not looked on as any way reprehensible or injurious, the female slaves will therefore *always* live in a state of prostitution [in the] . . . colonies."[277] Smith implies that slavery was not simply to satisfy economic desires run amuck—slavery was about predatory sexual impulses as well. Slavery provided black women to satisfy white men's lust. By stripping women of their humanity through slavery and reducing their being to a carnal body, that body becomes a plaything for white men's carnal cravings. Again, at the threat of repetition, when Thomas Jefferson and—likely—George Washington raped their slaves it was not a perversion of an already cruel game. Raping slaves was an integral reason the game ever existed.

As a side note, Smith remarks on the religious context of these acts of rape. After raping their slaves, "Their masters prayed for their thriving and multiplying in the same manner as for their cattle."[278] Again, Jefferson acts as a case in point: as a young man reflecting on Virginian ways with their slaves, he muses on the modern contentment slaveholders can find in singleness by raping slaves:

> For St. Paul only says that it is better to be married than to burn. Now I presume that if that apostle had known that providence would at an after day be so kind to any particular set of people as to furnish them with other means of extinguishing their fire than those of matrimony, he would have earnestly recommended them to their practice.[279]

Piety can prove remarkably predatory. And so Smith forces us to remember that a nation incapable of eliminating slavery found itself capable of reducing her women to objects to rape, and from objects to rape to milk cows. Smith forces us to remember that, if America was a Christian nation, the nature of her Christianity is known through both her lived life, prayer life, and the Jeffersonian twists to his words.

As Jefferson matures, his lusts only quicken. Shortly after beginning his sexual conquest of his fourteen-year-old slave Sally Hemings—half sister to his late wife and the aunt of his children—Jefferson recounts his encounter with "a 1699 painting of Abraham taking the young servant Hagar to his bed." The word that came to Jefferson's mind was "*delicious*."[280]

Smith needed more than one lecture to cover the topic. In his next lecture, he discusses the incredible death rates of the children of slavery. Even after two centuries of ripping Africans from their homeland, the colonies demand for new slaves continued to grow, not simply because the colonies expanded but because the colonies killed so many of the slave's children, and in particular, so many of the slave's daughters.[281]

Smith argues that the state of "prostitution"—that is perpetual rape—in which female slaves find themselves in is not conducive to reproduction, but even if they do bear children, "A child is a very delicate plant." Almost 50 percent of the children of the "middling ranks" perish before age five, and "neglect alone is the cause of this great mortality. And what children are so likely to be neglected as those of slaves[?]" Smith's question was one that did not receive much air time, but that couldn't be ignored. "It is found that by all these concurrent reasons the stock of slaves in the West Indies would be exhausted altogether in 5 or 6 years, so that in each year they must import about 1/5 or 1/6 of the whole."[282] Here again, a nation incapable of ending slavery proved capable of implementing the endless slaughter of its children.[283]

Smith closes his lecture by addressing slavery's impact on the working class and democracy itself: "I shall only observe farther on this head that slavery remarkably diminishes the number of freemen. That it must diminish the number of freemen is altogether evident, as a great part of the free will become slaves."[284] How so? "For it is all one," Smith writes, "whether one destroys the persons themselves or that which affords their maintenance."[285] Smith's basic argument to his students runs like this: In a slave society, rather than wealth promoting industry, wealth leads to the purchase of more slaves. As slavery expands, slaves begin displacing the working poor throughout the economy. If slavery is first and foremost a war against the slaves, it is secondarily an act of war against the working poor; against the families of the tanner, the baker, the ironsmith and every other worker who no longer possesses an avenue to employ their gifting within the society in which they live.[286] As one visitor from Scotland remarked about the vast trade of slaves at Mt. Vernon, Washington "has everything within himself—carpenters, bricklayers, brewers, blacksmiths, bakers, etc."[287]

In a land of slavery, freedom is a myth for the slave and working poor alike. And this is most true within a democracy that refuses to address the issue of slavery. "In a republican government it will scarcely ever happen that it should be abolished. The persons who make all the laws in that country are persons who have slaves themselves," Smith told his students. "These will never make any laws mitigating their usage. Whatever laws are made with regard to slaves are intended to . . . reduce the slaves to a more absolute subjection."[288] Smith proved an eerily accurate prophet of public policies. He impressed upon his students that to think of slavery without thinking of the continual raping of females, the death of children, the impoverishment of the community, and the demise of meaningful democracy is to refuse to think deeply about slavery at all.

After *The Wealth of Nations,* Smith became famous for heralding happy outcomes that arose from man pursuing their own interests through the unintended consequences of their industry. Despite the depraved desires and means that produced the colonies, and though the means misaligned the colonies from achieving their true potential, their discovery Smith cites as the "greatest and most important events recorded in the history of mankind." In the mind of Smith, the die was not yet cast in the colonies' fate. "What benefits, or what misfortunes to mankind may hereafter result from those great events," Smith wrote, "no human wisdom can foresee."[289] The colonies tied the world together. The fate of the colonies, what happened on their soils, in their economies, and to their people would be felt by every nation in the world. And it was this reality that made Smith feel that his project published in 1776 was of critical importance. The American project was simultaneously young enough to embrace his vision as an enthusiastic student and large enough for the impact of that experiment to be felt the world round. If the colonies would listen to his lectures and read his books, America possessed the potential to steer the modern world in a new direction.

— Equity Matters—

For Smith, it was critical for the colonies to not be deceived by fools who would lead them astray in their infancy. Of all the fools that Smith warns of, John Locke and his philosophies reigned supreme. Though Locke's thinking was original, the roots of his wisdom ran no deeper than the thin soil of the aristocratic imagination that knew no need of the truths of history and the real world.

Of all of Locke's foolishness, especially threatening was his teaching on taxes. "It is a rule laid down by Mr. Locke," Smith lectured his students, "as a principle that the people have a right to resist whenever the sovereign takes their money from them without their consent by levying taxes to which they have not agreed." The problem with Locke's principle is that it is not a principle anywhere in the world other than Britain, "and God knows it is but a very metaphorical consent which is here given."[290] Locke's philosophies missed the heart of the matter. Unlike aristocrats, for Smith the founding principle of a healthy government is not the preservation of property. "The power of the sovereign is in this case a trust reposed in him by the people; he is the great magistrate to whom they have promised obedience as long as he rules with a middling degree of *equity*." Rulers are not saints, but when they abuse equity "in a very violent manner . . . then undoubtedly he may be resisted."[291] For Smith the name of the game in a thriving society is equity.

Smith refused to wax philosophical on the necessity of equity, for equity is about morality and "morality, when traced to [its] foundation, turn out to be some Principles of Common Sence."[292] So Smith writes plainly: "No society can surely be flourishing and happy of which the far greater part of the members are poor and miserable." He continues: "It is but equity, besides, that they who feed, clothe, and lodge the whole body of the people, should have such a share of the produce of their own labour as to be themselves tolerably well fed, clothed, and lodged."[293] Equity equals well-being and it is through the well-being of laborers that the well-being of society itself is measured.

To achieve law and order, foolish folks—who like Locke lacked any social depth perception—desire to double the police force and get tough on crime. Yet, "we shall only observe on this head that those cities where the greatest police is exercised are not those which enjoy the greatest security." The truth of the matter, however, is that every crime has a story and what the stories tell is that crime thrives where "the greatest need is." People need their nickel to live on, and where they "cannot support themselves by work" they will "live but by crimes and vices."[294] Thus, for Smith, equitable commerce provides the only cure for a city's crime, for the share of revenue "determines in every country the general character of the inhabitants as to industry or idleness." For those who lament workers' laxity, Smith provides his readers a reminder of the workers' wisdom: "Our ancestors were idle for want of a sufficient encouragement to industry. It is better, says the proverb, to play for nothing than to work for nothing."[295]

Before minimum wages, the movement for workers' rights or equations that calculated living wages, Smith advocated that workers be both well paid and well rested.[296] For Smith, just wages were not found through balancing supply and demand but by balancing demand and necessity—in his words: "The money price of labour is necessarily regulated by two circumstances; the demand for labour, and the price of the necessaries and conveniences of life."[297] It was a well-paid workforce, rather than profitable corporations and wealthy elites, that made a nation wealthy in the long run. And encouraging a nation to strive towards equity, particularly within the colonies, was why Smith wrote with such urgency, clarity, and unforgettable images.

And so it was that Adam Smith attacked the self-deception of the rich, the wealthy, and their commercial and mercantile system. Smith decoupled wealth from virtue and the interests of the merchants from the interest of the community. He displayed how the wages rich folks paid their working poor led directly to the death of children, and depicted slavery as a war against the family and the freedom of the "free." The logic of the moderns may be wrapped in sheep's clothing, but Smith saw that inside such logic prowls a ravenous wolf.

~

In reading Smith's critiques of the rich and powerful, one cannot help but gasp at how accurately his critiques aligned with the vices of our Founding Fathers and the flaws of America's Constitution. Smith's critiques align perfectly with the social impact of Washington's Mt. Vernon, Madison's Mt. Montpellier, and Jefferson's Monticello and with the construction of a Constitution that provided more protection to the propertied minority than either the enslaved minority or the impoverished majority. Slowly but surely, Smith's readers realize that the deceptive logics of capitalism were well established long before Smith took pen to paper. Smith was many things, but the father of capitalism or an advocate for a corporate democracy he was not. If capitalism has one father, that father is much more likely Thomas Hobbes and his portrait of economics as a moral-free math. Nonetheless, Adam Smith is not well known for his prophetic retelling of history or his diagnosis of modern maladies, not because of historical inaccuracies or modern misdiagnosis but because these were not the ideas that intrigued Smith's readers the most. Hobbes's sinless history was much preferred to Smith's truthful history. Smith's readers proved remarkably uninterested in his diagnosis of society's sickness or his "attack on the commercial system."

What intrigued Smith's readers were the cures he prophesied over this sick system and the potential for his genius to empower the very project he critiqued so ferociously. Strangely enough, Smith's cures were very religiously rooted—rooted in the ancient soils of Stoicism—and it was selective parts of this religion that his readers took home and implemented into the political and economic machines, not to aim at equity, but to justify inequity. And though Adam did not father capitalism, he did father a morality that hardened society's heart to the realities capitalism produced. Here is how that happened.

THE STOIC DISCIPLE: & REWRITING THE WESTERN WORLD'S MORALITY

If the infamous skeptic David Hume is your best friend, the reputation of your piety is in pretty bad disrepair. When Smith praised Hume's peaceful defiance in the face of death, the clouds over his head concerning his own personal piety grew darker still. As Smith confessed, a "single . . . very harmless sheet of paper" memorializing his late friend Hume generated "ten times the amount of abuse" as *The Wealth of Nations*' "violent attack on the whole commercial system of Great Britain."[298] In his classroom, Smith attempted to remove prayer, and in his lectures and writings he routinely took Christians to task for false piety. When Christians joined the fight against slavery, he reminded his students that the clergy's fight flowed from their self-interest, not the virtues their piety produced. Yet, what seemed off the radar of his readers was that one could be quite pious without being Christian in any way.

Smith is not the forerunner of today's "spiritual but not religious." Smith would likely have seen such folks as superficial narcissists like John Locke. What made Locke superficial was that, despite his piety, he was not a disciple. Or in Smith's critique of Locke to his students: one without "any very strong affection to any particular sect or tenets in Religion, who cried up freedom of thought and Liberty of Concience in all matters religious or philosophical without being attached to any particular men or opinions."[299] To lack attachment is to hold a religion without form, backbone, or moral import. For Smith, religion is about discipleship, not self-expression.

Nonetheless, a religion that created uncommitted individuals rather than committed disciples was quickly becoming the norm in the modern world.[300] The superficial Christianity of modernity that Locke helped inspire, the one tailored to aristocratic desires, brought forth a new day in Christendom. Though it was hard to see at the time, Locke's aristocratic Christianity—a Christianity where pious whimsy replaced prophetic realism—paved the way for a religion that was Christian in name but Stoic in nature. Smith's Scotland proved the most fertile soil for this form of Christianity and placed Smith in the crosshairs of the religious phenomena of "Christian Stoicism."

Momma Margaret kept Smith in Kirkcaldy for his primary school years to receive his tutelage from Mr. David Miller[301]—a forerunner in integrating the teachings of Stoicism into Scotland's primary-school curriculum. Stoicism was a religion inspired by the merchant Zeno and refined in the imperial courts of Rome by folks like Seneca, Epictetus, and Marcus Aurelius.[302] Stoicism provided a morally rooted vision uniquely fashioned for a vibrant and thriving society that carried with it the paradoxical realities of immense wealth and suffering. Living wisely in a world of paradox was the faith's heartbeat. It is little surprise that, in the library that Smith left behind, was the 1670 edition of Epictetus's *Enchiridon*—a Stoic masterpiece and a likely remnant of his childhood readings.

Such readings were central to the type of curriculum Smith received in his earliest training. When Smith matriculated from Mr. Miller's burgh school to the University of Glasgow he came under the tutelage of Mr. Francis Hutcheson, one of the foremost theologians of Scotland's enlightenment and America's revolution, and a thoroughly committed disciple of "Christian Stoicism." In Adam Smith, Hutcheson found a profound student but not a convert to "Stoic Christianity." At no point in his writings does Smith claim Christianity in any form. But to say Smith rejected Hutcheson's Christian piety is not to say that Hutcheson's lecture hall and reading assignments did not leave their mark on him. They did. Mr. Miller and Mr. Hutcheson formed a very committed "and chaste disciple"—a disciple of Stoicism.

Francis Hutcheson's influence flows to the colonies through Timothy Dwight, President of Yale; William Small, of William and Mary; and John Witherspoon, President of Princeton. Witherspoon's writings followed Hutchison so closely that it bordered on plagiarism. Nonetheless, he proved "'probably the most influential teacher in the history of American education,' and Princeton under his tutelage produced a bumper crop of politician alumni: a U.S. president, a vice president, twenty-one senators, twenty-nine congressman, and twelve state-governors."[303]

When one reads Smith's first masterpiece, *The Theory of Moral Sentiments,* what bleeds through page after page is Stoicism untainted by Christian doctrine. It is not simply that *The Theory of Moral Sentiments* contains the fingerprints of Stoicism; it is that the Stoic tradition acts as the very foundation for the entire project. As Smith paints *The Theory of Moral Sentiments,* the Stoic tradition resurrects and the power of its presence begins shaping the reflexes of modern morality.

The Apostles in *Theory* were not St. Peter or St. Paul. The Apostles of *Theory* were Epictetus and Marcus Aurelius.[304] Stoicism made her disciples centered and rooted through "very sublime doctrines" that empowered a life of wisdom and virtue in a world of contradictions that too often produced haste, over-reaction, and self-destruction in the lives of those lacking wisdom. According to Stoicism, the ways of God and the ways of the world are one and the same and are benevolent. According to God's benevolent design, humanity is interconnected and only healthy within context of a community that calls forth the best of her members. Paradox plays a central role in Stoicism, for neither God's goodness nor his designs' benevolence always appear on the surface of things. When life roughs you up, God's goodness comes into question. But knowing God is good and his designs benevolent is necessary to navigate the trials of life with wisdom.

Clinging to God's goodness in a brutal world nurtures one's intimacy with God, deepens disciples' wisdom, and empowers them to slay the passions that war against reason. After slaying the rashness of their passions, Stoic disciples develop a moral depth perception that allows them to see through the eyes of God the deeper wisdom within the ways of the world, to see below the surface of things to the benevolent ecosystem that exists and is engineered for the flourishing of creation. This depth perception enables a way of life capable of navigating life's paradoxes by focusing on wisely handling the circumstances of life that are under their control and graciously enduring the uncontrollable. Stoicism is not simply static doctrines but a way of life that withstands life's storms with grace and dignity.[305]

From this rich religious tradition, Smith gleans the core principles of his philosophy.[306] Stoicism was the religion Smith attempted to write onto the soul of modern man to rid modernity of its self-destructive madness. After Smith, Stoicism slowly but surely shapes modernity's morality but in a way that ingrained modernity's vices rather than moderating them. For Stoicism itself is not a philosophy without its vices, and Smith's customizing of Stoicism for the needs of modern man only inflamed the philosophy's failures.

—Imaginary Friends—

Stoicism ignited the imagination of Smith in the same way that Yahweh and the Laws of Moses once inspired the Hebrew prophets of long ago. And like the prophets of long ago, Smith is not simply a recipient of a fixed religion but a participant in forming and critiquing the tradition itself in order to pass it forward to future generations. When Stoicism flows from Smith's pen, it carries with it the power of his imagination; and through Smith's imaginative nuancing of Stoicism, four critical convictions begin forming the soul of modern man: that impartiality is the highest morality, that self-interest fuels society's redemption, that time itself is a positive force in righting society's wrongs, and that justice is primarily retributive. The first two convictions come from Smith's imaginary friends—the impartial spectator and the invisible hand.

For all of his abiding reverence for the ways of the Stoics, what Smith is most critical of within the Stoic tradition was its tendency to esteem the apathy that resulted from the slaying of the passions. For Smith, apathy is a moral monstrosity. Yet apathy was not a flaw Smith found fatal, for "nature has proved a proper remedy and correction. The real or even imaginary . . . impartial presence of *the impartial spectator*, the authority of the man within the breast."

The impartial spectator was a stolen imaginary friend, first from Epictetus's *Dialogues* and then from Joseph Addison's *The Spectator*. But Smith places a bit more flesh on his imaginary friend, making him central to his project and customizing him to act as the cornerstone for the moral life. In *Theory of Moral Sentiments,* the impartial spectator is our conversation partner to process the things we see in the world, the ways of men, and how we should respond when life does its work on us. Our friendship with the impartial spectator empowers us to stand in *impartial* shoes and see the world from the perspective of a wisdom untainted by human dramatics.

And it is through intimacy with the impartial spectator that we become intimate with God—we become attuned to the voice he placed within us. "The wise and just man" is not only aware of the dictates of the impartial perspective, but "he really adopts them . . . he almost becomes himself that impartial spectator, and scarce even feels but *as that great arbiter* of his conduct directs him to feel."[307] The impartial spectator empowers us to see our world from the moral high ground of unbiased *neutrality*, and it was from this balanced perspective of neutrality that our emotions find their proper alignment, neither too callously apathetic nor too irrationally passionate. Impartiality seemed to provide the greatest ground for rationality, and the greatest rationality seemed to provide the greatest ground for morality. In time, neutrality itself becomes the platform for righteous reasoning and an ironically superior way of judging the world's ways.

Yet, surely to the chagrin of Smith, at a societal level impartiality and neutrality proved rather impotent antidotes to apathy. The prophetic tradition rooted righteous judgments, not in neutrality, but in a predisposition to protect the poor and marginalized. Perhaps impartiality produced more scientific approaches to societal inequalities, but it failed to even the playing field between rich and poor, male and female, black and white. The failure resided in impartiality's inability to produce intimacy. After all, it is diverse intimacies—not impartiality—that is necessary to address the injustices in a society divided by demographic differences. Rather than meaningful *solidarity*, impartiality too often created its own form of ignorance by promoting moral *superiority* under the guise of impartial neutrality. Racist inequalities produced by impartial judges, politicians, and preachers only perpetuated systemic failures while claiming a moral high ground.

Following Reconstruction, the nation embraced an impartial relationship to the South's racial injustice, in effect feeding black communities to racist wolves. "There was a time when Northerners . . . sought to give [African Americans] protection . . . against the prevailing sentiment of the South," declared President Taft. "The movement proved to be a failure." President Taft made clear that his embrace of Southern Racism was not a reflection of his own racism. "Personally," President Taft assured his audience, "I have not the slightest race prejudice."[308]

Smith's second imaginary friend: the invisible hand. Though the impartial spectator is Adam's favorite imaginary friend, the invisible hand proved to be America's. This imaginary friend Smith steals from Shakespeare's *Macbeth*. The work that Smith's invisible hand performs provides a portrait of a freely moving economy that harmonizes self-interested individuals into communities of mutual benefit. And it was this portrait of communities of mutual benefit empowered by self-interest that the economically minded—folks like Milton Friedman and the free market apologist from the University of Chicago—came to adore.

ADAM SMITH'S BUTCHERS, BREWERS, AND BAKERS

Your Meal Brought to You By:
The Free Market & Self Interest

What provided the invisible hand staying power was Smith's ability to replace an antagonistic relationship between virtue and vice in economics with a rationality whereby virtue and vice, in fact, complement. This remarkable ability proved transformational through his oft-quoted phrase: "It is not from the benevolence of the butcher, the brewer, or the baker, that we can expect our dinner, but from their regard to their own interest."[309] Following this alliteration, it proves difficult for Smith's readers to gather around a table without remembering his well-crafted phrase, which trains its recipients to see the power of self-interest in their daily life as the basic virtue that empowers even the most basic practice of fellowship—the breaking of bread and sharing of a meal. After Smith's writings, the power and benefit of impersonal exchange grew in the minds of economists who needed Smith's poetry to better understand what we too often take for granted in daily interactions. The clarity, poetry, and realism of this one alliteration possessed the power to overthrow an age-old conviction: lives of self-interest led not to damnation but to fellowship, redemption, and the proper alignment of society itself.

What distinguished Smith, however, was not simply his poetic realism concerning a daily interaction, but his ability to move his argument concerning the relationship between benevolence and self-interest from the daily grind of butchers, brewers, and bakers to encapsulate an entire system of economic exchange; his ability to endow his alliteration with cosmic potentiality. Self-interest converts to benevolence, not by human intentionality, but by the hocus-pocus of his imaginary invisible hand. In one of the most transformative paragraph's in the Enlightenment, Smith writes: "By directing that industry in such a manner as its produce may be of greatest value, he intends only his own gain, and he is in this, as in many other cases, led by an *invisible hand* to promote an end which was no part of his intention . . ." Smith continues: "By pursuing his own interests he frequently promotes that of society more effectually than when he really intends to promote it." And then Smith closes the paragraph noting the futility of fighting the system: "I have never known much good done by those who affected the trade for the public good. It is an affection, indeed, not very common among merchants, and very few words need be employed in dissuading him from it."[310]

On April 30, 1789, Washington addressed Congress for the first time: "No people can be bound to acknowledge and adore the invisible hand, which conducts the affairs of men, more than the people of the United States." Though the invisible hand came on Washington's lips, it was the hand of Madison—who had been reading *The Wealth of Nations* for his speech on import duties—that penned the address.[311]

For merchants and master manufactures, those who Smith trusted the least, the invisible hand provided such explanatory power for daily transactions that the figment of Smith's imagination was spoken of as if it were indeed both visible and tangible. Smith's ability to display how self-interest converts to a public good won him the chair of moral philosophy—not simply of Glasgow University—but of much of the Western world. Paradoxically, Smith's writings suffered severely from his own persuasive powers. It was this alliteration of butchers, brewers, and bakers, and this metaphor of an invisible hand, that made his readers deaf to almost everything else he said concerning the need for equity, the threats arising from the profits, the politics of merchants and master manufacturers, and the unjust wages that warred against working families.

One of the paradoxes of Stoicism was that though it warred against the passions, there was one passion that proved redemptive—self-interest. Of all the temptations Smith could toy with in the modern world, the passion of self-interest was perhaps the most toxic of all. Nevertheless, like the

Stoicism of old, Smith treats this passion as a paradoxical plaything and in so doing, when the interest of the powerful and the poor collided, Smith's philosophy seemingly sided with the wealthy and christened any atrocity induced by self-interest. Where the invisible hand received acceptance as a reality, the very pursuit of justice in the economic realm seemed as illogical as it was impossible. The poetics of Smith made the works of Hobbes that once seemed despotic all the more persuasive. Once upon a time, concepts such as unjust wages made sense, but after Smith, concepts such as unjust wages evaporated into a "freely" flowing market. Through Smith's genius, the economy overcame the restraints of morality; for economics was and is portrayed as existing outside the realms of morality in the same way that Greek gods existed outside the claims of time.

Smith's impartial spectator and invisible hand were hypnotic—providing a path for merchants to christen both their indifference to inequity and their self-interest. What made the logic of both *The Theory of Moral Sentiments* and *The Wealth of Nations* alluring to the affluent—particularly the affluent of America—was a selective reading that empowered each member of society to unabashedly pursue personal interest while at the same time removing any responsibility for the economic fallout from its power players. For those made drunk by Smith's alliteration and metaphor, the poor became "logically" responsible for the entirety of their predicament, while those who successfully sought their own gain received absolution. The more visible the hand grew in the mind's eye of business and political power players, the more invisible the poor and structural injustices became.

The invisible hand provided for the wealthy of the new nation Pilate's washbowl: a way to cleanse oneself of guilt by pretending they possessed no power to make the game more humane. Though the Judeo-Christian tradition relates the plight of the poor to the indifference of the powerful, after Smith such responsibility becomes insensible. Through Smith, the affluent received training *to not think, feel, or see* the ethical implications of their economic activity, their record profits, and their overabundance in a land of poverty.

Of course, what Smith's imaginary friends and alliteration failed to do was precisely what the moral philosopher was called to do—and that is to protect the well-being of those whom the system fails. If it is true that the butcher, brewer, and baker provided a good (i.e., our dinners) out of their own self-interest, it is also true that beef, brew, and bread go to rot, not due to a lack of hunger or thirst, but because the *best interest* of the hungry routinely fails to harmonize with the *self-interest* of the powerful. Malcolm X seared this routine failure on his readers by his retelling of his conversation in Mecca:

> [She] asked me, "Why are people in the world starving when America has so much surplus food? What do they do, dump it in the ocean?" I told her, "Yes, but they put some of it in the holds of surplus ships and in subsidized granaries and refrigerated space and let it stay there . . . until it is unfit to eat. Then [they] get rid of it to make space for the next surplus batch. . . ." Probably she thought I was kidding . . . I didn't go on to tell her that right in the United States there are hungry people.[312]

As Smith knew all too well, in the battle between the rich and the poor there are conflicts of interest rather than a harmony of self-interests. Nonetheless, rather than providing his readers a moral depth perception necessary for them to navigate these conflicts, Smith too often left his fingerprint on his disciples in their inability to think morally about society's most serious problems when self-interest failed to provide the prophesied redemption.

—Progressive Father Time, Retributive Lady Justice, & Benevolent Citizens—

If Smith's imaginary friends were not kind to the poor, if the impartial spectator failed to slay apathy, and if the invisible hand failed to harmonize the self-interest of the rich folks with the needs of the poor, Smith's understanding of time, justice, and how to provide for the poor only made matters worse. Smith committed himself to two Stoic lies and the ultimate Stoic self-deception. The Stoic lies resided in convictions regarding the nature of Father Time and Lady Justice; the Stoic self-deception resided in its convictions about the sufficiency of Benevolent Citizens to right a society's unjust ways.

First lie: Father Time is a progressive fellow. As a consequence of believing that the way things are reflect the benevolent ways of God, Smith and the Stoics believed that something in time itself moved history towards a greater and greater good and that the best path to justice is allowing nature to take her natural course. We are progressing towards a more benevolent society, not because we advocate for the broken and abused and work to rid society of inequalities, but because Father Time himself trots a progressive path. The greater the confidence in the progressive nature of Father Time, the stronger the paradoxical conviction becomes that the less we fight against the system's injustices, the more rapidly we progress towards a more equitable opulence. The argument runs like this: since the system is good and benevolent, any adjustment to the system to address its current dysfunctions will likely produce unintended consequences that will in turn produce injustices down the road. As Smith writes later: "A very considerable degree of inequality, it appears, I believe, from the experience of all nations, is not near so great an evil as a very small degree of uncertainty."[313] When dysfunction is witnessed, faith in the free market and Father Time is required. Haste makes waste.

Campaigning in 1903, President Theodore Roosevelt began promoting an impartial "square deal for the negro" to garner the African-American vote. To display his readiness to make a square deal real, the Justice Department investigated the South's convict leasing programs. Rather than facing what they found—a vast system of slavery reminiscent of the Old Confederacy—Roosevelt embraced injustice, retreated the investigations, and signed pardons for those convicted for enslaving generations of laborers. [314]

Smith, of course, placed his own signature on the conviction of Father Time's progressive tendencies by introducing into the conversation his conviction regarding the role of the division of labor. Smith believed that in the modern age, the age where machine and man partner for a previously unimaginable productivity, equity would gradually become the world's norm. There is in man, Smith argued, a "propensity to truck, barter, and exchange one thing for another."[315] The process is "very slow and gradual," but humanity learns to uniquely align talents in order to increase productive powers and, in time, well-organized societies increase in opulence. In the advent of where the division of labor is complemented by a partnership with machines "the great multiplication of the productions" means that soon "that universal opulence" will extend "itself *to the lowest ranks of the people*."[316] The division of labor within a free market, in Smith's mind, multiples the power of time's progressive tendencies.[317]

Smith believed his philosophies regarding the power of a progressive Father Time and the division of labor to provide for the poor were not cut from the fabric of fantasies. Smith's eyes focused on Holland, where his vision of a free market that produced low profits, high wages, and an equitable opulence, was already a reality.[318] Smith believed that through patience and the free market, the Dutch reality would become the English reality, the colonial reality,[319] the reality for which the world waited and towards which history strived. It was an inspiring vision and Adam made his case very convincingly, but he proved wrong and time failed to make the world more Dutch. And, in many ways, it was Smith's and the Stoic notions of justice he heralded that lost equity in its English translation.

The second lie: Lady Justice is about retribution. For the Dutch, and for philosophers such as Spinoza, justice was a proactive notion intertwined with the pursuit of equity and a positive peace.[320] Yet for Smith and the Stoics, "justice is upon most occasions, but a negative virtue, *and only hinders us from hurting our neighbour*."[321]

When justice is negative virtue, a society's vision of justice reduces to the tale of the fabled Little Bunny Foo Foo. Why did a Good Fairy turn Little Bunny Foo Foo into a goon? Was it because Little Bunny Foo Foo failed to care for other bunnies of the colony? No. Little Bunny Foo Foo was turned into a goon because he "went hopping through the forest, scooping up the field mice, and bopping them on the head." Even a Good Fairy cannot tolerate that in her forest. In the Western world that followed Smith's lead, justice reduced to not intentionally hurting others and turning her criminals into goons when they broke the law one too many times.

Rather than justice being about the care of widows, orphans, and restoring outcasts to community, Smith says flatly: "We may often fulfil all the rules of justice by sitting still and doing nothing."[322] Reversing the relationship so that indifference leads to justice rather than injustice proved a dangerous turn in the modern moral imagination. The more shaped by Smith's retributive understandings of justice a society became, the less able she grew to imagine that justice possessed restorative potential. No one embodied the inability to imagine the positive potential of a restorative justice more than one of America's most imaginative judges—Supreme Court Justice Anthony Scalia. "The racist concept of restorative justice," Scalia wrote in his previous life as a professor, "is fundamentally contrary to the principles that govern, and should govern, our society."[323] In a nation whose criminal justice proved complicit in cycles of injustice, in a nation that often imprisoned rather than protected her most vulnerable, Scalia failed to fathom the need for restorative justice. Tragically, throughout our history, rather than warring against poverty the U.S.'s retributive justice system warred—and wars—against the poor, for it lacked—and lacks—the imagination to do otherwise.

The great self-deception: Benevolent Citizens provide sufficiently for the poor. Neither confidence in a progressive Father Time nor a retributive Lady Justice answers the question of how a society practically responds to the problems of the impoverished in their midst. But Smith provides a solution—individual benevolence. "Generosity, humanity, kindness, compassion, mutual friendship and esteem," wrote Smith, "all the social and benevolent affections, when expressed in the countenance or behaviour, even towards those who are not peculiarly connected with ourselves, please the indifferent spectator upon almost every occasion."[324]

For Smith's students of history, private benevolence filling the void of society's systemic failures is a surprising suggestion. In Smith's lectures, it was after all the lords of feudalism who practiced *beneficia* and "by this means the lords secured the fidelity of their vassals."[325] According to Smith, feudal lords employed *beneficia* to perpetuate inequality, not to achieve an equitable society. Benevolence does what it is designed to do—ease the conscience of the powerful and employ the gratitude of the powerless to reinforce a broken social order. Though historically private benevolence proves a superficial solution to suffering resulting from public, systemic failures, superficial solutions rarely fail to satisfy the wealthy. In a free market, the only place where results fail to matter is how the economy provides for the poor.[326]

Thus the cause of the poor fell into the hands of new social players who conducted business like the feudal lords of old—the private philanthropists. Through philanthropy, the robber barons and titans of industry employed their wealth's might to ease the suffering of those the current social and economic structures failed. Despite a rhetoric of empowerment, too often benevolence functioned as social control to keep power in the hands of the powerful while providing the powerless little leverage in the very initiatives aimed at their uplift. The more poignant the need, the less sufficient personal benevolence proved. In the words of one social worker of a previous generation: "Trying to turn back this tide of distress through private philanthropic contributions is about as useless as trying to put out a forest fire with a garden hose."[327] From the days of feudal lords through the days of the titans of philanthropy, benevolence decoupled from the systemic pursuit of economic justice reinforced rather than redeemed the status quo.[328] "The negro race," wrote DuBois, "needed justice but is given charity . . . This nation will never stand justified before God until these things are changed."

~

Somewhat amazingly, Smith failed to see how the Impartial Spectator, the Invisible Hand, Father Time, Lady Justice, and Benevolent Citizens complemented one another in a way that made it nearly impossible for the poor to be grafted into their nation's opulence; that made it nearly impossible for the failures of the modern project he analyzed so incisively to be unwritten. Despite the historical impotence of benevolence to overcome systemic injustices, President George H. W. Bush turned the power of uncoordinated philanthropy into poetry through the "thousand points of light" phrase of his 1989 inaugural speech. "I have spoken of a Thousand Points of Light," Bush said with his well balanced touch, "of all the community organizations that are spread like stars throughout the Nation, doing good." Bush continued: "The old ideas are new again because they're not old, they are timeless: duty, sacrifice, commitment, and a patriotism that finds its expression in taking part and pitching in." To say that the Benevolent Citizens would provide a thousand points of light was also to commit to the night of poverty in the land of plenty. One aspect from Bush's speech was true. His ideas were old. Bush's philosophy of philanthropy was identical to President Hoover's and Adam Smith's.

A year before the stock market crash of 1929, President Hoover delivered his rugged individualism address: "We are nearer today to the ideal of the abolition of poverty and fear . . . than ever before in any land." When rugged individualism and unregulated self-interest failed, Hoover created the Emergency Committee on Employment Relief. "I have a remarkable job for you," Hoover told the director. "You are to feed the several million unemployed." "With what?" "That's what makes the job remarkable. If you had something to do it with, it wouldn't be remarkable."[329]

Unfortunately, there seems little Christian alternative to Stoic notions of justice in the thinking of white Christians on U.S. soils. Typical of the failure of Christian conviction to leaven Stoic thinking is a publication of Jerry Falwell's Liberty University, *Christian Perspectives: a Journal of Free Enterprise,* and its core conviction that "the combination of democracy and our capitalistic economy (free-enterprise) is the philosophical foundation upon which the practical solutions to almost all political-economy problems and issues must be based."[330] Despite the violence of American-styled democratic and economic systems on their brothers and sisters of color, white Christians too often see little wrong with the American game and believe their faith harmonizes with the injustices that are as American as apple pie. As white Christian leaders have become increasingly committed to the Stoic convictions regarding the nature of self-interest, time, and justice, the religion that is Christian in name has become increasingly Stoic in nature. Just as Epictetus and Marcus Aurelius replaced Peter and Paul in the works of Adam Smith, so does Adam Smith replace Jesus himself at the intersection of political and economic thinking for too many white Christians. In the arena of economics and politics, it is not that white Christians proved more or less moral than the surrounding culture; too often they simply proved no different.

A LETTER FROM BIRMINGHAM JAIL: TO STOIC NATION WITH A STONE HARD HEART

So it was that in a "Christian" nation, a nation ingrained with hard-hearted and racist ideologies, with politicians like John F. Kennedy and ministers like Billy Graham, that Martin Luther King Jr. sat in a Birmingham jail and began penning a letter. King addresses his letter to Christian ministers who proved as hard-hearted as the police and politicians who represented them, but he writes demanding an audience with the entire nation. Adam Smith and Martin Luther King diagnosed the modern predicament in remarkably similar fashions. What divided them was how to address modernity's evils. King's *Letter* reads as a manifesto against the morality that Smith worked to ingrain into America's soul.

For King, the impartial spectator was "the white moderate," those who Nixon later lionized as the "silent majority" and Falwell christened as the "moral majority." Unlike Nixon or Falwell, rather than this majority embodying the best of American morality, King believed their impartial silence led to an unspoken alliance with the forces of evil. King wrote with an eloquent fury: "The Negro's great stumbling block in the stride toward freedom is not the White Citizens Counciler or the Klu Klux Klanner, but the moderate who is more devoted to 'order' than to justice."

Graham biographer Grant Wacker recounts: "Though King did not specifically name him, Graham surely saw himself in King's crosshairs." Graham's response? He tells *The New York Times* that his "good personal friend," should "put on the brakes a bit." Graham refused to support the Civil Rights Acts of 1964 and 1965, and history is left to wonder what would have been possible had Graham, who was remarkably humble, learned from King rather than lectured him.[331]

King saw no invisible hand that coordinated the self-interests of whites with the interests of blacks. He saw instead a system that brutalized black fathers, mothers, and children through an unchallenged system that empowered the white majority to enforce unjust laws on minorities. Superficial solutions and "shallow understanding from people of good will is more frustrating than absolute misunderstanding from people of ill will," he wrote.[332]

For King, convictions concerning a progressive Father Time and a retributive Lady Justice only perpetuated America's original sin. "Time is neutral," wrote King, but "I am coming to feel that people of ill will have used time much more effectively than the people of good will." Then he moved to the heart of the matter: "We will have to repent in this generation not merely for the vitriolic words and actions of the bad people, but for the appalling silence of the good people. We must come to see that human progress never rolls on the wheels of inevitability." Where time is progressive and justice is retributive, the American Dream thrives, for the American Dream is a Stoic hypnosis. Smithian morality allowed America to dream all the deeper.

THE QUESTION OF CAIN: & INGRAINING THE SLAVEMASTER'S MYTH

And so it was that the moral philosopher of Glasgow became one of the most formative molders of modern morality. As a historian, Smith proved every bit the prophet. He saw clearly the threat of the nobility, the merchants, and the master manufacturers to society's common good and continually sided with the laborers and the poor. He highlighted the truths of history and social life that the aristocrats wanted to erase from the minds of the people. For Smith, history teaches us that the greatest temptation to stray from a path of equitable opulence was to allow merchants—whose interest always conflicted with those of the people—to shape political policies. The politics of the merchants was a politics of self-sabotage for the public. To the chagrin of free-market economists and the moguls of industry, Smith is neither their father nor their mouthpiece.

But the irony of Smith's work was that though his history and aims were prophetic, his theoretical solutions were thoroughly Stoic, producing a morality antithetical to prophetic aims. This tension between prophetic aims and Stoic means tore Smith's project asunder. Stoic philosophy was about the benevolence of the status quo and believed a challenge to the status quo always undermined the benevolence of the created order. For the prophet, the status quo was the problem not the solution. The task he undertook—to harness a project tailored to the interests of the Aristocrats and aim it towards an equitable opulence—was a project ill-suited for Stoic philosophy. In Smith, the deep paradoxes between prophetic and Stoic commitments produced almost schizophrenic ideas that only quickened and heightened the injustices he saw all too clearly.

With the nature of government and religion firmly in place through the lies written by Hobbes and perfected by Locke, Smith added the lies about the nature of justice. The lie that justice is retributive flowed straight from Smith's quill, while the lie that indifference to injustice was no threat to one's relationship with God was a lie that Smith wrote backwards—a working out of his logic that moved against the grain of his intentions. Smith's lie that redefined the nature of justice drove the lies about the nature of government and religion all the deeper into the modern soul.

The collective impact of Smith's philosophies was a way of thinking that made poverty all the more destitute and slave shackles all the more secure. Concepts Smith crafted to champion the dignity of the poor more often than not provided the merchants he distrusted with political power and justified the historical injustices he sought to bring to an end. A significant part of this tragedy results from the superficiality of his disciples—from Reagan and Rand to Falwell and Friedman, to Rand Paul and Paul Ryan—who have read Smith selectively and used his theories towards ends antithetical to their original aims. But another part of the tragedy is that Smith failed to grasp basic truths—the truth that Stoic philosophy never favored the people; the truth that Stoic philosophies imagined by a merchant and that were perfected to underwrite Rome's imperial power are antithetical to the pursuit of justice for the people; and the truth that the prophetic and the Stoic are at war and that anytime the Stoic wins equality loses.

Yet for all of Smith's failures, his moral vision was far more superior to the cultural common sense of those who heralded his philosophies. Somewhere along the line, we lost Smith's distrust of job creators, his urgency regarding the war of wages, how slavery was built to rape women and kill children, and how the only way out of the cycle of poverty, slavery, and crime was a commitment to equity. What we held onto was Smith's imaginary friends convinced of the morality of impartiality and self-interest and the Stoic lies regarding the nature of benevolent Father Time and retributive Lady Justice. What we held onto from Smith's brilliance ingrained the slavemaster's myth on America's soul—not by making slavery seem moral but by making indifference and taking a safe distance from the black cause seem acceptable to both secular and religious-minded people. Smith's attack on the commercial system only fortified the merchants, master manufactures and their politicians against the prophetic criticisms he leveled against them.

By the time Smith's philosophies filtered through his disciples, the only question that was left was from the original Adam's son Cain: "Am I my brother's keeper?" And, in America, the nation built on both rugged individualism and slavery, the answer was easy to anticipate. In a Christian nation, the only thing most Americans believe in more deeply than the power of Christ to forgive sin is the power of the market to end injustice. Yet, almost 250 years after Smith's famous bonfire of his unperfected works, we still wait for the free market to trickle the wealth of the prosperous down to the poor, believing that—with a little more time and money—faith will become sight.

5

Interlude

An Orbiting Cycle Creating Rational, Sentimental, and Hard-Hearted Citizens

THE LIES & AN ORBITING CYCLE

It proves difficult to overstate the differences in the world in which Thomas Hobbes was born in 1588 and the one in which Adam Smith was laid to rest in 1790. In Hobbes's time, imagining a world in which Christians *didn't* kill Christians in the name of Christ was nearly impossible. Christians killing Christians was the orbiting cycle of violence that flung the blood of its victims throughout Europe with no end in sight. Yet, by the time of Adam Smith's final bonfire, Christians killing Christians in the name of Christ was a rarity.

The brilliance of folks like Hobbes, Locke, and Smith slowed the cycle of religious violence until the "Wars of Religion" was the name of a bygone age of "irrationality." But if Hobbes, Locke, and Smith—and the enlightened way of life that they helped usher in—stopped the cycle of religious violence, they certainly didn't stop orbiting cycles of violence, nor did they stop Christians killing Christians and others. As the orbit of religious violence slowed, the orbit of "racial" violence accelerated. It is the violence of that orbit that we are now called upon to slow to a stop.

In the introduction, I argued that three lies were intertwined within "the trinity's" political and religious ideologies that coalesced into paradigms of political, economic, and religious thinking that keeps the orbiting cycle of racial violence, in the words of Willie Lynch, "spinning on its own axis forever." These paradigms produced broad-brush truisms and a cultural common sense that, when investigated up close and within the context of their primary sources, are actually finely stenciled ideologies performing sadistic work in society. Before moving into the final section, I want to revisit those three political and religious lies one last time, for they are lies we must un-write if we are to slow the violent orbit of our racist ideologies and begin imagining ways of life where intimacy and equity replaces enmity and indifference.

First, the political lies, lies regarding the purpose of politics, the morality of economics, and the nature of justice. The first political lie was that government is not about the pursuit of the common good or working to provide a more just balance to a community's inequalities. As outlined earlier, the roots of the rejection of the common good can be traced back Thomas Hobbes's *Leviathan*, where a totalitarian government seeks self-preservation by accumulating the world's resources. In Locke, Hobbes's ideas evolve into a democratic institutional form, as governments' goals reduce further from self-preservation via a political tyrant to the preservation of property via a small government. The concept crystalized in Locke's declaration that "the chief end" of "civil society . . . is the preservation of property."[333]

If small government provided an antidote to political tyranny, it did so while empowering another class of tyrants—the aristocrats. The Leviathan became corporate. Behind the idea of a small government was the lust for unmitigated power within the economically elite. For the rich of the earth, the appeal of small government is the freedom to plunder the poor of the earth—and the earth itself—without governmental checks and balances. Without a government to intervene to redistribute the concentration of wealth, the corporate titans became modernity's Leviathans, controlling both economic and political power. Thus the irony of small government is the incredible societal power entrusted to the economically elite.[334] Tyranny evolved, and we called it progress.

At the birth of a new nation, America's aristocracy—none more important than James Madison—designed a democracy that aimed to preserve property, creating a government more committed to protecting her inequalities than her people. In time, the aristocracy learned to argue that the only governmental good that needed doing consisted in deregulations and tax cuts. The suffering of slaves, the poor, and the marginalized were written out of the new political calculus. The lie that government is not about pursuing the common good became a foundational ideological lie of American politics.

The second lie centered on economics and also proved damning to the poor. It was that economics is a moral-free math, and man's equality need not translate to economic equity. Once the aristocracy sold the lie that government is impotent to bring good to the world, the economy was positioned to become the omnipotent provider of the world's deepest needs. The critical phrase that greased the logic's wheels was Hobbes's declaration: "The Value, or Worth of a man, as of all things [is] his Price . . . And as in other things, so in men, not the seller, but the *buyer* determines the Price."[335] Hobbes's equating the scientific value of man to his role within the economic engine provided humanity a utilitarian value perfectly tailored to strip the poor of human dignity. No longer are the poor understood as the priceless children of God. They are expendable components of an economic engine. The poor play an economically rigged game, and if they failed to beat the odds, God's children were reimagined as economic drains. Locke's lie that the government was about the preservation of property helped institutionalize a morality-free economic math in free-market form. As the elite concentrated the wealth of the world into their pockets, the governments protected, rather than rectified, the inequalities that sick economies engineered. As Adam Smith wrote: "Civil government, so far as it is instituted for the security of property, is in reality instituted for the defense of the rich against the poor."[336] The lies about the nature of government and economics interlocked in Hobbes's and Locke's philosophies to write the dignity of the oppressed people out of *both* political and economic considerations.

The final political lie: justice is retributive. When neither the government nor the economy intentionally seek to provide basic needs for hordes of people, more lies are needed to reinforce society's sadistic work. Thus, the concept of justice went through a great evolution during the Enlightenment. Hobbes, Locke, and other Enlightenment thinkers thinned out notions of justice into contractual arrangements. Reducing justice to paperwork displayed the depth—or the lack thereof—of the Enlightenment thinkers' commitment to exercise justice on behalf of those their philosophies abused. Without the commitment to exercise, justice's intellectual and institutional muscles atrophied. Nowhere is the atrophy of justice more clear than in the Stoic writings of Adam Smith when he wrote that "we may often fulfil all the rules of justice by sitting still and doing nothing."[337]

Rather than tying justice to care for the least of these or the restoration and redemption of the fallen, the final lie reduced justice to punishing those who break the rules. When we learned to limit justice to retribution for rule breakers, we failed to learn how to question the brokenness of the rules themselves. And when the rules of the game crucified the vulnerable and their children, our notions of justice did exactly what the Enlightenment designed them to do—brutally enforce the status quo. And that is the kicker, as our ability to think about justice atrophied, the systems of justice became accomplices to the works of injustice. From denying the humanity of Dred Scott, to upholding the constitutionality of Jim Crow, to prisons that turned black and brown in a colorblind age, our system of justice twisted the laws of the land into nooses that strangle the life out of black and brown people and communities. At the color line, America's justice system historically and systemically raped and rapes Lady Justice with no end in sight.

And so it goes. The Enlightenment sowed lies about the very purpose of government, the morality of economics, and the nature of justice into the soul of the American experiment. When America harmonized its desires for freedom, liberty, and justice with the teachings of Willie Lynch, it produced the land of the American Dream. But an indispensible component of that dream is its obliviousness to the nightmare of an orbiting cycle of racialized violence within the land of milk and honey. When racism was common sense, the violence needed no explanation; when racism was no longer politically correct, white folks convinced themselves that the racial tragedies were coincidental rather than contrived. After examining these three political lies, we see why American democracy failed to achieve racial justice. America designed her democracy to perpetuate racial injustices and economic inequity.

Politics was only part of America's racial problem. Before the Enlightenment, our ideas about God shaped society's thinking about the role of government, economics, and justice. The Enlightenment reversed the way the river flowed so that everything we said about religion harmonized with the Enlightenment's political philosophies, including the projects of colonization, capitalism, and racial inequality. From her inception, America's white pulpits brought religious zeal to the orbiting cycle of racialized violence, making the cycle all the more furious and intractable. The pulpits failed to produce a prophetic solidarity with the dispossessed across racial lines, and a white Christianity arose on America's soil that possessed few prophetic bones in her body.[338]

The white church followed the train track of religious lies the Enlightenment had laid down. The first religious lie that shaped America's white church was that Christians could be in right relationship with their God without being in right relationship with the broken and abused of their society. The lie contradicted both the Old and New Testaments, and Hobbes's fingerprints are all over it. Here's how the perversion played out: Since humanity is primarily rational and not relational, religion needs to produce holy *knowledge* not holy *relationships*. As Hobbes quips: "All that is NECESSARY to Salvation, is contained in two Vertues, Faith in Christ, and Obedience to Laws."[339] Centering religion in individualized knowledge—or faith in Christ—and obedience to rulers allowed the White Church, whether liberal or conservative, to reduce to a space for white Christians to commune with God with no need for the wisdom, knowledge, or intimacy with their black and brown brothers and sisters. When religion reduced to loving on Jesus and obeying the powerful, the faithful became willingly complicit in the injustices their society's perpetuated, confusing such complicity with piety.

The second lie tightly aligned to the first: religion is about the salvation of the soul. This lie was Locke's, as he labored to institutionalize enlightened ideas regarding religion in ways that protected and perpetuated society's social divides. "The *only* business of the Church," as Locke said, "is the salvation of souls; and *it no way* concerns the commonwealth, or any member of it."[340] A faith that provides little to no room for the poor, widows, and orphans in its thinking easily wraps religion around individual selves and souls. Unsurprisingly, Christianity became an increasingly introspective and individualistic thing, oblivious to the world and unable to translate Scripture's social convictions to the world's most basic and earthy needs. Erudite Christian leaders proved capable of translating Paul from Greek to English, but few possessed the relationships necessary to translate Paul to the political and racial problems of their day. That, they thought, was not their job.

The third lie: indifference to injustice is no threat to one's intimacy with God. In biblical traditions, indifference to injustice means one really doesn't know the Bible's God, and it leads Jesus to damn the indifferent to "the eternal fire prepared for the devil and his angels."[341] The religious tradition that celebrates indifference is Stoicism, and thus the writing of this lie fell to the Stoic disciple Adam Smith. Smith never intended to act as a forefather of any Christian movement. He was, however, very interested in accelerating the influence of Stoic morality into Christian culture. As the masses of America's white Christians exchanged the prophetic tradition for his Stoic morality, Smith became a Founding Father for the white American Church. In this swap, self-interest replaced self-sacrifice, impartiality replaced solidarity, and confidence in the progressive ways of time displaced the need to partner with God in the struggle to bring His Kingdom to earth.

Rather than self-sacrifice, solidarity, and laboring for God's Kingdom, impartiality and "benevolent affections" acted as the pinnacle of the moral life. Even within the lives of committed Christians, impartiality and benevolence failed to awaken the apathetic lulled to sleep through self-interest and partiality. Instead, "Christian" instincts proved remarkably indifferent to injustice. In America's white Christianity, Adam Smith proved more persuasive in forming morality than the prophets, Christ, and the early church combined. With this new morality, benevolent white Christians provided themselves safe distance from the pain, suffering, and rage of their black brothers and sisters and became kindly cogs in the orbiting cycle of racial violence. When religion no longer revolved around relationships and the creation of the beloved community, white churches often seemed more dedicated to the logics of their race than their redeemer.

As our nation continued to promote economic and political policies that placed black and brown people on American-made crosses, white Christians refused to stand in solidarity with God's black and brown children. Instead, they empowered politicians who made a living deprioritizing black dignity. Like the wheels of the bus, the orbiting cycle of racial violence went round and round, round and round. After examining theses three religious lies, we see why America's white Christianity failed to achieve racial justice. America's white Christianity was designed to perpetuate racial injustices.

~

Long after the slave ships like the *Jesus of Lübeck, the Trinity, Bartholomew,* and *John the Evangelist* lowered their sails, the American experiment continued to infuse life into these lies. On American soil, the orbiting cycle of racialized violence lead to slavery, Jim Crow, mass incarceration, and a war against immigrants. This cycle produced and was then perpetuated by folks who proved remarkably rational, strangely sentimental, and thoroughly hard-hearted.

The orbiting cycle began spinning in the colonies. The Declaration of Independence failed to slow the orbiting cycle down because we fought the Revolution, at least in part, to speed the cycle up. The Emancipation Declaration removed the axis of slavery from the orbiting cycle, but rather than committing to racial equity, the nation committed herself to another racial axis, Jim Crow segregation. Looking back, we are shocked at this racial depravity and to the extent of our obliviousness to how deeply ingrained racism is in our national experiment.

For those with depth perception, it was predictable. "The law and the sword cannot abolish the malignant slaveholding sentiment," wrote Frederick Douglass during the Civil War. "Pride of race, prejudice of color, will raise . . . [and] the slave having ceased to be the abject slave of a single master, his enemies will endeavor to make him the slave of society at large."[342] Over the next one hundred years, Douglass's depth perception proved prophetic. Jim Crow's pitiless rule—from convict leasing programs to the New Deal's racist edges to Truman, Eisenhower, and JFK's remarkable indifference—attempted to perpetuate racial divisions and inequalities by modern twentieth-century means.

For the Union, the Civil War was first about national unity not slavery. As Lincoln himself made clear, "If I could save the union without freeing any slave I would do it."[343]

SLOWING THE ORBIT

Nonetheless, the next pivot in racial relations arose as Ms. Parks sat and brought the civil rights movement into public view. Jim Crow slowly began to crumple, and after a decade of boycotts, protests, sit-ins, and martyrdom, the Civil Rights Bills of 1964 and 1965 put an end to Jim Crow segregation and provided the right to vote, removing the axis around which Southern-styled racism spun. In many ways, 1965 brought an end to Phase I of the civil rights movement, which sought to empower minority communities by removing obstacles to participate in American society. Phase I re-wrote the books of law, and in re-writing them fundamental changes began in American life.

Yet, the victory of what King referred to as the Second Emancipation Proclamation was met by white backlash that equaled the first Emancipation. In *Where Do We Go From Here?*, published soon after the signing of the Civil Rights Bill of 1965, King writes: "white backlash had become an emotional electoral issue . . . as political clowns had become governors . . . their magic achieved with a 'witches' brew of bigotry, prejudice, half-truths and whole lies." White backlash was not limited to the voting booth but became incarnate in the martyred bodies of civil rights workers. "The swift and easy acquittals that followed for the accused," King wrote, "shocked much of the nation but sent a wave of unabashed triumph through Southern segregationist circles. Many of us wept at the funeral services for the dead and for democracy."[344]

Through tear-filled eyes, King's vision moved beyond fighting segregation and Phase I's push for participation and full citizenship to fighting the more entrenched forms of racism above the Mason–Dixon Line. The vision moved King to confront America's most segregated city—Chicago.[345] From the hood to the suburbs, Chicago's toxic racism was obvious in radical inequalities that separated black and white lives. Chicago's racism, however, was so enmeshed in the laws that it was almost invisible. Unsurprisingly, the racism that existed between the letters and lines of Chicago's laws proved no less lethal than the laws that spelled out Southern racism.[346] King wrote that the violence and vitriol of Chicago's suburbanites rivaled anything experienced below the Mason–Dixon Line. King was bewildered.

Chicago changed King even if King didn't change Chicago. After Chicago, King saw that the lies that formed America's faith and politics, the lies that empowered the orbiting cycle of racial violence, no longer needed the axes, like slavery and segregation, that the South had so long provided upon which to spin. The orbiting cycle was so ingrained into the hearts and minds of America that it performs its work just as effectively in a colorblind age, crucifying poor folks on both sides of the color line while concentrating its violence on those with black and brown skin. King continually spoke of "a triple pronged sickness that has been lurking within our body politic from its very beginning . . . racism, excessive materialism and militarism."[347]

Chicago taught King that the nature of the future fight of the civil rights movement, what he later referred to as Phase II, was not against the brazen racism of the Bull Connors of Birmingham but the ideologies of the refined racism of the white moderate that he attacked in his "Letter from Birmingham Jail." After Chicago, King saw that the fight for the civil rights movement must radicalize. Phase I of the fight for justice was a fight for participation via the abolition of segregation. Phase II of the fight for justice, the more radical fight King envisioned, was a fight for equality via the abolition of poverty. King saw, with a clarity that we yet lack, that "the curse of poverty has no justification in our age. It is as socially cruel and blind as the practice of cannibalism at the dawn of civilization . . . the time has come for us to civilize ourselves by the total, direct and immediate abolition of poverty."[348]

King understood racism in America was and is about producing people with the ability to justify and protect the inequalities—economic, educational, judicial—that define our lives together. King began believing that only by attacking the inequalities that racist lies were intended to protect could the power of their spells be broken.

An Orbiting Cycle
Creating Rational, Sentimental and Hard Hearted Citizens

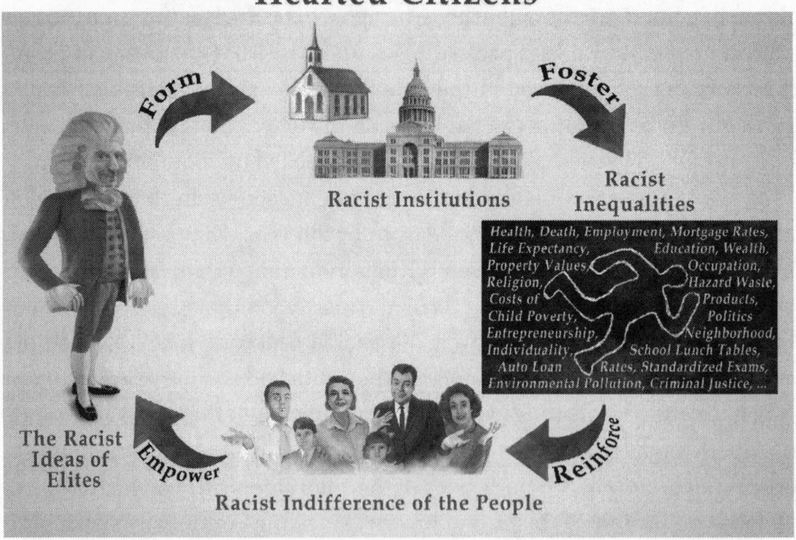

This is how the orbiting cycle operates. The Racist ideas of the elite—ideas that employ racial differences to protect their wealth and promote their power—form institutions. Racist institutions—underfunded schools, racially biased courtrooms, and racial employment lines—foster racial inequalities. But here is the kicker, for kind but hardhearted people, racial inequalities *legitimize racist ideas and reinforce* the indifference that is the primary symptom of the people's racism. Rather than eliciting compassion and solidarity, racial inequalities drive racist lies all the deeper and further empower the racist lies of the elite.

And the cycle spins and spins and spins, and as these ideologies are spun through time and space, from one generation to the next, racist *ideologies* harden into racist *convictions*. Here is the difference: ideologies are ideas held by idealists and are employed for personal gain. Convictions are ideas that possess the convicted even when these ideas lead to self-destruction. When de-humanizing ideologies become convictions, we need more than education. What we need is an exorcism.

~

As we move on from how our unholy ghosts were imagined, institutionalized, and ingrained into the American system, we move to the ongoing work of slowing down this orbiting cycle by exorcising our racial demons. If we can reject the notion that poor children in the wealthiest society in history should go hungry and uneducated, expect incarceration, and never rise above the poverty they are born into, then we must fundamentally rethink the ideologies that underwrite the rules of our relationships and life together. If we can rethink and rewrite our relationships and the rules of the game, then we can change the game's possibilities. Rewriting America's relationships and rules was never easy work, but it has happened. Since rethinking and rewriting the rules has happened, we must bear the responsibility of knowing that—despite what our eyes see and ears hear—it must happen once more.

As we begin to reconsider the possibilities of politics and religion in America, we will revisit once more that era in which the rules were rewritten. On issues of race and equity, the Kennedy era elicited only desperation and hopelessness among those longing for a new day. Yet on the heels of Kennedy's reign, a brief window opened during the first years of the Johnson administration, and the nation began learning to see itself through the eyes of the victims of America's racialized violence. For a brief but illiminating moment, the nation entered into a period of vulnerability and began to learn from the brilliant faith and politics of the Prophetic Black Church.

America's vulnerable learning from the Prophetic Black Church did not long endure. "It is an aspect of their sense of superiority," lamented King regarding the short attention span of white America, "that the white people believe they have so little to learn." For King, the failures of both liberal and conservative thinking came from their shared belief in the sufficiency of white wisdom. For King, white wisdom was white obliviousness.

Thus, after revisiting the era when America proved humble enough to learn from the victims of her racial violence, I desire to return my readers to sit at the feet of the Prophetic Black Church to nurture that vulnerability once more. For those who desire to follow in King's footsteps and to continue the work of uprooting racist cycles and breaking the grip of white supremacy, there is no better instructor than the institution that initiated the work to begin with. Till the end, King believed the best way to lean into the work of slowing down the orbiting cycle of racial violence was to enter into the institution on American soils born from the suffering of slaves and designed to exorcise America's unholy ghosts.

After the movement the Church birthed, after the ongoing sacrificial faithfulness of churches like Charleston's Mother Emanuel, we find ourselves without excuses for our superficial understandings of the brilliant faith and politics of the Prophetic Black Church. The time for superficiality has passed.

6

Because They Are Hard

Rewriting the Rules

CAMELOT

Standing behind the podium of the sun-soaked stadium at Rice University in Houston, Texas, John F. Kennedy looked like a Brooks Brothers model who only incidentally happened to be one of the most powerful men on earth. On the bandstand behind the podium sat an integrated gathering of Texas's leaders, but the audience in front of Kennedy pictured Texans' commitment to their segregated way of life. As was typical for Kennedy, he displayed no interest in ruffling racist feathers that September day.[349]

The President cozied up to his audience with the charm through which he attained his power. "We meet at a college noted for knowledge, in a city noted for progress, in a State noted for strength," he began, "and we stand in need of all three, for we meet in an hour of change and challenge, in a decade of hope and fear, in an age of both knowledge and ignorance." The challenge he spoke of was the challenge to outwit gravity itself and place a man on the moon.[350] He recognized the enormity of the challenge that lay before NASA. We did not know yet what we needed to know and had not developed the materials spaceships demanded. The race to space promised to be costly and entailed the price of passing through the failures we could not yet see but that progress always entails. Space travel is not a cheap—"50 cents a week for every man, woman and child in the United States"—and there would be no free rides. "However, I think we're going to do it, and I think that we must pay what needs to be paid."

The speech was a thing of beauty, and it rooted the logic behind America's ambition in the race to space in its most powerful poetic punch: "We choose to go to the moon in this decade and do the other things, not because they are easy, *but because they are hard* . . . because *that* goal will serve to organize and measure the best of our energies and skills, because *that* challenge is one that we are willing to accept, one we are unwilling to postpone, and one which we intend to win."[351] The crowd roared. Only JFK could close the gap between Camelot and Texas.

The image of Camelot for the Kennedy Presidency was solidified by Jacqueline Kennedy's interview with *Life*'s Theodore White a few weeks after JFK's life was snuffed out by a sniper's bullet. But the image of Camelot was apt and carried with it both the enchantment—and disenchantment—with the Kennedy Presidency. The Kennedys' and their friends were some of our nation's most brilliant and beautiful people, and they were positioned to bring their idealistic ambitions into reality through their collaboration. But the other side of Camelot was its distance, detachment, and indifference to the problems that haunted most Americans—and black and brown Americans in particular.

"At night," Jacqueline remembered, "before we went to sleep, Jack liked to play some records . . . The lines he loved to hear were: *Don't let it be forgot that once there was a spot, for one brief shinning moment that was known as Camelot.*" The interview encapsulated how she wanted history to remember the husband she loved and lost: "There'll be great Presidents again . . . but there'll never be another Camelot."

In the months leading up to the speech, in places like Birmingham, Albany, and Amercus, Kennedy's administration refused to challenge the Klan and segregationists' brutal assault on civil rights workers. Instead of using their executive muscle against segregationists, the Kennedys often used their power to bless the harassment and imprisonment of those in the movement. When civil rights entered into Kennedy's calculus at all, it entered through the lens of a utilitarian political calculus aimed at perpetuating the power he held and still had little idea how to use. King lamented: "It is a difficult thing to teach a president."[352] For King, Kennedy was "not even fit for office," as time and again, Kennedy proved ready "to accommodate to injustice to maintain his political balance."[353] When it comes to race, Camelot proved as thoroughly possessed by racist ideas as Trumpland.

In the summer prior to "Because They are Hard," Mrs. Marion King had given birth to a still-born child after being beaten by a sheriff while bringing food and clothing to those imprisoned due to their protests. Rather than prosecuting the sheriff, the Kennedy Administration backed local prosecutors' imprisonment of civil rights workers for "seditious conspiracy."

Better than any speech, "Because They are Hard" captured the paradox of the Kennedy Presidency's inspirational but tone-deaf nature. For Kennedy, defeating gravity was realistic politics, politics worthy of readjusting the federal budget to achieve. Feeding and educating the poor, bringing down racial discrimination and empowering the poor, these were neither realistic aims nor Camelot's primary concerns. In Camelot, space travel and the things of the heavens was much more intoxicating than poor folks and the things of the earth. Kennedy embodied aristocratic politics made modern.

A year and three days after "Because They Were Hard," four girls were murdered in the bombing of the 16th Street Baptist church in Birmingham. It was the twenty-eighth racially motivated bombing that nonetheless generated no meaningful movement from the Kennedy White House. During the girls' eulogy, King saw clearly through tear-stained eyes. He declared that their murders said something "to every minister of the gospel who has remained silent" in the face of Kennedy's federal government that "has compromised with the undemocratic practices of southern dixiecrats and the blatant hypocrisy of right-wing Republicans." What did the girls bloodstained dresses say? "They say to us that we must be concerned with not merely *WHO* murdered them, but about the system, the way of life and the philosophy which *PRODUCED* the murderers."[354] The philosophies that produced the murders traced back to racist philosophies shared by the Founding Fathers and every president from Washington to Kennedy.

MLK understood that when you live in a nation ready to blow up little girls in Sunday dresses, the time has come to direct the nation's passions, efforts, and resources to righting the nation's racial wrongs with the same intensity that the nation was pursuing space travel. King saw that the time had arrived to rewrite national budgets and policies and to begin a fundamental realignment of the American experiment. Following JFK's tragic death that embodied the nation's unraveling, this is precisely the journey the nation began.

REWRITING THE RULES: WHEN THE BELOVED COMMUNITY INSPIRED A GREAT SOCIETY

The direction of the American experiment hung in the balance with how America responded to Kennedy's assassination. It was not clear what kind of President the country was getting when LBJ placed his hand on the Bible aboard Air Force One on the Dallas runway and swore the oath of office.[355] What became clear within the first hours following Kennedy's last breath was that LBJ possessed a clear vision. He desired to "out Roosevelt Roosevelt" in his fight against poverty and to "out Lincoln Lincoln"[356] in righting racial wrongs. Rather than unraveling, under the leadership of LBJ and MLK, the nation entered into a period that began binding the wounds of inequity and racism as they rewrote the nation's rulebook.

When Air Force One took off from Dallas, the nation unknowingly entered into a period of time that proved that rewriting the rulebook was possible. Equally striking, MLK and LBJ proved that white pastors, Congress, and presidents could learn from the visionary Prophetic Black Church and implement her insights into the ways of the world. King referred to the work as building the Beloved Community; LBJ referred to it as building the Great Society. When these leaders pushed in the same direction, walls between the possible and impossible began to fall.

In popular culture, MLK's legacy centers on the beauty of his dream and the baritone of his voice, but he was much more than that. MLK possessed a prophetic edge that frightened our land and earned him the title as "the most dangerous negro"[357] in the eyes of the FBI. He was a "scholar's scholar"[358] and as fierce a prophetic critic of Christianity and democracy as our nation has ever known. He excoriated politicians and preachers alike. He wrote of "tears of love" that he shed over "his most pervasive mistake"[359] in trusting that the righteous, self-sacrifice of black Christians would inspire white Christians to stand in solidarity with the movement and repent of the nation's racist and unjust ways. The heartbreaking truth, King learned, was that in times of trial white Christians proved "no better than strangers even though we sing the same hymns in worship of the same God."[360] White preachers preached a false religion. "Any religion," wrote King in the magazine *The Christian Century*, "that professes to be concerned about the souls of men and is not concerned about the slums that damn them, the economic conditions that strangle them and the social conditions that cripple them is a spiritually moribund religion awaiting burial."[361] The inconvenient truth MLK saw was that white Christians too often prove "to be more white than Christian."[362]

If King didn't spare the rod on white Christianity and his fellow preachers, he certainly did not spare the rod on the character of our democracy at large. He watched the drama of Kennedy's assassination unfold on TV from Atlanta. He was horrified. "This is what's going to happen to me. . . This is such a sick society."[363] As early as 1957, King saw with clarity that the struggle he led concerned the very soul of the nation and the integrity of democracy. "In short," King wrote, "this crisis has the potential for democracy's fulfillment or fascism's triumph."[364] When a nation sided with the forces of segregation and inequality, their democratic ideals were but a mask on a fascist face. It was the work of the Beloved Community to unmask the fascist.

The radical King was the president's preacher as LBJ entered office. LBJ's politics aimed much lower than his predecessor. For LBJ, politics was less about spaceships and more about the things of this earth and addressing the needs of those suffering in the homeland. Politics, for LBJ, was about knowing whose "ass to kiss" and whose "nuts to cut," and how to get the deals done and legislation signed to reframe the American way of life on a more just foundation. Politics was more like the Colosseum than Camelot. From his time mastering the Senate, LBJ earned a reputation of viciousness. But what was "revealed," in Robert Caro's famous words, from the moment LBJ took office was that intertwined with his viciousness was a commitment to those excluded from America's prosperity. When the reigns of power came to his hands, he planned on using them, and he knew where he wanted to go.

LBJ's knowledge of poverty came from first-hand experience of growing up poor in the Texas Hill Country. In his first job after college, he taught Hispanic students who came to school hungry, and he learned about poverty sharpened by a racial edge: "They knew even in their youth the pain of prejudice," Johnson said. "They never seemed to know why people disliked them. But they knew it was so, because I saw it in their eyes."[365]

President Johnson worked to keep Kennedy's administration committed to his cabinet as the nation transitioned between two leaders. Camelot's brain trust warned Johnson to take it slow on civil rights or risk losing reelection. Failing to understand why not to fight for what he believed in, now that he sat in the most powerful seat, Johnson asked: "Well, what the hell is the Presidency for?"[366] In his first State of the Union Address, Johnson let the Congress and the world in on his ambitions:

> Let this session of Congress be known as the session which did more for civil rights than the last hundred sessions combined . . . as the session which declared all-out war on human poverty and unemployment . . . which finally recognized the health needs of all our older citizens; . . . and as the session which helped to build more homes, more schools, more libraries, and more hospitals than any single session of Congress in the history of our Republic . . . The richest nation on earth can afford to win it. We cannot afford to lose it.[367]

So much for Camelot's political calculus. Before the State of the Union Address, Johnson started the ass-kissing and nut-cutting, and within only a few months what was dead legislation under Kennedy showed signs of life. "We would have beaten President Kennedy, but now I won't predict [the outcome]," reported the leader of the opposition, Senator Russell. "Now it will be three times harder . . .[Johnson] knows more about the uses of power than any man."[368]

Russell, a close friend of Johnson, received an invitation to the White House for lunch and a swim. When time came to talk business, Johnson made clear he meant business: "Dick, you've got to get out of my way. If you don't, I'm going to roll over you." "You may do that," Russell replied. "But it's going to cost you the South and the election." "If that's the price I have to pay," Johnson answered, "I'll pay it gladly."[369]

From the moment Johnson took office, he worked with an urgency that equaled King's. For the first time in U.S. history, a president entered office ready to go all in on the battle against poverty *and* racism. LBJ believed the time was ripe, the window of opportunity was short, but that the rulebook could be rewritten to transform the lives of everyday folks through the eradication of evils that haunted the nation since its inception.

MLK worked the streets and LBJ worked the congress. The preacher politicked and the politician preached. On March 25, 1964, LBJ brought his sermonic power to the Rose Garden as he faced off with 150 leaders of the Southern Baptist Convention.[370] The heart of LBJ's sermon was equal parts warning and invitation. After lightheartedly establishing common ground through his Southern Baptist roots, LBJ's sermon turned remarkably candid. He was going to pass the Civil Rights Bill. Southern Baptists could help. Over the next few months, history would be rewritten and Southern Baptists needed to choose on which side of history to stand. "No group of Christians has a greater responsibility in civil rights than Southern Baptists," LBJ said. Yet, often preachers were the problem as "teachers of injustice and dissension . . . sowing half-truths and untruths wherever they find root."[371] Like a prophet of old, LBJ drew a line in the sand and invited the religious leaders to join him on the right side of history. Yet the historical significance of that moment in the Rose Garden was not the conversion of Southern Baptists. The significance of that moment was that a president was indeed all in for civil rights. Perhaps for the first and last time in U.S. history, pandering to racist religious leaders for permission was no longer part of the president's political calculus.

In 1964, LBJ and the civil rights movement passed a Civil Rights Bill that brought down segregation and reordered the nation's life together. That November, Johnson won reelection in a landslide. 1965 witnessed the passage of another Civil Rights Bill that protected the right of African Americans to vote. And it wasn't just about the rights of African Americans. Thanks to the selfless sacrifices of civil rights workers and a nation suddenly vulnerable to their message, an environment emerged where bills protecting and providing for the dignity and decency of human life began ripping through Congress. Johnson signed the Elementary and Secondary Education Act, providing federal aid to "5 million educationally deprived students." He signed the act establishing Medicare at Truman's Presidential library and passed a pen to Truman so that the former President could be the first to enroll in the program for which he had fought so long. Ninety percent of the 19 million elderly soon followed suit within the next few months. Medicaid was covered in the same bill. In what became known as the "fabulous 89th Congress" more legislation was passed that improved life for poor folks on both sides of the color line through education, health, and environmental protections than the rest of U.S. history until that point combined.[372]

~

To trace the history of what made the transformational timeframe of 1964, 1965, and 1966 possible to its beginning is to walk through the doors of the Prophetic Black Church and into her sanctuary. That sanctuary provided the only safe place in the nation to unlock and unleash the gifts, talents, and brilliance of black folks. That sanctuary nurtured a vision within a persecuted people that things could, should, and must be different in our nation. As time passed, a conviction developed in that holy space that the transformation that must come could only come through a self-sacrificial readiness to enter more deeply into their persecution. By bringing the holy truths held safely in the sanctuary into the dangers of the streets, the church began wading even deeper into their persecution in order to break the chains that bound them and bring the nation into a closer harmony with the Promised Land they saw in their mind's eye. The movement challenged the unholy ghosts of Mississippi, Alabama, and Georgia in order to challenge the unholy ghosts in the halls of power in Washington, DC. King and his church saw that the truths held in their sanctuary must be written into the books of law that ruled the land.

It was a long road from Ebenezer Baptist in Atlanta to Dexter Avenue Baptist in Montgomery to 16th Street Baptist in Birmingham to Brown Chapel AME in Selma, but after a decade of taking it to the streets, after a decade of facing prisons and martyrdom, President LBJ stood in his first address to Congress. "We have talked long enough in this country about civil rights. We have talked for one hundred years or more," President Johnson declared. "It is time now to write the next chapter, and to write it in a book of law."[373] As the nation reached its breaking point following the sacrifices at Selma, LBJ declared to Congress and the nation that "the real hero of this struggle is the American Negro . . . His actions . . . protests . . . courage . . . awakened the conscience of his nation. His demonstrations have been designed to call attention to injustice . . . provoke change . . . stir reform . . . And who among us can say that we would have made the same progress were it not for his persistent bravery and faith in America."[374]

THE OTHER SIDE OF THE MOUNTAIN: VIETNAM AND FIFTY+ YEARS OF DOMESTIC WAR

Neither MLK nor LBJ stayed on the mountaintop long. And they departed in two different directions. The dividing line was neither the Watts riot of 1965 nor the white backlash that their mountaintop experience inspired. The line between their paths was a war in the backwaters of Vietnam.

After Watts and Chicago, King's radical edge sharpened, and he could no longer domesticate his commitment to nonviolence by excluding its implications from international affairs. He began seeing war, and the war in Vietnam in particular, for the madness it was. Unable to remain silent, he mounted the pulpit at the Riverside Church in New York in 1967 and outlined points for his stand against the nation's madness. King said what he saw from the mountaintop inspired his stand against the war. He said his nonviolent fight possessed no backbone if he failed to challenge the "greatest purveyor of violence in the world today: my own government." King said his "commitment to the ministry of Jesus Christ" demanded he speak. Finally, he said, "I share with all men the calling to be a son of the living God. Beyond the calling of race or nation or creed is this vocation of sonship and brotherhood. Because I believe that the Father is deeply concerned, especially for His suffering and helpless and outcast children, I come tonight to speak for them."[375]

Under Truman and Eisenhower, America's misconceived commitment to Vietnam was relatively minor. Under Kennedy the commitment became major. But under Johnson the U.S.'s role became monstrous. Almost as if viewing the future unraveling of his Presidency in a crystal ball, President Johnson huddled his advisors shortly after his landslide election:

> I've just been elected and right now we'll have a honeymoon with Congress . . . But after I make my recommendations, I'm going to start to lose the power and authority I have . . . that's in the nature of what the President does. He uses up capital. Something is going to come up . . . something like the Vietnam War or something else where I will begin to lose all that I have now. So . . . I want you guys to get off your asses and do everything possible to get everything in my program passed as soon as possible, before the aura and the halo that surround me disappear . . .[376]

Johnson believed both that the U.S. could afford "guns and butter" and that a liberal democratic president could not afford to look soft on foreign affairs and expect to move the needle on domestic issues. The Vietnam War became like a drug for President Johnson, a political narcotic he desired to manipulate in order to empower his agenda and presidency. Like most addicts, it is difficult to pinpoint when the narcotic transformed from a servant to a dictator within Johnson's presidency.

Just as Johnson sought MLK's support for the Great Society, he sought Billy Graham's support for escalating the Vietnam War. The Johnson White House became Graham's hotel, and after touring Vietnam at the president's invitation, Johnson received the public endorsements from Graham he desired. Though Graham never supported Johnson's efforts on civil rights, he rarely failed to lend support for his efforts in Vietnam.[377]

Ironically enough, King's steadfast commitment to the poor and suffering, the commitment he shared with LBJ on domestic issues but that King extended to the soils of Vietnam, cost him his alliance with the President. At a time when both the war and the president were incredibly popular, King's protest cost him most of the alliances that undergirded the movement. The nation followed LBJ to Vietnam and the pursuit of a Beloved Community and Great Society was, one agonizing bomb at a time, blown asunder with the families of Vietnam.

When destroying innocent families in other nations is deemed a political necessity, it is not a long road to deeming the destruction of families within one's own borders a political necessity as well. Building a Great Society while piling up bodies in Vietnam proved impossible. President Johnson's addiction to Vietnam not only cost him his office, but, more importantly, it tore both nations asunder. As the bombs falling on Vietnam slowed, the battle against America's vulnerable on the home front began heating up. The Great Society began disintegrating into a time of domestic unrest. Following Johnson, a president rose to power who morphed the War on Poverty into the War on Drugs. The illusory political necessities that justified the war in Vietnam returned home through America's domestic policies that took aim on black and brown families. One policy at a time, the vision of the Beloved Community was abandoned for a racialized vision of law and order.

~

The nation never recovered from the cultural chaos that reached fever pitch during LBJ's Presidency.[378] It is in this chaos that we now live and move and have our being. Between Nixon and Trump, the culture wars played out with varying degrees of intensity. In that nearly fifty-year window, we made nearly no progress in pursuit of a Beloved Community or a Great Society. After LBJ, most changes in the laws of our land heightened the United States' inequality and sowed the lies that ushered America's unholy ghosts even more deeply into our nation's soul.

Outside of the Prophetic Black Church, it often seems that Phase II of King's beloved community and a land of equity was entombed with him. Americans, both liberals and conservatives, distanced themselves from the politics of the Prophetic Black Church and the radical equalities and nonviolence that the vision of the beloved community demanded. In the infighting between white liberals and conservatives, the nation lost the radical wisdom and grace of King's tradition.

The most striking example of a president distancing himself from the Prophetic Black Church was President Obama. Obama began distancing himself due to the remarks of his pastor—Jeremiah Wright, a Vietnam veteran—over Vietnam. Eventually, Obama broke away from his church of over twenty years. More important than Obama's thoughtful critiques of Wright was his decision to divorce himself from his congregation and to remain unaffiliated with the Prophetic Black Church throughout his presidency.[379]

Though no religious or political philosophy provided more inspiration or practical transformation in righting our society's wrongs than the Prophetic Black Church, no religious or political philosophy was so quickly abandoned. Over the last fifty years, we grew tone deaf to the lessons of the Prophetic Black Church. This deafness is not because the basic ingredients of the Prophetic Black Church's faith and politics lost its power but because, during the times of testing and challenge, the nation lost her way because she lost her nerve. Liberals' optimism cooled to cynicism, solidarity reduced to sentimentality, and the opportunity for a second American Revolution joined the list of squandered opportunities in America's racial history.

At the close of chapter 1, I argued that if the Nixon era of law and order closed the door to King's radical revolution and our vulnerability to the vision of the Prophetic Black Church, perhaps President Trump provides an opportunity to reignite the movement's labor of love for the heart, soul, and laws of the land. For our closing considerations, we enter into the sanctuary of the Prophetic Black Church to consider the distinctive ingredients of the tradition's faith and politics, ingredients that empowered her prophets to carry a cross that transformed our nation. As the transformations that came to our nation from 1964 to 1966 proved, when Americans humble themselves enough to learn from those she oppresses, nothing is then impossible. These then are ingredients that began the movement and that continue the movement in churches located throughout America's forgotten neighborhoods. We begin with the organizing principle of faith and politics.

GOD'S BABIES: FROM DEPRAVITY TO DIGNITY

Our journey into the brilliance of the Prophetic Black Church starts in the dust. In Genesis, God gathers dust and imprints his image on it, creating humanity in his image and likeness. Genesis is, admittedly, an odd place to begin a critique of race, religion, and politics in American life. It is not, however, too much to say that the interpretation of this ancient story proved as formative for life within the American order as any scientific, political, or economic breakthrough. The interpretation of this story forged the *organizing principles* of America's political and religious logics. It is in challenging the implications of this story that the Prophetic Black Church begins to challenge the lies that formed America's unholy ghosts.

From Christendom's influence, the Western world long believed in human depravity—that the human experience is marred by sin and that our lives were now lived east of Eden. Yet it was the modern project, as seen in Hobbes, that made human depravity an organizing principle of our life together. Depravity is not a Christian fantasy. It is, however, a terrible organizing principle for any religion or society. When depravity acts as an organizing principle, other depraved principles—like those I attempted to detail—are produced and intertwine, and political thinking finds itself operating within a matrix of lethal lies without an exit. The matrix provides hypnotic logic that empowers the spellbound to look upon the world's manmade tragedies as if they are unavoidable necessities of modern society and dream that nothing can or should change.

On American soils, it was the Prophetic Black Church that provided the most poignant challenge to the matrix's hold on our national imagination and to the callouses that covered our hearts. From the same sands of Genesis, a radically different religious and political vision rose up in the sanctuary of the Prophetic Black Church. Rather than highlighting human depravity, Genesis revealed to slaves and their descendants that we are God's children endowed with a God-given dignity. In the Prophetic Black Church, humanity's "is-ness" did not reside in her rationality or depravity but in the richness of her relationships—in its fundamental identity as God's beloved child and in our relationships as brothers and sisters. And it became the quest of the church to reclaim human dignity, intimacy, and interconnectedness in a society that fostered enmity, segregation, and individualism.

In sermons and writings, Martin Luther King referred to our basic human dignity as "somebodiness." We are God's babies, broken but beautiful. In this church, human depravity did not diminish her dignity. In a world that attempted to "thingify" God's children—to instill a "nobodiness" into the mind, heart, and soul—the Prophetic Black Church worked to root "somebodiness" into her members. It was this conviction about humanity's God-given dignity that empowered the church to dream of a different future and hold the nation accountable for its historical and contemporary atrocities.

Thus, King and the Prophetic Black Church demanded that the nation square her politics, economics, and religious energies with the principle of human *dignity*. By exchanging depravity for dignity as the cornerstone that should shape America's political and economic life, the logic that justified hunger amidst abundance was seen as the depraved nonsense it was. With dignity as the cornerstone for political, economic, and religious thinking, the prophets of the church refused to judge America's ideologies by the warm fuzzies they illicit in the hearts and minds of the mainstream. The righteousness of America's ideologies are known by their fruit—by the results they produce on those living on the margins. When America's politics, economics, and religion are judged by the most vulnerable among us, what is revealed is that we need a new cornerstone for our life together.

When MLK spoke, particularly towards the end of his life, about the sickness of capitalism, about guaranteeing incomes, and comparing poverty to cannibalism, he sounded as if he had lost his sanity because he no longer saw the world through American illusions. If he was out of touch with reality, it was because he could see a world that others could not. He saw a world where we *didn't* kill the children of Vietnam in the name of democracy; where food *didn't* go to waste to protect abstract economic *principles* amidst the *tangible* hunger and needs of *people*; where religious folks *didn't* seek the safety of the sidelines as their brothers and sisters were crucified for the color of their skins. King saw the world as it should be as clearly as he saw the world as it was; as clearly as he saw the caskets of the girls following the Birmingham church bombing, Jimmie Jackson's casket in Selma, and the grotesque inhumanity of those in power who brought back enough caskets from Vietnam to build a mountain—not to mention the caskets they left behind.

And in seeing the world as it should be from the mountaintop, King saw a world he couldn't unsee regardless of how it conflicted with America's commitments. And as he did from the beginning, so he did to his last days: he refused to limit his struggle to what the smallest minds deemed possible in times afar off. King began imagining what it would look like for America to square itself with the principle "somebodiness" for everybody. The more radical this worldview made King, the more reticent the nation proved to work to bring King's dreamland to America's heartland. As his contemporary James Baldwin lamented: "White Americans are not simply unwilling to effect these changes; they are, in the main, so slothful they have become, unable to envision them."[380]

By attempting to write the conscience of the Prophetic Black Church onto the stone tablets of America's hearts, minds, and laws, King sought to give his nation eyes unblinded by their own lies. "I once was blind," the gospel declares, "but now I see." Eyes hurt the first time they see. Light is a very violent thing for those who live in darkness. In the Prophetic Black Church, regaining one's vision provides a sorrow wrapped in, to use Tolkien's phrase, a joy as poignant as grief.[381] Once we begin seeing our world truthfully, as it is and as it should be, we begin seeing the matrix of our nation from the vantage point of those crucified by our lies. In America, redemption comes through the communities that bear the cross. It is from communities littered with American-made crosses, from America's Harlems, South Sides, Comptons and Fifth Wards, that the light of revelation shines on America's soul.

Not until we see our world as King saw our world can our lies lose their grip on our lives; not until we see our world as King saw our world can we that see that things can and must be radically different, not only in the

New Jerusalem, but in New York, Chicago, Los Angeles, and Houston. And once we can see a world in which the war in Iraq did not happen; where we begin burying guns rather than continuing to bury victims; where inner-city schools bring life not death to students' dreams; where rather than repeating the racism of Falwell, Dobson, and Graham, white pastors begin learning from churches like Mother Emanuel in Charleston—not until we learn to see these impossibilities in our mind's eye will we be able to break the matrix's hold on our life.

The tragic truth of the matter is white folks are often reticent to *learn* and *change.* After tracing the partisan divide between white evangelicals and black Protestants following the civil rights movement, historian Mark Noll—who himself identifies as a white evangelical—writes:

> In light of these dramatic partisan differences keyed to race and religion, it is pertinent to remember one more fact documented by a wealth of polling—that the two identifiable groups standing closest to each other on religious belief and moral practice are white evangelicals and black Protestants.[382]

Nonetheless, when it comes to a readiness to learn from the Prophetic Black Church, white evangelicals are the tragic epitome of white people's refusal to learn from the Prophetic Black Church. Partisan politics is always about navigating between imperfect options, and what is clear is that single-issue voting robbed the evangelical voting block of the moral depth perception that navigating imperfect options always entails. Ironically, when it comes to race and equity, throughout our nation's history white evangelical Christians often proved the greatest obstacle to a more "Christian" nation. But if white evangelicals are the *epitome* of the rule that white folks refuse to learn from black wisdom—and the Prophetic Black Church in particular—they are not the *exception.* Throughout our history rife with racial strife, when it came to the struggle to bring racial equity, white conservatives and liberals, white Christians and secular folks, always had more in common with one another than with King and the vision of the Prophetic Black Church.

Baldwin lamented the racism of missionaries who reduced men and women to souls to save and objects of charity. But for Baldwin, the counterpart of the American missionary was the American liberal who "could deal with the Negro as a symbol or victim but had no sense of him as a man."[383]

"*My* friends," writes Rev. Michael Eric Dyson to the white folks he loves, "what I need you to do—just for starters—is not act. Not yet. Not first. First I need you to see." A hard truth is that when the desire to help overrides a readiness to learn, the good-hearted often remain within the orbiting cycle of racialized violence and repeat all the racist ways of the missionaries of old. Philanthropy, volunteering, and random acts of kindness by themselves fail to heal Americans of racism.

The truth is one can engage in all those benevolent actions at an animal shelter. Something deeper is needed to break the grip of white Supremacy and the power of racist ideas. In the Prophetic Black Church, the first step in the exorcism of America's unholy ghosts is a *relational learning* that empowers us to see through the self-deceit that justified false superiorities and inferiorities within the same body. It is only *after* we see all of God's children as indispensible ingredients of the Beloved Community; only *after* protecting the dignity of the last becomes our first political priority, and *after* the fears of the first become our last political priority that we can participate in the process of healing a divided nation. When human dignity acts as the cornerstone for our life together, relationships based on equality replace relationships of charity, changing the way we see the world and tilling the ground in preparation for new ideas and possibilities. The conviction that we are God's babies has lost no political power or relevance.

PROPHETIC PROTEST: FROM SENTIMENTALISM TO SOLIDARITY

It was the conviction regarding human dignity that inspired King's dream, but in the minds of prophets, the dream was always a double-edged sword that wielded both inspiration and accountability. Throughout American history, no space acted as a more powerful conduit for prophetic protest than the pulpit of the Prophetic Black Church. As white politicians and preachers perpetuated America's racial crisis in implicit and explicit ways, prophetic protest in the Black Church provided vocal chords to those who our nation desired to suffer in silence. There is no better paradigm for prophetic protest than the tradition of black preaching. Born from intimate—rather than abstract—relationships with those who suffer, prophetic preaching uses protest to shape the life of citizenship and discipleship, providing an antidote to the temptation towards indifference, and to forging the spine that truthful living requires.

There is a distinctive and transformative flavor to the prophetic protest that flows from the pulpit. Prophetic protest is held within the flames of a furious solidarity with God's rage and within the tears of a vulnerable solidarity with God's love. Prophetic protest is flavored by what Paul refers to as the fruits of the Spirit—love and joy, peace and patience, kindness and goodness, faithfulness and gentleness, and self-control. These fruits coalesce into a grace-filled gratitude that, like the fiery bush that signified God's presence to Moses long ago, burns brightly without being consumed. Through this fire, Prophetic protest places flesh onto the fury of a God who is love. It is that love-filled rage and rage-filled love that demarcates the tradition that King embodied.

When I moved into the inner city, my father failed to understand the fury overtaking me. Yet he saw something only someone with his wisdom sees, and he provided me a gentle warning in a manner that only a loving father or mother can. His warning was that fury without love never redeems. His warning has haunted me ever since.

Lives of prophetic protest require that paradoxical flavor. Rage is a poison if there is no love, while love without rage—in a nation like ours—is invertebrate. From the luxury box, white folks confuse cynicism with rage and sentimentalism with love. But the truth is that cynicism and sentimentalism are rage and love's opposite. It is intimacy and solidarity that produce rage and love. Cynicism and sentimentalism freely operate under delusions of false superiorities fostered at a safe distance from the sacrifices of a redemptive struggle. Both cynicism and sentimentalism prove too cheap for redemption's work. It is, of course, easy to reduce intimacy and solidarity to word games that produce neither. For white folks, it is one thing to gain fluency in discussions of white privilege. Yet, the tragedy of the conversation concerning white privilege on the lips of white folks is how rarely that fluency translates into rewriting white life and segregated orbits; rewriting where white folks live, where they send their children to school, where they worship, and from whom they learn. Too often white conversations of white privilege inspire acts of semantics and politically correct posturing, not lives of solidarity.

This is the truth of the matter: the reason that the orbiting cycle of racial violence continues to spin and spin and spin is because too often white America proves unable to see the faces of their children in the faces of black and brown children, see their brothers and sisters faces in the faces of their black and brown communities, or see their parents faces in the faces of the black and brown elderly. Whether in Camelot or in Trumpland, semantics fail to stop white folks from seeking haven in segregated orbits, neighborhoods, schools, and churches. If this were not so, black and brown lives and communities would no longer be deemed expendable and political realities would be forced to adjust to a new calculus of family values.

The question that faces white America during this time is whether or not white America is ready to learn a new way of being human by repeating the audacious loyalty of Ruth to Naomi, "Your people shall be my people." Until the lives of white Americans say to their brothers and sisters, black and brown: "Your heartbreak shall be my heartbreak. Your anger shall be my anger. Your hopes shall be my hopes. Your neighborhood shall be my neighborhood, your teachers shall be my teachers, and our children shall be brothers and sisters" we will continue to perpetuate the domestic war that has been with us since our nation's inception. With rare exception, our nation continues to fail to produce white folks with enough courage or wisdom to follow the Prophetic Black Church into the fire and tears of prophetic protest through lives of solidarity.

But that is not because an invitation is absent. "Black and white people don't merely have different experiences," writes Dyson, "we seem to occupy different universes."[384] The Prophetic Black Church and the civil rights movement they inspired provided and continue to provide an invitation to our nation to break out of segregated orbits and into this different universe; they provide an invitation to move our ideals from semantics to solidarity. The prophetic protest of the Black Church acts as an invitation to exchange cynicism and sentimentalism for love made flesh; to exchange a luxury-box logic concerning race, faith, and politics for a wisdom forged from the fiery furnace of the long struggle.

Meaningful relationships across the color line rarely begin on grounds of ideological purity. Within the Prophetic Black Church, relationships begin and are fostered by a pursuit of a way of life that attempts to bring to life shared convictions by living in such a way that love, mercy, dignity, equality, resurrection, and redemption make sense in the here and now. In the Prophetic Black Church tradition, the question is not if white friends are racist but if white friends are ready to learn a different way of being human. It is that readiness to live and work and worship with folks of questionable purity that provides the Prophetic Black Church its prophetic edge.

With his remarkable vulnerability, MLK built alliances with those ready to lean into the movement's call. The love-filled rage and rage-filled love of his followers was perhaps his leadership's greatest achievement. "A genuine leader," King declared as folks attempted to blunt his fury, "is not a searcher for consensus but a molder of consensus."[385] Yet if King's prophetic edge sharpened, if King refused to blunt his fury, he also refused to blunt his vulnerability. One of the geniuses of King was his recognition that his movement required a diversity of thinking, gifts, and resources. He was ready to have his heart broken time and time again in order to incorporate folks from diverse backgrounds into his movement and use to their gifts to bring the Church's vision to life. With allies like Stanley Levinson, Rabbi Joshua Abraham Heschel, and Harris and Clare Wofford, King worked across racial, religious, and political lines to form a coalition capable of challenging America's original sin and most intractable injustices.[386]

King understood that moving the needle on any point of racial inequality, from the prison, education, and health systems to job, housing and banking markets, requires aligning assets—talents, relationships, and resources—of diverse people to a shared vision. Though King learned the dangers of overestimating the readiness of white folks to join in his movement and share with his community's suffering, he believed that refusing the risks inherent in diverse intimacies was not prophetic. Despite his disillusionment with white folks in general and white Christians in particular, King held fast to his vulnerability and sought to engraft Americans across racial and religious divides into the holy struggle.

Admittedly, King saw tragically little light in the lives of those on the other side of the color line. But in the darkness, sometimes the lightening struck and King witnessed what reason and experience tells us is impossible. Engraftment into prophetic protest happened and a few blinded eyes began to see. A solidarity occurred that threatened America's system of apartheid. Until his dying day, King fought with the end in mind: "The end," King declared as the movement got underway, "is reconciliation . . . redemption; the end is the beloved community."[387] From a young age, King's life was intimate with bouts of darkness, but the darkness did not overcome him.[388] Until his dying day he stood by his commitment to live his life under the light of the truths revealed when the lightening struck and the thunder rolled.

The dark night of the soul that covered America following King's assassination feels unending for those whose lives are wrapped up in the pursuit of racial justice. The truth, however, is that during this dark night of the soul every now and then lightening strikes. Business people of different backgrounds, colors, and creeds take up a community's anger and pain and use their gifts to revitalize communities on the brink. Lightening strikes, and educators radicalize and dedicate their lives to the great giftedness of marginalized students. Lightening strikes, and academics ply the tools of their trade to trace the driving factors of inequality in order to design public policies that replace poverty with equity. Lightening strikes, and good-hearted folks develop the backbone that their good hearts require. The night is dark, but the struggle continues, and these types of miracles happen everyday.

In America's at-risk communities, the Prophetic Black Church often acts as the lightening rod to address communities' systemic inequalities. And this conduit of prophetic protest provides a paradigm for those seeking to stand in solidarity against America's unholy ghosts. It behooves America to learn from the fury and rage and the love and kindness of the Prophetic Black Church's protest and refuse to allow our tears to extinguish the flames of our rage or the flames of our rage to evaporate our tears of love. It is the readiness to live within these flames and tears and through the dark nights illumined by lightening that begins refining what King referred to as "the strength to love." The strength to love—in King's sense—is not innate but wrought; the strength to love is not born of individual effort but from communal commitments; the strength to love is not measured by the depth of sentimental feelings but by the fire in the bones produced by solidarity with those who suffer.

FACES OF FLINT: FROM SELF-INTEREST TO SELF-SACRIFICE

Faces of flint is an image taken from the prophet Isaiah who writes from the perspective of the suffering servant: "For the Lord God will help me . . . therefore have I set my face like a flint, and I know that I shall not be ashamed."[389] It is an image that struck me as a child and that continued with me as I read of the unflinching sacrifices of those of the civil rights era. For both commentators and participants, one of the most troubling aspects of the civil rights movement was the readiness of leaders to sacrifice themselves and those who followed them to white America's most ravenous wolves. Bob Moses provided the quiet and intense leadership of the

Student Non-Violent Coordinating Committee's Mississippi voter registration drive of 1963. The drive witnessed six killed, five hundred beaten or arrested, and thirty-five churches burned. Moses summarized all his critics within a single sentence. His movement was "an attempt to get some people killed so the federal government will move into Mississippi." It was perhaps the one point upon which Moses and his critics agreed.[390]

The jury is still out on whether the civil rights victories won proved worthy of the sacrifices made. The fiercest critic arose from within the ranks. Stokely Carmichael, one of the movement's most dedicated disciples and decorated veterans—a man who stands with few peers for the sacrifices he made for our nation—began the search for alternatives: "This is the 27th time I have been arrested and I ain't going to jail no more!," Carmichael declared. "The only way we gonna stop them white men from whuppin' us is to take over. We been saying freedom for six years and we ain't got nothin'. What we gonna start saying now is Black Power!'"

The search for an alternative to non-violent self-sacrifice in the path to achieving justice continues. In the conclusion of *Stamped from the Beginning*, Kendi promotes an antidote to the racist ideas that shaped the American experiment. "Antiracists merely have to have *intelligent self-interest*," Kendi writes, "and to stop consuming those racist ideas that have engendered so much unintelligent self-interest."[391] I am sure Kendi is right in calling for the time to stop consuming racist ideas. It is time to turn off Fox News, which shrinks the minds and hardens the hearts of so many that I love. It is time to stop confusing Dobson's or Falwell's empires with the pursuit of Christ's Kingdom. Jesus, after all, epitomizes the demographic without a place in Dobson's and Falwell's politics—for he was neither conservative, white, nor wealthy. It is time to stop pretending Bill Maher's secular fundamentalism and intellectual superiority proves less racist in practice than the white supremacy he falsely believes he is above.

Yet, what strikes me in Kendi's remedy is not his recommendation to unplug from the consumption of racist ideas, but his attempt to redeem self-interest through intelligence. Of anything in Kendi's masterpiece, there is nothing I wish were true more than his conviction that intelligence possesses the power to redeem self-interest. Yet there is nothing that I believe is more false than the hope for self-interest to provide a humanizing lens through which to live our lives. On the dark nights throughout our national history, lightening rarely travels through people who live lives of intelligent self-interest. Instead, lightening resides within people of different colors, politics, and creeds possessed by their convictions even when it means incredibly costly self-sacrifice. If racist ideas form convictions that possess racist folks even when the ideas prove self-destructive, anti-racist ideas also form convictions that take possession of anti-racist folks even when these ideas fail to harmonize with an intelligent self-interest. A rich and truth-filled life cannot revolve around self-interest, intelligent or otherwise.

Being American makes self-interest seem more innate in our humanity than self-sacrifice. But it is not. Self-sacrifice is an integral part of the humanity we share and is perhaps *the* integral virtue required to regaining the humanity we lost while living under the spell of racist logics. If we can give up on the myth that self-interest is more innate in our nature than self-sacrifice, perhaps we can also give up on the myth that we are rational rather than relational creatures. The truth is that the lens of self-interest often perverts and rarely rightly aligns our lives with the costs associated with loving our friends, spouses, parents, children, siblings, and enemies. A lens that perverts relationships is simply a poor lens for anti-racist work.

And if self-interest fails to provide a lens through which we can navigate our relational lives, its failings only multiply when it enters into costly pursuit of King's vision of equity, for self-interest produces a dysfunctional relationship to suffering. Living through the lens of self-interest leads to superficiality because we live too cheaply and avoid the suffering that confronting the lies within ourselves and our world always entails. The calculations of intelligent self-interest always take place within too short a timeframe, demand return on investment, and only operate in the realm of the possible. If the lives of those committed to justice —Harriet Tubman, Malcolm X, W. E. B. Dubois, Ida B. Wells, James Baldwin, Marian Wright Edelman—teach us anything, it is that the commitment is for a lifetime and produces mixed results. No one who actually moved the needle in the fight limited themselves to the realm of the possible. As Baldwin wrote his nephew, truthful living is simply risky business: "One can give nothing whatever without giving oneself—that is to say, risking oneself."[392] Dubois word-smithed it differently while pointing to the same necessity: "The true joy of living dwells in that Higher Life . . . In that higher life, my friends, there are three things: Work, and Love, and Sacrifice—these three things—but the greatest of these is Sacrifice."[393] To enter into the struggle and stay in solidarity for the long-term is to do so despite the imperfect calculations of self-interest.

When self-sacrifice elicits lightening—when gifts, talents, and relationships align to make meaningful differences in the lives of underserved communities—we see for brief moments and with tantalizing clarity a picture of a holier American dream. But the tragedy of lightening is not simply its brevity, but that when the darkness returns what we saw in the lightening strike with tantalizing clarity fails to align with what the future actually holds. The prophetic feels illusionary. It is not the struggle up to the mountaintop that destroys the spirit. It is the descent back to the valley where so little has changed despite the sacrifices, strivings, and struggles to bring a new day.

The frontlines of the struggle reveal the terrible secrets behind the curtains of the halls of power. On the frontlines, one sees that the carpenters of American-made crosses are intelligent, relatively well-informed politicians only interested in perpetuating their own power. An equally disturbing truth is this: the businessmen and preachers who are capable of aligning the politicians' self-interest to the standards of human dignity might be less informed but prove no less self-interested. And when the self-interest of politicians and businessmen and preachers fail to harmonize with the dignity of America's most marginalized, racist rhetoric evolves to war against the marginalized in more modern ways. It is not a lack of knowledge regarding the impact of public policy that perpetuates today's inequalities; it is that the marginalized are considered political playthings and fail to inspire the political will to do what can, should, and must be done.

The truth is that we are free to begin doubling our investment in pre-K and elementary funding for deeply at risk students, and no investment would provide a greater long-term return. There would be failures and there would be successes, but when the failures harmonize with racist instincts and small successes fail to dazzle, it is an investment we refuse to make for the long term. The truth is that we are free to stop separating children from hard working parents and to stop exporting mothers and fathers working to provide food and shelter who pose no threat to our nation. Yet because we lack the ability to empathize with the fight for poor people to survive—the very fight for survival that drives immigration—we insist on enforcing legalities designed to fail for all involved. The truth is we are free to begin emptying our prisons of nonviolent criminals whose sentences crystalize the racial depravity of our system. With the money saved by early release, we can provide guaranteed income as well as opportunities for job training and education. Instead, taxpayers pay big bucks to pour salt on our nation's most grievous wounds. None of this is that complicated, but it is costly, for it exchanges the hypnosis of the American dream for the vision necessary to end uniquely American nightmares.

If the dreams of inner city students too often go to die in schools designed to fail, the dreams of those who labor to make our nation more equitable too often go to die in the halls of power designed to enforce our nation's inequalities. Funerals for dreams are costly dirges. The question of those who stand in solidarity with King's movement is how many funerals one can bear without losing the poignancy of one's convictions and commitments, how many funerals can one endure until, in Langston Hughes's words, the struggle "is a broken winged bird that cannot fly."[394] How do we keep our hands on the plough in a field that so stubbornly refuses an equitable harvest? Of all the lessons the Prophetic Black Church offers in the struggle towards a more perfect union, I believe the greatest lesson is the endurance the Prophetic Black Church embodies. Their faces became like flint, and their hands never left the plough.

Reconstruction during President Grant's tenure embodied the challenges of endurance in the pursuit of racial justice. As the Ku Klux Klan rose throughout the South, Attorney General Amos Akerman desired to commit the nation to fight the Klan and protect African Americans in the South. Instead, Grant wearied of the fight and fired Akerman. In the endless struggle, the general who defeated the Confederate Army reduced to becoming the first—but certainly not the last—to employ presidential power to protect the Klan.[395]

The brilliance of the community that stayed in the trenches, embraced the necessity of self-sacrifice, and continued to shine a light of love into our nation's most neglected communities continues to shape our society's most prophetic voices. As inner cities imploded, inequalities rose, and Chicago-styled racism infected both parties of the two party system, the Prophetic Black Church stayed within the crucible of the struggle, serving the poor and the marginalized, and attempting to get her nation to exchange its heart of stone for a heart of flesh. Just as Willie Lynch was not created *ex nihlio*, neither were today's most prophetic voices, voices like Ibram X. Kendi,[396] Michelle Alexander,[397] and Ta-Nehisi Coates.[398] These voices, as often as not, preach outside of the Church's sanctuary and often provide a different line of vision and convictions than those who gather under steeples. Yet their work carries with it flavors of the wisdom and incisive insights of the institution that not only traveled to the mountaintop but returned back to the valley to reside where the racial wars raged on.

In 1958, King published *Stride Toward Freedom: The Montgomery Story.* In *Stride,* the brilliance and beauty of the Prophetic Black Church was in full force: "We will match your capacity to inflict suffering with our capacity to endure suffering. We will meet your physical force with soul force." King entered into his preaching cadence:

> We will not hate you . . . Do to us what you will and we will still love you. Bomb our homes and threaten our children; send your hooded perpetrators of violence into our communities and drag us out on some wayside road, beating us and leaving us half dead, and we will still love you. But we will soon wear you down by our capacity to suffer. And in winning our freedom we will so appeal to your heart and conscience that we will win you.[399]

In time, the light of King's optimism concerning his ability to wear out racists dimmed even as his idealism hardened into convictions that he refused to relinquish. But if King overestimated his reach in his hope to transform the minds, hearts, and lives of white folks, perhaps he underestimated how his example empowered the church he left behind. Through the Prophetic Black Church and those who stand in solidarity with her Movement, a light continues to shine in the struggle to restore humanity to a nation that gained the world but lost its soul. The Prophetic Black Church wars on with grace, joy, and dignity, for though the struggle has yet to defeat America's lies, America has yet to defeat the Prophetic Black Church.

There is no failure in lives that align with truths yet to come into fruition. Yet there is light in those lives that signals that the darkness has not overcome our world. In lives of self-sacrifice, in the lives of struggling grandmothers and grandfathers, mothers and fathers, brothers and sisters, teachers, preachers, and lovers rays of redemption, resurrection, and reconciliation challenge the darkness of the night. In these lives, faith, hope, and love become real long before they become sight. And so week after week, Gospel choirs take their stands, preachers take their pulpits, and congregants take their pews knowing that there is a wisdom in lighting candles while whistling in the dark.

WHAT REMAINS? FROM SPECTATORS TO PARTICIPANTS

As I began researching the racial edges of the Enlightenment in grad school, I came across an apropos quote from Ludwig Wittgenstein: "We must begin with the mistake," Wittgenstein counseled, "and transform it into what is true. That is, we must uncover the source of error; otherwise hearing the truth won't help us . . . To convince someone of what is true, it is not enough to state it; we must find the *road* from error to truth."[400] By bringing together the philosophers of the Enlightenment and how they influenced our shared history and life together with the prophets of the Black Church, I aimed not at *answers* to our racial crisis but a different *angle* to see our predicament and to imagine our way forward. If *America's Unholy Ghosts* offers her readers anything, I hope it is a unique angle that offers a line of vision regarding our nation and our places within it.

For most of my adult life, I have lived as an affluent white man amidst black and immigrant poverty. Often against my own wishes, I began seeing race's critical and often vicious role in how we think about the nature of religion, politics, and the radical inequalities that mark this American life; I began seeing how ideologies I held sacred touched ground in my city to destroy the vulnerable of my neighborhood. It has proven a long journey in learning what I never wanted to know. Simultaneously, it has proven a journey in learning what I needed to know in order to survive even a modest attempt to live with integrity in a nation like ours.

I set about writing *America's Unholy Ghosts,* in part, to share truths of this American life that communities of privilege sought to conceal from folks like me and that folks like me try to conceal from ourselves. Those blinded by whiteness today are neither willing participants nor innocent victims of America's unholy ghosts. We are what Baldwin described "as the slightly mad victims of [our] own brainwashing."[401]

In dissecting the interconnectivity between race and inequality and religious and political ideologies, the question I desired to place before those who stood outside of the struggle for justice was our place and role in perpetuating the racial lies and segregated ways of life we inherited. For too long, most white folks considered themselves passive spectators to the racial animosity within our nation rather than participants whose lack of intentionality makes our nation all the more ingrained with racial inequity. Our place within our nation's history of racial tension is a question with consequences our children, their communities, and our nation cannot dodge—even if we do. I wrote with the fragile hope that if I helped a few readers see the matrix in which we live they might be better positioned to understand themselves as participants capable of weaving different patterns into the communities we call home.

As critical as it was to me to call into question the ways we perpetuate racism and inequality, equally critical for me was questioning from whom we might learn ways of living against the grain of the American way. In the 1960s, the attempt to weave a different pattern was referred to as a counterculture. As black churches challenged white superiority through a civil rights movement, another movement rose to the surface within the white communities to provide an internal critique of white life. Young white kids thirsted for a countercultural movement, and their movement produced a moment called Woodstock. Jimi Hendrix played Woodstock, but he was one of the few blacks to attend. He played to a 95-percent white audience.[402] Tragically, the hippies' world of love and hedonism often proved as racist as the Jim Crow and fundamentalist morality they believed they rejected. Too often, white countercultures produce enclaves of whiteness rather than incubators of solidarity. In time, most hippies exchanged their tie-dyed T-shirts for a more corporate getup and felt free to pursue the American dream with a conscience cleansed by the civil rights movement for which too many sacrificed too little.

Hippies did get some things right, not least of which was their rejection of the Vietnam War.[403] I believe, however, that if we learn anything from the hippies of the sixties and the movement they birthed, it is that white countercultural instincts need to learn from their brothers and sisters of color. Children of white heritage often prove to be superficial authors of righting the wrongs that shape our nation. I believe that hippies made our nation better in some ways. I also believe that in largely missing the civil rights movement, they largely missed the domestic potential of their moment.

There is something tragic in missed opportunities. Those moments in history where we ask ourselves what if . . . The history of race relations in the United States is such a history. What would have happened had hippies chosen solidarity with the civil rights movement and its self-sacrificial ways? What if poor whites had understood that perpetuating slavery and race-hate was designed to perpetuate white poverty and self-hate? What if we had displayed the same unmitigated tenacity in the pursuit of justice as had been demonstrated in space travel? It is dangerous to open the door of the mind to see what could, should, and must be, for once that door is unlocked it is a very difficult door to close.

When we imagine the nation as King dreamed it—an America after the uprooting of racism, materialism, and militarism—we stand in Kennedy's shoes as he spoke of going to the moon. Kennedy understood that no one knew what we needed to know and that no one possessed what we needed to possess in order to accomplish NASA's mission. But Kennedy, with remarkable foresight, understood that only by making the commitment to defeat gravity could we learn what we needed to learn and develop the resources space travel demanded. In "Because They are Hard," Kennedy provided no answers to space travel. Instead, he provided a commitment that the end of the journey to the moon was not the disappointment, set backs, and heartache along the way. The end of the journey was landing on the moon.

If it is true that our nation finds herself amidst a cultural crisis at the intersection of race, faith, and politics resulting from the civil rights revolution that was never resolved, then perhaps the future remains in the hands of those King referred to as "the creatively maladjusted." The greatest blessing in our nation today is that the desire for fundamental changes has returned to the fever pitch through which the civil rights movement inspired the Great Society. The greatest challenge of today is that the unending nature of the domestic war within our nation normalized our lies and though we have come to the breaking point, our self-deception continues to cloud our vision of what could and should be. One day at a time the clarity LBJ and MLK provided dissipated from America's mainstream imagination of what could and should be possible within our communities, cities, and nation. Such murkiness makes it all the more difficult to wring redemption from our cultural crisis.

I do not know if America will ever grow vulnerable again to the message of the Prophetic Black Church or if the fight against racism and inequality will ever be remotely as effective as her fight against gravity. "Race isn't rocket science," wrote Christopher Edley. "Race is harder than rocket science."[404] In many ways, our nation's journey to equity began long ago. Rather than beginning in presidential proclamations, the journey began in the songs of slaves and continued through a church that chose to embrace the cross rather than submit to our nation's racial status quo. Today, the journey continues through the Prophetic Black Church and a remarkable remnant of gifted writers, researchers, and practitioners across racial and religious divides. If I wrote to those on the sidelines of the struggle, I also wrote to this tradition and that remnant with the modest hope that some might find within my writings fuel for their own fire that empowers their journey through the present darkness to the dawning of a new day.

I understood from the outset that many readers likely thirsted for a more secular alternative to King's prophetic vision of seeing humanity as interconnected children of God. Yet it is not clear to me that secularism provides the antidote to the sickness within white America's soul. The past few years of our nation's life together stirred many poignant emotions in white America. Relationships within families grew more difficult across political divides. White Christians' relationship to their faith and churches began changing as well. Though many doubled down on familiar formulas and pretended that nothing was wrong with the disciples these formulas formed, others simply exited the church all together. And yet what struck me as odd was how easily white folks—both secular and religious—reduced Christianity to the hypocrisies of white Christians and how little they felt the need for black wisdom.

Nonetheless, as I worked on *America's Unholy Ghosts*, my worldview shook as well. As racist politicians, preachers, and policemen continued to fill the headlines, and as racist people easily forgave their racist words and deeds without the need for repentance, I read and reread, wrote and rewrote, about the sickness that resided within our nation and her churches. After turning my attention to the civil rights era, I saw more clearly how today's crisis was but a broken record of racist logics and a tragically repetitive history. More often than not, the work made me more intimate with the darkness and the questions became immensely personal. Many of my most important relationships proved more difficult to navigate, and I began to understand the exodus of many of my generation from the church at a deeper level than I desired.

Yet, in this disorienting time of soul searching, what remained clear to me was that those navigating our nation's chaos most redemptively and lovingly were often my friends of color whose world was shaped by the tradition that formed Martin Luther King. The more I read King and watched those who embody the tradition he championed during this time, the more clear it became to me that the counterculture that our nation needed resided in the Prophetic Black Church; that the instincts fostered in the Prophetic Black Church provided an antidote to the instincts fostered by our culture at large. Again, this is not because the Prophetic Black Church is any less riddled with human failings, but rather because it possesses—or put more accurately is possessed by—a love- and truth-filled vision that restores a humanity that our crisis threatens to extinguish. I started writing out of the conviction that the work that has taken place within the souls of black folks desperately needs to take place within the souls of white folks as well. The more I read, witnessed, and wrote, the deeper that conviction grew.

If this time of cultural crisis deepened my commitment to the religious and spiritual life, it also deepened my commitment to my nation. For a long time the term patriotism seemed so broken and abused, so tied to a hardhearted nationalism, that it was difficult for me to employ. After studying the sacrifices of those who gave their lives for our nation in times of domestic war, I began seeing that if patriotism is to love your neighbors and enemies within your community, your city, and your nation, and if there is no greater act of love than the readiness to lay down your life for others, then I should pray to mature into that kind of patriotism. So if we use the term patriotism, perhaps we can use it to communicate our commitment to making our nation more worthy of our children by committing to a way of life that measures every citizen as God's beloved child.

What remains after the exorcism of America's unholy ghosts? Faith—but not a faith reduced to obedience to racist rulers and to knowledge of religious formulas. Hope—but not a hope limited by white fears and what the smallest minds deem possible. Love—but a love that rejects false superiorities by embracing a radical solidarity. I understand our nation's wounds will not be healed by a faith, hope, and love that fails to transform the societal systems and lifestyles that segregate the American way. But to the extent that faith, hope, and love are insufficient virtues for the needed radical racial revolution, perhaps they are also equally indispensible.

The question, it seems to me, is not whether a radical racial transformation is possible—probability was never on the prophetic side of history—but on which side of history we chose to stand. And the answer to that question is in our hands. We are not spectators of this cultural crisis. We are participants.

Finis.

Acknowledgments

The truth is I love to write, but love needs encouragement. To that end, I begin by thanking two of my first encouragers in writing: Dr. Kavin Rowe and Rev. Marty Troyer. Kavin is one of the most remarkable teachers I ever encountered, and though his critiques of my writing during my final year at Duke Divinity School were scorching, I never knew a more constructive critic. He requested a copy of my final paper, and he invited me to his office where he encouraged me to continue to read and write following my studies at Duke. The next semester I began reading the Enlightenment thinkers I analyzed in this book. Without Kavin's encouragement, this book would not have happened. Marty Troyer is Houston's most famous Mennonite and once blogged regularly for the Houston Chronicle. Rather than monopolizing his platform, Marty invited his friends to write and included me in on the opportunity. The blogs became my way of expressing my love of writing. The blogs helped me to grow as a writer, and without those blogs my love would likely have died.

Four institutions played a critical role in this book—two churches and two colleges. The first is Pleasant Hill Missionary Baptist Church, which integrated me into their family and forever changed my life; a special thanks to Rev. Harvey Clemons Jr., who opened Pleasant Hill's door. Following my time at Pleasant Hill, Truett Theological Seminary at Baylor University provided me an opportunity to be a Visiting Scholar. A special thanks to Dean Todd Still of Truett who provided me space to think, research, and write during the 2016–2017 school year. During this time, Free Indeed Ministry's Rev. Johnny Gentry III provided me a platform for my work and research, and Rev. Ann Rolle provided helpful readings of early drafts of this project.

The final institution I am indebted to for writing and researching this project is the University of St. Thomas's Center for Faith and Culture, where I serve as a Visiting Scholar of Race, Religion, and Politics. A special thanks to Ft. Donald Nesti and Ft. Chris Valka who made room for me at the Center and provided helpful readings of the first draft of the manuscript.

Four readers provided chapter-by-chapter responses and sacrificed their limited time to make the manuscript stronger and to pick me up when I felt like I had reached the end of my rope. A special thanks to two dear friends and a teacher—Dr. Phillip Luke Sinitiere, Dr. Michael O. Emerson, and Dr. Richard Lischer. The final of the four readers who provided chapter-by-chapter feedback was my sister-in-law Ali Mullen who found time to read the manuscript despite the demands made by my niece and nephew. For reading my manuscript, she is officially my favorite Mullen in Indiana.

The University of St. Thomas hosted reading circles of various scholars, students, and practitioners. The reading circles also made me more courageous in seeking feedback from others I admire. The feedback provided the foundation for the improvements made between the first and final draft. Those readers not previously mentioned include: Rev. Chris Hartwell, Rev. Dr. Steve Bezner, Dr. Mirela Oliva, Dr. Angela Ravin-Anderson, Bishop Michael Rinehart, Monica Hatcher, Dr. Angela Bell, Dr. Sergio Arispe, Dr. Andrew Tuch, Stephan Fairfield, and Callie Thomas. The title was shaped from feedback from a friend I refer to lovingly as "Grandma" but who is known to the world at large as Rev. Kevin Gardner-Sinclair.

I am deeply grateful to the Cascade team of Charlie Collier, Matthew Wimer, Jimmy Stock, and Jim Tedrick who brought this book to life. I hope it proves worthy of their confidence and investment, and I am thankful that my book managed to enter into the line of books with their fingerprints. A special thank you to Rev. Michael Pickett, my long time friend and partner in crime, for his assistance with many of the graphics and illustrations.

Lastly, my family. My children: Naomi and Roger. This writing demanded I dive deeply into a world of disturbing ideas that racialized our nation. Throughout this writing, ya'll's daily lovable ridiculousness made room for sunshine amidst the darkness. The light of our household was not overcome. Finally, the reader that matters most to me—my wife Sarah. Sarah, you read and re-read and re-read. If this makes you proud, I am more than satisfied. My friends wonder how I convinced a woman of such beauty, wisdom, grace, and strength to marry me. But you and I know. It is not a mystery. I was very lucky.

Notes

1. King, "Three Evils of Society."

2. The term Prophetic Black Church will be utilized to refer to the church that was organized by slaves, sought to foster her members' relationship to God, and that works to right America's relationship to the poor and marginalized by upholding the dignity of all of God's children.

3. "Peculiar institution" was a term used for slavery in the nineteenth century, coined by Vice President John C. Calhoun and employed within a mythology that sought to justify slavery as a necessity of southern life and the natural outgrowth of racial differences. Stamp, *Peculiar Institution*, 7.

4. Crump, "5 years after Trayvon Martin's death, what has nation learned?"

5. An impressive array of scholars provide deeper analysis of the racialized murders of this era, including Eddie S. Gaulde, Wesley Lowery, Marc Lamont Hill, Christopher Lebron, Keeanga-Yamahtta Taylor, Carol Anderson, and Phillip Luke Sinitiere.

6. Dyson, *Tears We Cannot Stop*, 5.

7. Johnson, "To Fulfill These Rights."

8. King, *Testament of Hope*, 478.

9. King, *Testament of Hope*, 328.

10. Nixon, Address Accepting the Presidential Nomination.

11. Tyson, *Blood Done Signed My Name*, 111.

12. Assisting in this illusion was the emergence of America's freeway systems that happened to coincide with the fall of segregation. As legal segregation fell, the freeways allowed white America to retreat to the suburbs, and overpasses allowed their travelers to bypass urban realities. For the few who stayed in the center city, the white enclaves became ever more elite and economically exclusionary.

13. For more analysis on media and race, see the chapters "The News Media and the Racialization of Poverty" and "Media Distortions: Causes and Consequences" in Gilens, *Why Americans Hate Welfare: Race, Media and the Politics of Anti-Poverty Policy.*

14. The facts of the politicians proved faulty, but at the time fear clarified racist convictions concerning the work that needed doing. Those in power were gonna get tough on crime and teach those in the inner city—poor black and brown folks—their lesson for forsaking personal responsibility.

15. For a thorough analysis of church segregation, see Emerson and Woo, *People of the Dream*; Emerson and Smith, *Divided by Faith*; and Shelton and Emerson, *Black and Whites in Christian America*.

16. For a brilliant but flawed analysis of Reaganomics and Clintonomics, see

"Reaganomics vs. Clintonomics, 1981–2000" in Nester, *A Short History of Industrial Policy*, 222–62. Nester roots the ideological differences among Reaganomics and Clintonomics in the same ideologies that separated Thomas Jefferson and Alexander Hamilton. A fundamental flaw of the work is how Nester fails to see the similarities between the actual tax codes that tied Reagan and Clinton together.

17. *Wall Street Journal,* "President Elect Obama."; Wise, *Between Barack and a Hard Place.*

18. By 2013, Houston experienced 288 consecutive jury acquittals of police shootings despite the fact that 1 in 5 police shootings in Houston are of unarmed civilians. Pinkerton. "Bullet Proof Part I."

19. See the *Washington Post*'s online database: https://www.washingtonpost.com/graphics/national/police-shootings/ and Kendi, *Stamped from the Beginning*, 1. The collective body count of those injured or killed by gun violence annually exceeds 40,000. In 2015, there were 13,473 fatalities and 27,016 injuries. "Past Summary Ledgers," Gun Violence Archive, accessed January 28, 2019, http://www.gunviolencearchive.org/past-tolls.

20. "Poverty," The Working State of America, accessed January 28, 2019, http://www.stateofworkingamerica.org/fact-sheets/poverty.

21. See Goza et al., *New HISD Chief Must Tackle Challenge of Fifth Ward Poverty.*

22. Montero, *A Changing of the Guard at Houston's Disciplinary School.*

23. Pager, "Mark of a Criminal Record."

24. Obama, "Charleston Eulogy for Clementa Pinckney."

25. See Ira Kratznelson's *When Affirmative Action Was White* and *Fear Itself* for more analysis.

26. Kendi, *Stamped from the Beginning,* 1.

27. Kendi, *Stamped from the Beginning,* 1.

28. Kendi, *Stamped from the Beginning,* 5.

29. Kendi, *Stamped from the Beginning,* 9.

30. Moyers, "What a Real President Was Like."

31. "In 1964, just three years after Barack Obama was born, about two-thirds of all persons locked up in the nation's jails were white, while a third were persons of color, mostly African American. By the early 1990s, those numbers had essentially flopped." Wise, *Between Barack and a Hard Place,* 56.

32. Alexander, *The New Jim Crow*, 98. Alexander cites research from Human Rights Watch, "Punishment and Prejudice: Racial Disparities in the War on Drugs." Leading this explosion are seven states whose drug incarcerations are over 80 percent African American, though African Americans are a minority that uses drugs at statistically lower rates. The seven states are: Maryland, Illinois, South Carolina, North Carolina, Louisiana, Virginia, and New Jersey.

33. Alexander, *The New Jim Crow,* 84 & 112–19.

34. Alexander, *The New Jim Crow*, 119.

35. Coates, *Between the World and Me*, 103, 146.

36. FitzGerald, *The Evangelicals,* 487, 512.

37. Martinich, *Hobbes: A Biography*, 2.

38. The Hobbes family included two alehouse owners—Edmund and Robert Hobbes—and though the family ties are difficult to connect, it seems that Thomas Sr. was in their alehouses more than his church. Noel Malcolm, "A Summary Biography of Hobbes," chapter 1 in Sorell, *The Cambridge Companion to Hobbes*, 15.

39. For the preeminent biography of Thomas Hobbes, see Martinich, *Hobbes: A*

Biography.

40. To avoid confusion, Leviathan will carry two meanings in this work. One is the book Hobbes writes and will be italicized—*Leviathan*—the other Leviathan is the authority figure with all power that Hobbes imagines in his book and will not be italicized.

41. Hobbes, *Leviathan,* 19.

42. Ironically, Bertrand Russell claims that the most influential philosopher since Aristotle is none other than John Locke.

43. Hobbes, *Leviathan,* 100.

44. Hobbes, *Leviathan,* 80.

45. Hobbes, *De Cive,* 14 (I.II).

46. Hobbes, *Leviathan,* 80–81.

47. Hobbes, *Leviathan,* 86.

48. Hobbes, *Leviathan,* 27. Importantly, this is the work of false religion.

49. "In a time when all politics aims at cutting taxes for the rich, it is important to remember that politics once had the highest of aims of pursuing the greatest of all goods—as Plato put it—politics seeks to bring humanity to 'the completest possible assimilation to the gods.'" Wolin, *Politics and Vision*, 265.

50. Hobbes, *Leviathan,* 44.

51. Hobbes, *Leviathan,* 42.

52. Following the logic of slaying the relational aspects of reason, philosophy itself morphs from the love of wisdom to the infallible power of reason.

53. For a better understanding of whiteness in a more contemporary sense, see David Roediger's *Working Towards Whiteness: How Americas Immigrants became White: The Strange Journey from Ellis Island to the Suburbs.*

54. Some founding fathers—such as Washington—did not wear wigs. Instead, they powdered their hair to a more pristine whiteness.

55. See John Locke's *Fundamental Constitution of Carolina* for an example.

56. Dorrien, *The New Abolition,* 191

57. Kendi, *Stamped from the Beginning,* 82, 311.

58. Hobbes, *Leviathan,* 19.

59. The image of Leviathan is a biblical depiction of Pharaoh from the book of Job.

60. Hobbes, *Leviathan,* 247. The rhetoric of "all other contentments" will evolve into John Locke's "life, liberty and the pursuit of property" before evolving further into the Declaration of Independence's "life, liberty and the pursuit of happiness."

61. Hobbes, *Leviathan,* 132.

62. Hobbes, *Leviathan,* 190.

63. Hobbes, *Leviathan,* 101.

64. Hobbes, *Leviathan,* 103; emphasis mine.

65. Trattner, *From Poor Law to Welfare State,* 23.

66. Brands, *Traitor to His Class,* 237.

67. Blackmon, *Slavery by Another Name,* 216.

68. See Putnam, *Bowling Alone.*

69. See "Facts about povery and hunger in America," accessed Janury 28, 2019, www.feedingamerica.org/hunger-in-america/impact-of-hunger/hunger-and-poverty.

70. Hobbes, *Leviathan,* 98.

71. One way of understanding America's ever-evolving racial oppression—from slavery to convict leasing programs to Jim Crow and the New Jim Crow—is as Hobbesian ways of managing equality.

72. Hobbes, *Leviathan,* 98.

73. Hobbes, *Leviathan,* 118.

74. Fain, *The Destruction of Black Wall Street.*

75. Hobbes, *Leviathan,* 79.

76. Hobbes, *De Cive,* 31.

77. One of the more breathtaking examples of predatory paperwork was the convict-leasing programs that popped up following the Civil War that perpetuated slavery for tens of thousands of people for well over another fifty years. The story of how African Americans were arrested under false pretenses and forced to sign contracts that reduced them to slaves is harrowingly chronicled in Blackmon, *Slavery by Another Name.*

78. Hamilton, *Report on Pubic Credit*; Feldman, *The Three Lives of James Madison.* 293–300; Chernow, *Alexander Hamilton,* 295–308.

79. Hobbes, *Leviathan,* 79.

80. As Hobbes put it, "The publique worth of a man, which is the Value set on him by the Common-wealth by offices of Command, Judicature, publike Employment; or by Names and Titles." (*Leviathan,* 73).

81. Hobbes, *Leviathan,* 181.

82. Hobbes, *Leviathan,* 75.

83. Hobbes, *Leviathan,* 189.

84. Hobbes, *Leviathan,* 245.

85. Hobbes, *Leviathan,* 73.

86. Coates, *Between the World and Me,* 10.

87. Hobbes, *Leviathan,* 154; emphasis mine.

88. For further analysis, see Robert Bernasconi and Anika Maaza Mann, "The Contradictions of Racism: Locke, Slavery, and the Two Treatises," in Valls, ed., *Race and Racism in Modern Philosophy,* 89–107.

89. In time, it was a logic that would strike back, even on its most committed prophets. Writing in wake of the stock market crash of 1929, Thomas Wolfe pens *You Can't Go Home Again.* He writes that the moguls of the time "were all victims of an occupational disease—a kind of mass hypnosis that denied to them the evidence of their senses . . . the men who created this world in which every value was false . . . saw themselves, not as creatures tranced by fatal illusions, but rather as the most knowing, practical, and hard headed men alive [yet] were so little capable of facing hard reality and truth that they blew their brains out or threw themselves out the window" (166–67).

90. The journey of corporations enjoying the benefit of personhood in the Supreme Court begins with *Trustees vs. Dartmouth College* in 1818 and more poignantly in the 1886 case *Santa Clara v. Southern Pacific,* when oral arguments extend the 14th amendment to protect corporations.

91. Thankfully for my father and myself, Roy failed to slay cupid. Two months after Mom graduated, Mom married.

92. "Dissolution Of Common-wealths Proceedeth From Imperfect Institution." (Hobbes, *Leviathan,* 237). Perfecting institutions was the goal of education. Yet, "perfecting" would find a very specific meaning in Hobbes's system.

93. Hobbes, *Leviathan,* 250.

94. Hobbes, *Leviathan,* 46.

95. Hobbes, *Leviathan,* 510.

96. In *Behemoth,* Hobbes says almost the exact same thing: "The core of rebellion, as you have seen by this, and read of other rebellions, are the Universities; which

nevertheless are not to be cast away, but to be better disciplined . . . such as are fit to make men know that it is their duty to obey all laws whatsoever that shall by the authority of the King be enacted." See Borot, "History in Hobbes Thought, in Sorrell, *The Cambridge Companion to Thomas Hobbes*, 319.

97. Hobbes, *Leviathan*, 249.

98. Hobbes, *Leviathan*, 157. The allegory is God questioning Adam about why he disputed rather than obeyed.

99. Hobbes, *Leviathan*, 249.

100. Hobbes, *Leviathan*, 250.

101. One of Hobbes's first works was a translation of Thucydides's *Peloponnesian War*. The work proved pivotal in Hobbes's intellectual development, convincing him that history teaches citizens political science in ways more powerful than abstract philosophy and that the purpose of the discipline of history is training citizens in obedience.

102. Hobbes, *Leviathan*, 577.

103. Hobbes argues that the closest parallel to the education he envisions is that of the synagogue. Yet the striking difference in historical training in these two institutions is the telling of history. In the synagogue, since the goal is train the young to honor God, the sins of the forefathers are remembered so that they would not be repeated. In the university, since the goal is faithfulness to the Leviathan, the sins of the forefathers must simply be edited out of history. Who the telling of history is designed to serve—God, the people, or the king—makes all the difference.

104. The logo of the Masonic lodge in Danville, Virginia.

105. An indication of this decline is found in Robert Putnman's observation of the irony that, "The average college graduate today knows little more about public affairs than did the average high school graduated in the 1940s." (*Bowling Alone*, 35).

106. See Dewey's *Democracy and Education*.

107. For the realities of taxes and the colonies, see Terry Anderson and Peter J. Hill's *Birth of a Transfer Society*. For a more thorough analysis of the impact of America's dependence on slavery and England's move towards abolition in inciting the revolution, see Horne, *The Counter Revolution of 1776: Slave Resistance and the Origins of the United States of America*. Horne writes: "The embodiment of colonial secession, George Washington, may have spent more time overseeing 'his' enslaved African than he did supervising soldiers or governmental officials . . . John Adams . . . earned handsome fees as legal counsel for slaveholders against the enslaved . . . John Hancock, whose large signature . . . was somehow appropriate as he was one of Boston's largest slaveholders.

108. Unsurprisingly, in the South, the justification for the Civil War that arose after the war—states' rights—rather than the justifications that inspired the war—slavery—traveled through time in textbooks often inspired more by the politics of regional loyalty than the facts of history. But the South's style of telling history is not simply regional. It is distinctively Hobbesian. It is distinctively American. See Dew, *Apostles of Disunion: Southern Secession Commissioners and the Causes of the Civil War*.

109. Chernow, *Washington*, 492–93.

110. Coates, *Between the World and Me*, 26–27.

111. In time, the prophetic tradition itself is re-engineered into a visions of the future unconnected to the injustices of the present.

112. "True Religion—Feare of power invisible, feigned by the mind, or imagined from tales publiquely allowed, And when the power imagined is truly such as we imagine, TRUE RELIGION" (Hobbes, *Leviathan*, 67).

113. "Lastly, Obedience to his Lawes. . . is the greatest worship of all. For as Obedience is more acceptable to God than sacrifice" (Hobbes. *Leviathan,* 356).

114. Hobbes, *Leviathan,* 425.

115. Hobbes, *Leviathan,* 93.

116. Throughout American history, there exists exceptions to this rule within white leadership, from William Lloyd Garrison to Henry Ward Beecher and Harriet Beecher Stowe, but despite such exceptional leadership the Church was and continues to be defined by its failures at the intersection of race and social justice.

117. Allitt, *Religion in America Since 1945,* 152.

118. "Preachers are not called to be politicians . . . If as much effort could be put into winning people to Jesus Christ across the land as is being exerted for the present civil rights movement, America would be turned upside down for God" (Falwell, *Falwell: An Autobiography,* 312).

119. Falwell, *Falwell: An Autobiography,* 311–15.

120. Hobbes, *Leviathan,* 270.

121. Hobbes, *Leviathan,* 88.

122. Hobbes, *Leviathan,* 100.

123. Hobbes, *Leviathan,* 145.

124. Hobbes, *Leviathan,* 221.

125. Hobbes, *Leviathan,* 129.

126. Hobbes, *Leviathan,* 88.

127. Many political commentators believe that Kennedy lost to Nixon based largely off of Nixon's poor presence in front of the TV camera. Nixon hired Ailes to alleviate that liability and turn his TV appearances into a strength. See Perlstein, *Nixonland,* 234–35, 302–4.

128. With roots that travel back to 1949, the Federal Communications Commission required TV and Radio productions to protect bipartisan perspectives for their audience. The Fairness Doctrine was overturned in 1987. Later legislation protecting the doctrine was vetoed by Reagan.

129. Hobbes, *Leviathan,* 242.

130. Hobbes, *Leviathan,* 146.

131. Granston, *John Locke: A Biography,* 1.

132. Granston, *John Locke: A Biography,* 480.

133. Granston, *John Locke: A Biography,* 3.

134. "The curriculum that Locke was required to follow differed hardly at all from that which had irritated the young Thomas Hobbes fifty years before and both reacted to it the same way" (J. R. Milton, "Locke's Life and Times," in Chapell, ed., *The Cambridge Companion to John Locke,* 6).

135. Locke and Hobbes both believed the world's quagmire was rooted in Aristotle's the "Schoolmen's" philosophy; they both root their philosophies in the precise use of words; they both immersed themselves in the study of other cultures and developed their thinking with the colonial experiment in mind; and they both believed that through the precise use of words, morality and politics could achieve the certainty of geometry.

136. In truth, Hobbes granted the Leviathan few privileges that Locke refused the aristocracy. From the perspective of the poor, differences between Locke and Hobbes were less in who was empowered to oppress them—a governmental Leviathans or the wealthy elite.

137. "Boyle theorizes that 'unblemished' light is white—an idea that inspires Locke's

Puritan companion Sir Isaac Newton's *Optics*. The racial imagination follows Boyle from the sciences into his political forays in the council for Foreign Plantations that promotes slavery for the sake of English empire" (Kendi, *Stamped from the Beginning*, 46, 50.)

138. Locke will pen the *Fundamental Constitution of the Carolinas* and sit on the Board of Trade becoming one of the most informed and supportive philosophers of the slave trade. Locke also moves his fascination with slavery from the political to the theological. The last writing of John Locke is on St. Paul; in these writings, Locke is still hot at work reconciling slavery with Paul's teaching, a work of dubious exegetical integrity.

139. Cranston, *John Locke: A Biography*, 107.

140. Cranston, *John Locke: A Biography*, 107 .

141. This is not to suggest that Locke was the first to suggest a separation was needed between political practice and policies and religious convictions. William Cavanaugh's chapter "The Invention of Religion" in *The Myth of Religious Violence* provides a more thorough history of writers who predate Locke suggesting solutions similar to Locke's. What I am suggesting is the logic of Locke proves more persuasive in time than those of his era who argue the same point.

142. Locke, An Essay Concerning Human Understanding, 55.

143. Locke, *An Essay Concerning Human Understanding*, 477.

144. Locke, *An Essay Concerning Human Understanding*, 57–58. For Locke, though we cannot know everything, we can know somethings, and as we seek to know what we can know we find that the mind is mighty enough to perform the practical work that needs doing.

145. Romans 1:20.

146. "Thus the first capacity of human intellect is that the mind is fitted to receive the impressions made on it; either through the senses by outward objects, or by its own operations when it reflects on them" (Locke, *An Essay Concerning Human Understanding*, 120).

147. Locke, *An Essay Concerning Human Understanding*, 60.

148. David Armitage, "John Locke: Theorist of Empire?" in *Empire and Modern Political Thought*, ed. Sankar Muthu, 84–111.

149. "The actions of men," Locke says are, "the best interpreters of their thoughts" (Locke, *An Essay Concerning Human Understanding*, 75).

150. Locke, *An Essay Concerning Human Understanding*, 91.

151. The practicality of the philosophic trinity is important to keep in mind. In an age where philosophers often prove less than practical or politically engaged, it is important to remember that in the times of Hobbes and Locke philosophers feared what they wrote might lead to their death. These philosophers were intimately intertwined with the political struggles of their day. In fact, many of Locke's most important works were penned anonymously precisely because they were written under the fear of death.

152. Locke, *An Essay Concerning Human Understanding*, 339–40.

153. The term Locke employes is "species," for the larger organizational buckets that our minds categorize different animals and objects into such as dogs, cats, and, of course, humans.

154. Locke, *An Essay Concerning Human Understanding*, 403.

155. Chernow, *Washington*, 470, 484.

156. Locke, *An Essay Concerning Human Understanding*, 403.

157. Locke, *An Essay Concerning Human Understanding*, 459.

158. Locke, *An Essay Concerning Human Understanding*, 500–501.

159. Jefferson, *Notes on Virginia*, Query XIV, 1785.

160. McCoullough. *John Adams*, 330.

161. Kendi, *Stamped from the Beginning*, 82.

162. Kendi, *Stamped from the Beginning*, 210.

163. Kendi, *Stamped from the Beginning*, 210.

164. As *The New Jim Crow* so painfully shows, long after Dred Scott the Supreme Court continually qualified the value of black lives by upholding the racist administration of the laws of the land in order to protect the stability of unjust systems. Perhaps as powerful as any case Alexander sites was 1987's McCleskey vs. Kemp where the court upheld racially biased sentences fearing the unraveling of too many verdicts across the nation, for "taken to its logical conclusion, [Warren McCleskey's claim (of racism)] throws into serious question the principles that underlie our criminal justice system." In a land declaring innocent until proven guilty, black lives continue to be declared guilty of being expendable.

165. Locke, *Political Writings*, 262.

166. Locke, *Political Writings*, 264.

167. Wolin, *Politics and Vision*, 267 (quoting from Locke's *Travel and Sojourn in France*).

168. Locke, *Political Writings*, 393.

169. Locke, *Political Writings*, 304.

170. "The business of laws is not to provide for the truth of opinions, but for the safety and security of the commonwealth, and every particular man's goods and person. And so it ought to be" (Locke, *Political Writings*, 420).

171. Locke, *Political Writings*, 432.

172. It is important to note that this, for Locke, is no attack on Christianity or the critical place for faith in the life of the ruler. "Magistracy does not oblige him to put off either humanity or Christianity," wrote Locke. "But it is one thing to persuade, another to command, one thing to press with arguments, another with penalties . . ." (Locke, *Political Writings*, 395). The eviction notice from the political arena that Locke pens for religion is not aimed at undermining Christian piety but at placing it on a more sure foundation by protecting Christian piety's better angels from the main temptations to which Christendom's fallen angels succumbed since the times of Constantine.

173. In the words of Locke, "It is the duty of the civil magistrate . . . to secure . . . every one of his subjects in the just possession of these things belonging to this life. If anyone presume to violate the laws . . . established for the preservation of these things, his presumption is to be checked by fear" (Locke, *Political Writings*, 394).

174. Locke, *Political Writings: The Second Treatise of Government*, 334.

175. Critical to Reagan's rise to power was demonizing those on welfare, who in reality were often the elderly and disabled. In order to demonize, Reagan relied on myths like welfare queens, and in so doing paints a picture of lazy and hypersexual blacks as the image of welfare recipients in the minds of conservatives. In a frighteningly brilliant word play, Reagan states: "We should measure welfare's success by how many people leave welfare, not by how many are added." What makes Reagan's quip brilliant is that everyone agrees with it, just not with how to do that. Reagan's most devastating critique of the welfare system was his "Radio Address to the Nation on Welfare Reform," February 15, 1986. The problems of poverty resulted from neither unjust wages nor a lack of opportunity nor the prison system nor the broke education system. The problem of the poor was a welfare system that pays folks to not work and incentivizes the break up of

families; the problem was that the liberals war on poverty created poverty.

176. Reagan, "The President's News Conference," August 12, 1986.

177. Brands, *Reagan,* 545.

178. Bivens, "The Top 1 Percent's Share of Income."

179. Locke, *Political Writings: The Second Treatise of Government,* 309.

180. Locke, *Political Writings: The Second Treatise of Government,* 276.

181. Two of the most famously wealthy presidents in American history were FDR and JFK. A pillar of Roosevelt's wealth—from the Delano side—was the opium industry, while Kennedy's wealth traces back to dubious dealings in liquor during prohibition. One not need look further than the Roosevelts and Kennedys to complicate the illusion that linked extraordinary wealth with extraordinary work ethics.

182. Locke, *Political Writings: The Second Treatise of Government*, 288 (emphasis mine).

183. Locke, *Political Writings: The Second Treatise of Government,* 297.

184. This is at the heart of America's tax code, where the burden falls on labor for those who work, while the wealthy are able to live from their investment and income produced from capital that is taxed at less than half the rate of income from labor.

185. An example of this irony is the fight for free tuition at public colleges. Children of the rich are under no threat of "entitlement" if their folks can afford to pay for their education, but the children of the poor are if the state covers their tuition. Only because our logic is broken do we believe access to education is related to the wealth of students' parents.

186. Madison, *The Federalist Papers. No. 10,* in Hamilton et al., *The Federalist Papers,* 42, 47.

187. Locke, *The Reasonableness of Christianity,* 24 (emphasis mine).

188. In *A Letter Concerning Toleration,* Locke lawyers the divorce between the church and the state by redefining the nature of each.

189. Locke, *Political Writings: A Letter Concerning Toleration.* 412.

190. Hobbes attempted this move, but he wrote obedience to the tyrant into the equation and rooted religion in fear rather than piety. Though it can be argued that the definitions prove to play out the same way historically, the differences in images again prove definitive for the purposes of persuasion.

191. Locke, *Political Writings: A Letter Concerning Toleration,* 395.

192. Locke, *Political Writings: A Letter Concerning Toleration,* 410.

193. Locke, *Political Writings: A Letter Concerning Toleration,* 410.

194. Locke, *Political Writings: A Letter Concerning Toleration.* 290.

195. Romans 8:36 and Revelations 5:6.

196. Locke, *Political Writings: A Letter Concerning Toleration,* 392.

197. Locke, *The Reasonableness of Christianity,* 30.

198. Locke, *Political Writings: A Letter Concerning Toleration,* 390.

199. Critical to the evolution of the separation of church and state was Lockean disciple James Madison's *The Memorial and Remonstrance* that more perfectly tailored Locke's thoughts for the American context. See Feldman, *The Three Lives of James Madison,* 63–67.

200. "In the South, local whites forced Moody to choose between racial integration and public popularity—Moody chose popularity . . . With Moody, southern whites had everything they wanted, a northern religious leader who capitulated to southern racial etiquette, who refused to chastise them for slavery . . ." (Blum, *Reforging the White*

Republic, 141).

201. The 2010 "Restoring Honor Rally" featured Fox News and included Christian leaders James Dobson and Jerry Falwell Jr. The rally celebrated the power of faith in public life while ignoring inequality and racism. Veterans of the movement considered the event "sacrilege." FitzGerald, *The Evangelicals*, 597.

202. Douglass, "Oration of Frederick Douglass."

203. Marsden, *Jonathan Edwards*, 62; Bailey, *Race and Redemption*, 61–62; and Stinson, "The Other Side of the Paper."

204. Hobbes, *The Elements of Law*, 23.8.

205. Locke, *Some Thoughts Concerning Education*, 8.

206. Locke, *Some Thoughts Concerning Education*, 70.

207. Locke, *Some Thoughts Concerning Education*, 34.

208. Locke, *Some Thoughts Concerning Education*, 34.

209. Locke writes *Essay on the Poor Law* from his position as the commissioner the of the Board of Trade and Plantations.

210. Hamilton, *Report on Manufactures*, Chernow, *Alexander Hamilton*, 376.

211. Locke, *Essay on the Poor Law and Working Schools*, 1697.

212. Cranston, *John Locke*, 115.

213. Locke, *Political Writings*, 304.

214. Locke, *Political Writings*, 272.

215. Locke, *Political Writings*, 355.

216. Locke, *Political Writings*, 230 (emphasis mine).

217. Ketcham, *James Madison*, 12.

218. Tyson, *Blood Done Signed My Name*, 37.

219. Coates, *The Case for Reparations*.

220. The supremacy of Virginia within the context of the revolutionary context was stated most succinctly by the second president, John Adams, in reflecting on the selection of young Jefferson to author the Declaration of Independence, referred to as "the Frankfort advice, to place Virginia at the head of everything" (Meacham, *The Art of Power*. 102).

221. Locke, *Essay Concerning Human Understanding*, 620.

222. Bourne, *The Life of John Locke*, 252.

223. Phillipson, *Adam Smith: An Enlightened Life*, 9.

224. Smith, *The Wealth of Nations*, 654.

225. Phillipson, *Adam Smith*, 3.

226. "In the University of Oxford, the greater part of the public professors have, for these many years, given up altogether even the pretense of teaching" (Smith, *The Wealth of Nations*, 821).

227. Smith seems to have hit it off with Voltaire, whose bust he purchased while admiring the genius from afar. One of the many things they agreed on was that Shakespeare left much to be desired. Voltaire famously remarked "that Hamlet was the dream of a drunken savage and that Shakespeare had good scenes but not a good play" (Rae, *The Life of Adam Smith*, 368). Smith could not describe his feelings on the subject any better, so he simply quoted Voltaire.

228. Smith's friendship with Hume was carefully managed. During Hume's life, he failed to support him in pursuing a post at the University of Glasgow and also refused to provide a helping hand in publishing Hume's writings on religion following Hume's passing. The decisions, however, likely contained more than Smith's desire to avoid

controversy. They likely included deep philosophical differences on how to approach matters of religion.

229. Phillipson, *Adam Smith*, 262.

230. "He regarded Pascal's moving analysis of the nature of human wretchedness as the work of a 'whining moralist'. . . Such writers had famously written for an intelligent, educated, and generally well-born elite, and they had only occasionally looked beyond their rarefied private world to that of ordinary human beings who were engaged in the pursuit of wealth, power and self-esteem, blissfully unaware of their wretchedness" (Phillipson, *Adam Smith*, 61).

231. Phillipson, *Adam Smith*, 7.

232. "I have heard him say, that he employed himself frequently in the practice of translation, (particularly from the French), with a view to the improvement of his own style: and he used often to express a favourable opinion of the utility of such exercises, to all who cultivate the art of composition" (Stewart, *Account of the Life and Writings of Adam Smith*).

233. Smith, *Lectures on Rhetoric and Belles Lettres*, 21.

234. Smith, *Lectures on Rhetoric and Belles Lettres*, 56.

235. Smith, *Lectures on Rhetoric and Belles Lettres*, 57.

236. Smith, *Correspondence of Adam Smith*, 251.

237. Smith, *Lectures on Jurisprudence*, 207.

238. Smith, *The Theory of Moral Sentiments*, 85. I quote here from *Theory* to encapsulate a more lengthy argument from his lectures.

239. Protecting citizens and their property is but a means to the end goal of creating a healthy, interconnected and vibrant society. When politics confuse means with ends, it becomes as superficial as society's elite who lack the ability to imagine a society where all are empowered to flourish and man's equality produces a commitment to equity.

240. Smith, *The Wealth of Nations*, 771.

241. Smith, *The Wealth of Nations*, 444.

242. Feldman, *The Three Lives of James Madison*, 137, 212.

243. Smith, *Lectures on Jurisprudence*, 208.

244. Smith, *Lectures on Jurisprudence*, 24.

245. Smith, *Lectures on Jurisprudence*, 261. The result was ruin of the nobility and gave raise "to the absolute power of the king."

246. "So far from being the only bastion against despotism, as Montesquieu [and Locke] had thought, Smith would believe that aristocracy posed a continuing threat to justice, sociability, and the progress of civilization" (Phillipson, *Adam Smith*, 112).

247. Rand, *Philosophy*, 10.

248. Smith, *Lectures on Jurisprudence*, 217.

249. He told his students that though the wealthy benefit an "equitable society," it is neither their virtue, nor their wisdom, that makes them beneficial. Smith's equation is as follows: The wealthy *can* be of benefit by making heavy investments in capital, capital *can* promote the division of labor, the division of labor *can* promote high wages for workers. The actual value of the wealthy, in Smith's philosophy, is continually measured by wages of the working class.

250. Smith, *Lectures on Jurisprudence*, 340. (The context is comparing the poor to the savage.)

251. Smith, *Lectures on Jurisprudence*, 401.

252. Smith, *The Wealth of Nations*, 287.

253. "In raising the price of commodities the rise of wages operates in the same manner as simple interest does in the accumulation of debt. The rise of profit operates like compound interest" (Smith, *The Wealth of Nations*, 287).

254. Smith, *The Wealth of Nations*, 113.

255. Smith, *The Wealth of Nations*, 287. One of the more influential aspects of *The Wealth of Nations* was its critique of monopolies; his critique of profits is much neglected. This is because both critiques are anchored in the impact on the common good; and as the modern project matures, merchants realize that monopolies warred against their interests while profits only warred against the common good.

256. Friedman, *Capitalism and Freedom*, 113.

257. Smith, *The Wealth of Nations*, 662.

258. Smith, *The Wealth of Nations*, 287.

259. Smith, *The Wealth of Nations*, 287.

260. Smith, *The Wealth of Nations*, 663.

261. Smith, *The Wealth of Nations*, 288.

262. Smith, *The Wealth of Nations*, 75.

263. Smith, *The Wealth of Nations*, 76.

264. Smith, *The Wealth of Nations*, 76.

265. Smith, *The Wealth of Nations*, 76.

266. Smith, *The Wealth of Nations*, 77.

267. Smith, *The Wealth of Nations*, 76.

268. Ingraham. *Our Infant Mortality Rate*. September 29, 2014.

269. See fact sheets available at http://www.houstonfoodbank.org/hunger/researchresources/. Two thirds of the food bank's 800,000 clients are working families. Almost half of the clients are children.

270. Smith begins his treatment of the colonies by recalling the colonies of Greece and Rome. Whereas Grecian colonies were inspired by population increases and "necessity," Roman colonies were inspired by what he coyly calls utility: "The people became clamorous to get land, and the rich and the great, we may believe, were perfectly determined not to give them any part of theirs. To satisfy them in some measure, therefore, they frequently proposed to send out a new colony . . . the interest which prompted to establish them was equally plain and distinct [Greeks and Romans colonies] derived their origin either from irresistible necessity or from clear and evident utility. The establishment of the European colonies in America and the West Indies arose from no necessity" (Smith, *The Wealth of Nations*, 601).

271. Smith, *The Wealth of Nations*, 601.

272. Smith, *The Wealth of Nations*, 613.

273. Smith, *The Wealth of Nations*, 601.

274. Smith, *The Wealth of Nations*, 678.

275. Smith, *Lectures on Jurisprudence*, 175–82.

276. Smith, *Lectures on Jurisprudence*, 175.

277. Smith, *Lectures on Jurisprudence*, 179.

278. Smith, *Lectures on Jurisprudence*, 180.

279. Jefferson, *Letter to William Fleming*, March 20, 1764.

280. Meacham, *The Art of Power*, 235.

281. "As it is for the labour of the slaves that the masters desire to have them, so it is chiefly male slaves which they procure as they are most able to sustain a great degree of hard labour. The women are not of such strength, and are therefore not much coveted.

They are never desired for propagating, for as it is always much cheaper to bye an ox or a horse out of a poor country where maintenance is cheap than to rear them in a rich one, so is it much cheaper to bye a slave from a poor country than to rear them at home" (Smith, *Lectures on Jurisprudence*, 193).

282. Smith, *Lectures on Jurisprudence*, 193–94.

283. One of the more tragic modern examples of the war over wages is the convict-leasing programs that were inaugurated in the years following the Civil War. In *Slavery by Another Name* Douglas Blackmon analyzes the work that enslaved generations of African Americans throughout the south for generations following the Emancipation Proclamation. Mass arrests on faulty charges feed a prison system that rented out its victims to industrialist. The death rates of the programs were staggering: "In the first two years that Alabama leased its prisoners, nearly 20 percent of them died. In the following year, mortality rose to 35 percent. In the fourth, nearly 45% were killed" (Blackmon, *Slavery By Another Name*, 57).

284. Smith, *Lectures on Jurisprudence*, 194.

285. Thus, the distinction between killing someone and robbing them of the means to feed, shelter, and clothe themselves is nil in Smith's mind.

286. "We may see from this that slavery amongst its inconveniencies has this bad consequence, that it renders rich and wealthy men of large properties of great and real detriment, which otherwise are rather of service as they promote trade and commerce" (Smith, *Lectures on Jurisprudence*, 198).

287. Chernow, *Washington*, 142. The fuller context of Chernow's reflections on Mt. Vernon eerily harmonize with Smith's musings on the impact of slavery on the working poor: "For the rest of his life, Washington grappled with the dilemma of having too many slaves, whose numbers only increased . . . At the same time he increasingly trained his slaves to perform a multitude of skilled tasks, producing a workforce of artisans proficient in diverse crafts."

288. Smith, *Lectures on Jurisprudence*, 181.

289. Smith, *The Wealth of Nations*, 675.

290. Smith, *Lectures on Jurisprudence*, 323.

291. Smith, *Lectures on Jurisprudence*, 317. In the same lecture—Tuesday, March 22nd, 1762—Smith associates the Hobbesian notion that a people have no right to resist with the view of divine monarchial right of the Tories: "The calm, contented folks of no great spirit and abundant fortunes which they want to enjoy at their own ease, and don't want to be disturbed nor disturb others" (320).

292. Smith, *Lectures on Rhetoric*, 55.

293. Smith, *The Wealth of Nations*, 90.

294. Smith, *Lectures on Jurisprudence*, 333. The comparison Smith makes is between Paris and London. London was larger with a relatively small legal code, and yet London was a peaceable city. Paris, on the other hand, possessed a large police force and criminal code, but "hardly a night passes in Paris without a murder or a robbery in the streets." In looking at the two cities, one should think from this "that the more of police there was in any country the less was the security."

295. Smith, *The Wealth of Nations*, 365.

296. "The liberal reward of labour, therefore, as it is the effect of increasing wealth, so it is the cause of increasing population. To complain of it is to lament over the necessary effect and cause of the greatest public prosperity" (Smith, *The Wealth of Nations*, 93). "If masters would always listen to the dictates of reason and humanity, they have frequently

occasion rather to moderate than to animate the application of many of their workmen. It will be found, I believe, in every sort of trade, that the man who works so moderately as to be able to work constantly not only preserves his health the longest, but, in the course of the year, executes the greatest quantity of work" (Smith, *The Wealth of Nations*, 94).

297. Smith, *The Wealth of Nations*, 97.

298. Smith, *Correspondence of Adam Smith*, 251.

299. Smith, *Lectures on Rhetoric and Belles Lettres*, 56.

300. This truth, however, was not yet an open secret as a culturally Christian lingo acted as the primary language of the pious tongue.

301. Phillipson, *Adam Smith*, 19.

302. It is important to note that Epictetus was a slave. Nonetheless, he is a slave that knows the imperial throne room and is an incredibly brilliant and beautiful (if harsh) mouthpiece of imperial logic. Think Clarence Thomas, Ben Carson, or Thomas Sowell as comparable, incredible intellectuals from an oppressed people who nonetheless took on the logic of the empire. For more analysis of Seneca, Epictetus, and Marcus Aurelius as philosophers, see Kavin Rowe's *One True Life: The Early Stoics and Christians as Rival Traditions*.

303. Noll, *America's God*, 103–13; 229–38. Meacham, *The Art of Power*, 18; Chernow, *Alexander Hamilton*, 47.

304. "The independent and spirited, but often harsh Epictetus, may be considered as the great apostle of the first of those doctrines: the mild, the humane, the benevolent Antoninus, of the second" (Smith, *Theory of Moral Sentiments*, 288).

305. Thus, the wise man learns to embrace the hand he is dealt and to play it to the best of his ability, for in the long run life is more about the skill of the players than the cards. The disciple focuses solely on what is under their control, slays the passions that war against living wisely, and ingrains the virtues of wisdom and prudence into their life to rise above life's circumstances. And when a disciple master's that which under their control, they realize the elegance of the game God crafted and praise the benevolent God for participating in such a beautiful world. A Stoic needs no sunglasses to hide his eyes while playing his hand, for he is the player ready to look the dealer in the eye without fear.

306. From Zeno, Smith learns that the benevolent power of self-interest is woven into the very grain of the universe and most effectively and efficiently leads to self-preservation and thus harmonizes with the ecosystem of God's designs. From Seneca, he learns to think of life as art and the storms of the world as that which calls forth man's most priceless truths as a sea captain whose art "is not made worse by any storm." From Epictetus, he learns to live with man's end in mind and to consult an impartial spectator in order to navigate life with wisdom. From Marcus Aurelius, Smith learns "That which is not good for the bee-hive, cannot be good for the bee" for "all things are linked and knitted together, and the knot is sacred."

307. Smith, *Theory of Moral Sentiments*, 147.

308. Taft, Inaugural Address, March 4, 1909.

309. Smith, *The Wealth of Nations*, 15.

310. Smith, *The Wealth of Nations*. 485.

311. Feldman, *The Three Lives of James Madison*, 260–63.

312. X, *The Autobiography of Malcolm X*, 329.

313. Smith, *The Wealth of Nations*, 889. Here Smith is writing on taxes and the need for clarity for what people can anticipate paying. I employ the quote here because it embodies the principle of the free market approach to pursuing justice.

314. Blackmon, *Slavery by Another Name*, 157–67, 170, 295.

315. Smith, *The Wealth of Nations*, 14. "To truck, barter exchange is unique" to humanity—"nobody ever saw a dog make a fair and deliberate exchange of one bone for another with another dog."

316. Smith, *The Wealth of Nations*, 12.

317. As much as any report in the young nation, Hamilton's aforementioned *Report on the Subject of Manufactures* in 1791 brings to life Hamilton's conviction concerning the centrality of the division of labor in America's future economy. For the report, Hamilton intimately studied *The Wealth of Nations* and Smith's influence is felt throughout. See Chernow, *Alexander Hamilton*, 376.

318. "The province of Holland, on the other hand, in proportion to the extent of its territory and the number of its people, is a richer country than England. The government there borrows at two per cent, and private people of good credit at three. The wages of labour are said to be higher in Holland than in England, and the Dutch, it is well known, trade upon lower profits than any people in Europe. The trade of Holland, it has been pretended by some people, is decaying, and it may perhaps be true some particular branches of it are so. But these symptoms seem to indicate sufficiently that there is no general decay. When profit diminishes, merchants are very apt to complain that trade decays; though the diminution of profit is the natural effect of its prosperity, or of a greater stock being employed in it than before" (Smith, *The Wealth of Nations*, 105).

319. During his diplomatic assignment in 1780, future President John Adams was as equally impressed with the Dutch as Adam Smith. Holland was: "The greatest curiosity in the world . . . Their industry and economy ought to be examples to the world" (McCullough, *John Adams*, 247).

320. A couple of quotes from Dutch philosopher Spinoza: "Peace is not an absence of war, it is a virtue, a state of mind, a disposition for benevolence, confidence, justice" (quoted in Gregor, *A Natural History of Peace*, 4). More explicitly: Those things, which beget harmony, are such as are attributable to justice, equity, and honourable living. . . . "Men are also gained over by liberality, especially such as have not the means to buy what is necessary to sustain life. . . providing for the poor is a duty, which falls on the State as a whole, and has regard only to the general advantage" (Spinoza, *On the Improvement of the Understanding*, 239).

321. Smith, *Theory of Moral Sentiments*, 82.

322. Smith, *Theory of Moral Sentiments*, 82.

323. Scalia, *The Disease as Cure*, 153.

324. Smith, *Theory of Moral Sentiments*, 39.

325. Smith, *Lectures on Jurisprudence*, 464.

326. In an exchange with a then-young Bernie Sanders regarding public responsibility for the impoverished, the previously mentioned Friedman individualizes responsibility, removing the care for the poor as a measure of economic or governmental effectiveness. "Government doesn't have responsibility," Friedman responded, "people have responsibility, you and I have responsibility." Individual, rather than collective, actions provide the foundation for the formula of Friedman's social responsibility. The only problem with the equation is that it is designed to fail.

327. Trattner, *From the Poor Law to Welfare State*, 273.

328. Dorrien, *The New Abolition*, 234.

329. Piven and Cloward, *Regulating the Poor*, 51.

330. See the cover of *Christian Perspectives: A Journal of Free Enterprise*, vol. 2, no. 3

(Winter 1989).

331. FitzGerald, *The Evangelicals*, 205; Wacker, *America's Pastor*, 120–36.

332. King, *A Testament of Hope*, 295.

333. Locke, *Political Writings*, 304.

334. Though Adam Smith hopes the teachings within *The Wealth of Nations* help level the wealth and bring power back to the people, his critiques of society's new Leviathans were largely ignored. Instead of bringing the dawning of a new day of an opulent equity, his philosophies regarding the magical powers of an invisible hand deepened the conviction that non-intervention in things economic is the primary domestic good of a good government.

335. Hobbes, *Leviathan*, 73 (emphasis mine).

336. Smith, *Wealth of Nations*, 771.

337. Smith, *Theory of Moral Sentiments*, 82.

338. One of the most significant failures of America's self-righteous reading of Scripture was white Americans conflating their identity with Scripture's Israel even while playing the role of Egypt and Pharaoh in the lives of people of color.

339. Hobbes, *Leviathan*, 542.

340. Locke, *Political Writings*, 412 (emphasis mine). When Locke writes, "Neither the use nor the omission of any ceremonies, in those religious assemblies, does either advantage or prejudice the life, liberty, or estate of any man," what is revealed to the reader is that the conviction concerning the effect of baptism on the relationship between slave and slavemaster was not the original genius of the South, but the outworking of the liberal project.

341. Matthew 25:41.

342. Noll, *God and Race in American Politics*, 43.

343. Lincoln, *Letter to Horace Greenly*.

344. King, *A Testament of Hope*, 556.

345. "King was tackling the most rigidly segregated city in America. In the previous ten years, efforts by individual black families to move into all-white neighborhoods had ignited arson, bombings, and more than a dozen riots. The living "arrangement" was maintained by the Chicago Board of Realtors" (Kotz, *Judgment Days*, 366).

346. See Coates, *The Case for Reparations*.

347. King, "Three Evils of Society."

348. King, *A Testament of Hope*, 617.

349. The first African-American student began classes in the graduate school of Rice University only the month before Kennedy's speech at the university. Two Rice Alumni then sued the school for breaking its commitment to segregation. The first African-American undergrad at Rice University began in 1965, four years after University of Georgia, three years after the University of Mississippi and two years after the University of Alabma. For more on the integration of Southern universities, see Levingston's *Kennedy and King: The President, The Pastor and the Battle Over Civil Rights*.

350. "No nation," counseled the President, "which expects to be the leader of other nations can expect to stay behind in the race for space."

351. Kennedy, Address at Rice University, September 12, 1962.

352. Levingston, Kennedy and King, xi

353. Garrow, *Bearing the Cross*, 220.

354. King, *A Testament of Hope*, 221.

355. "What they knew about him—besides his southern roots and accent, the

'magnolia drawl' that raised the hackles on liberal necks—was his southern record, a twenty-year record that had begun with his arrival in Congress in 1937 and lasted through 1956, on civil rights: a perfect 100 percent record of voting against every civil rights bill that had ever made it to the floor, even bills aimed at ending lynching, and a record, moreover, as a southern strategist, protégé of the chieftain of the mighty Southern Caucus, Richard Brevard Russell. . . But although the cliché says that power always corrupts, what is seldom said, but what is equally true it that power *reveals*. When a man is climbing, trying to persuade others to give him power, concealment is necessary: to hide traits that might make others reluctant to give him power, concealment is necessary: to hide also what he wants to do with that power; if men recognized the traits or realized the aims, they might refuse to give him what he wants. But as a man obtains more power, camouflage is less necessary" (Caro, *The Passage of Power*, xiv).

356. Kotz, *Judgment Days,* 134.

357. Sullivan, FBI Memo: "Communist Party, USA, Negro Question." August 30, 1963. See Capaccio, "MLK's speech attracted FBI's intense attention."

358. Kotz, *Judgement Days*, 47.

359. King, *A Testament of Hope,* 344, 345.

360. King, *A Testament of Hope,* 608.

361. King, *A Testament to Hope,* 38.

362. King, *A Testament to Hope,* 577.

363. Kotz, *Judgement Days,* 3.

364. King, *A Testament of Hope,* 472.

365. Kotz, *Judgment Days,* 312–13.

366. Kotz, *Judgement Days,* 38.

367. Johnson, State of the Union Address, January 8, 1964.

368. Kotz, *Judgement Days,* 97.

369. Kotz, *Judgement Days*, 38.

370. Falwell, *Falwell,* 312.

371. Johnson, Remarks to Members of the Southern Baptist Christian Leadership Seminar, March 25, 1964.

372. Johnson, Remarks on the Accomplishments of the 89th Congress, October 15, 1966

373. Kotz, *Judgement Days*, 33.

374. Kotz, *Judgement Days*, 311.

375. King, *A Testament of Hope*, 231–34.

376. Kotz, *Judgment Days*, 260.

377. FitzGerald, *The Evangelicals,* 244.

378. See the preface to Rick Perlstein's *Nixonland.*

379. Powell, *Following Months of Criticism, Obama Quits His Church.*

380. Baldwin, *The Fire Next Time*, 85.

381. "The fairy tale "does not deny the existence of . . . sorrow and failure . . . it denies (in the face of much evidence. . .) universal final defeat . . . giving a fleeting glimpse of Joy, Joy beyond the walls of the world, poignant as grief" (Tolkien, *On Fairy Stories*, 22).

382. Noll, *God and Race in American Politics,* 9.

383. Baldwin, "Transcript: James Baldwin Debates William F. Buckley (1965.)"; Baldwin, *The Fire Next Time,* 58.

384. Dyson, *Tears We Cannot Stop,* 3.

385. King, *A Testament of Hope*, 595.

386. See Dorrien, *Breaking White Supremacy*, 301.

387. Dorrien, *Breaking White Supremacy*, 301.

388. As a child, King attempted suicide twice by throwing himself out of a two-story window. Dorrien, *Breaking White Supremacy*, 258.

389. Isaiah 50:7 (KJV). In the Christian tradition, the suffering servant prefigures Jesus as the Christ.

390. Kotz, *Judgement Days,* 175. Moses continued: "The way some of us feel about it is that in our country we have some real evil, and the attempt to do something about it involves enormous effort—and enormous risks." For folks like Moses, the embracing the cross provides a better alternative to living at peace with America's violence and harmonizing one's life with her lies.

391. Kendi, *Stamped from the Beginning*, 504.

392. Baldwin, *The Fire Next Time,* 86.

393. Dorrien, *The New Abolition,* 296.

394. Hughes, "Monotony," in *The Collected Poems of Langston Hughes,* 31.

395. McFeely, *Grant,* 367–74

396. Kendi's parents "were student activists and Christians inspired by Black liberation theology." See www.ibramxkendi.com/aboutibramxkendi/.

397. Alexander's relationship to the church is complex. The child of interracial Christians, several churches refused to marry her parents, creating a tension-filled relationship between Alexander's family and the Christian faith. Nonetheless, in 2016 Alexander entered Union Theological Seminary as a visiting professor. In her sign-off from social media, Alexander posted: "At its core, America's journey from slavery to Jim Crow to mass incarceration raises profound moral and spiritual questions about who we are, individually and collectively, who we aim to become, and what we are willing to do now. I have found that these questions are generally not asked or answered in law schools or policy roundtables. So I am going to a place that takes very seriously the moral, ethical and spiritual dimensions of justice work," Facebook, September 14, 2016, https://www.facebook.com/168304409924191/posts/i-am-taking-a-long-break-from-social-media-but-tonight-i-want-to-thank-the-heinz/1090233291064627/.

398. Coates, a committed atheist, was raised in a non-religious household. Thus, Coates's intersection with the Prophetic Black Church tradition was at the "Mecca"—Howard University, a school thoroughly shaped by the influence of the Church. For a detailed history of that intersection, see Dorrien's *Breaking White Supremacy*.

399. King, *A Testament of Hope*, 485.

400. Wittgenstein, *Remarks on Frazer's Golden Bough,* 1.

401. Baldwin, *The Fire Next Time,* 102.

402. Perone, *Woodstock,* 40. Interestingly, the largest other demographic at Woodstock were those who refused to be identified by race.

403. I began studying the Christian responses to war in graduate school and was stunned to find my Southern Baptist tradition on a lower rung of the moral totem pole than hedonistic hippies.

404. Emerson, *Healing the Brokenness Series.*

Bibliography

Alexander, Michelle. *The New Jim Crow: Mass Incarceration in the Age of Colorblindness.* New York: The New Press, 2012.

Allitt, Patrick. *Religion in America Since 1945: A History*. New York: Columbia University Press, 2003.

Anderson, Terry L., and Peter J. Hill. *The Birth of a Transfer Society.* New York: University Press of America. 1989.

Baldwin, James. *The Fire Next Time.* New York: Vintage, 1963.

———. "Transcript: James Baldwin Debates William F. Buckley (1965)." Cambridge University's Union Hall. *Blog#42*, https://www.rimaregas.com/2015/06/07/transcript-james-baldwin-debates-william-f-buckley-1965-blog42/.

Bailey, Richard A. *Race and Redemption in Puritan New England.* New York: OxfordUniversity Press, 2011.

Bivens, Josh. "The Top 1 Percent's Share of Income from Wealth Has Been Rising for Decades." Economic Policy Institute, April 23, 2014, https://www.epi.org/publication/top-1-percents-share-income-wealth-rising/.

Blackmon, Douglas A. *Slavery by Another Name: The Re-Enslavement of Black Americans from the Civil War to World War II.* New York: Anchor, 2008.

Blum, Edward J. *Reforging the White Republic: Race, Religion, and American Nationalism* 1865–1898. Baton Rouge: Louisiana University Press, 2005.

Bonhoeffer, Dietrich. *Letters and Papers from Prison.* New York: Touchstone, 1971.

Bourne, Henry Richard Fox. *The Life of John Locke: Vol. I.* New York: Harper, 1876.

Brands, H. W. *Reagan: A Life.* New York: Anchor, 2016.

———. *Traitor to His Class: The Privileged Life and Radical Presidency of Franklin Delano Roosevelt.* New York: Anchor, 2008.

Bush, George H. W. Address Accepting the Presidential Nomination at the Republican National Convention, New Orleans, August 18, 1988. *C-Span*, https://www.c-span.org/video/?3848-1/george-hw-bush-1988-acceptance-speech.

Capaccio, Tony. "MLK's speech attracted FBI's intense attention." *The Washington Post*, August 27, 2013, https://www.washingtonpost.com/politics/mlks-speech-attracted-fbis-intense-attention/2013/08/27/31c8ebd4-0f60-11e3-8cdd-bcdc09410972_story.html?noredirect=on&utm_term=.2d0a2e3980a1.

Caro, Robert A. *The Years of Lyndon Johnson: The Passage of Power.* New York: Vintage, 2010.

Chapell, Vere, ed. *The Cambridge Companion to Locke.* New York: Cambridge University Press, 1994.

Chernow, Ron. *Alexander Hamilton*. Penguin, 2004.

———. *Washington: A Life*. New York: Penguin, 2010.

Coates, Ta-Nehisi. *Between the World and Me*. New York: Spiegel and Grau, 2015.

———. "The Case for Reparations." *The Atlantic*, June 2014, https://www.theatlantic.com/magazine/archive/2014/06/the-case-for-reparations/361631/.

Cranston, Maurice. *John Locke: A Biography*. New York: Oxford University Press, 1985.

Crump, Benjamin. "5 years after Trayvon Martin's death, what has nation learned?" *USA Today*, February 23, 2017, https://www.usatoday.com/story/opinion/policing/spotlight/2017/02/23/trayvon-martin-george-zimmerman-anniversary-policing-the-usa/98168962/

Dew, Charles B. *Apostles of Disunion: Southern Session Commissioners and the Causes of Civil War*. Charlottesville: The University of Virginia Press, 2001.

Dewey, John. *Democracy and Education*. New York: The Free Press, 1916.

———. *Experience & Education*. New York: Touchstone, 1938.

———. "The Motivation of Hobbes's Political Philosophy." In *Thomas Hobbes in His Time*, edited by Ralph Ross, Hebert W. Schneider, and Theodore Waldman, 8–30. Minneapolis: University of Minnesota Press, 1974.

Dorrien, Gary. *Breaking White Supremacy: Martin Luther King Jr. and the Black Social Gospel*. New Haven: Yale University Press, 2018.

———. *The New Abolition: W. E. B. DuBois and the Black Social Gospel*. New Haven: Yale University Press, 2018.

Douglass, Fredrick. "Oration of Fredrick Douglass," *American Missionary* 39 no. 6 (June 1885) 164.

Dyson, Michael Eric. *Tears We Cannot Stop: A Sermon to White America*. New York: St. Martin's, 2017.

Emerson. *Healing the Brokenness Series: How Race Works in Contemporary America*. Oct. 24, 2011.

Emerson, Michael O., and Christian Smith. *Divided by Faith: Evangelical Religion and the Problem of Race in America*. New York: Oxford University Press, 2000.

Emerson, Michael O., and Rodney M. Woo. *People of the Dream: Multiracial Congregations in the United States*. Princeton, NJ: Princeton University Press, 2006.

Fain, Kimberly. "The Devastation of Black Wall Street." *JSTOR Daily*, July 5, 2017, https://daily.jstor.org/the-devastation-of-black-wall-street/.

Falwell, Jerry. *Falwell: An Autobiography*. Lynchburg, VA: Liberty House, 1997.

Feldman, Noah. *The Three Lives of James Madison: Genius, Partisan, President*. New York: Random House, 2017.

FitzGerald, Frances. *The Evangelicals: The Struggle to Shape America*. New York: Simon and Schuster, 2017.

Foley, Duncan K. *Adam's Fallace: A Guide to Economic Theology*. Cambridge, MA: The Belknap Press of Harvard University Press, 2006.

Friedman, Milton. *Capitalism and Freedom*. Chicago: The University of Chicago Press, 2002

Hatch, Nathan O. *The Democratization of American Christianity*. New Haven, CT: Yale University Press, 1989.

Garrow, David J. *Baring The Cross: Martin Luther King, Jr. and the Southern Christian Leadership Conference*. New York: Perennial Classics, 1986.

Gilens, Martin. *Why Americans Hate Welfare: Race Media, and the Politics of Antipoverty Policy*. Chicago: The University of Chicago Press, 1999.

Goetz, Rebecca Anne. *The Baptism of Early Virginia: How Christianity Created Race*. Baltimore: John Hopkins University Press, 2012.

Goza, Joel, Ruth Lopez Turley, and Jay Kumar Aiyer. "New HISD Chief Must Tackle Challenge of 5th Ward Poverty." *Houston Chronicle*, April 11, 2016, https://www.houstonchronicle.com/opinion/outlook/article/New-HISD-chief-must-tackle-challenge-of-5th-Ward-7241140.php.

Gregor, Thomas, ed. *A Natural History of Peace*. Nashville: Vanderbilt University Press, 1996.

Hamilton, Alexander. *Report on Public Credit*. January 9, 1790. Online: http://www.wwnorton.com/college/history/archive/resources/documents/ch08_02.htm.

———. *Report on Manufactures*. December 5, 1791. Online: http://www.let.rug.nl/usa/biographies/alexander-hamilton/report-on-manufactures---submitted-to-congress-december-5-1791.php.

Hamilton, Alexander, et al. *The Federalist Papers: A Collection of Essays in Favour of the Constitution, as Agreed Upon by the Federal Conventionm September 17, 1787*. Mineola, NY: Dover, 2014.

Hobbes, Thomas. *De Cive*. Whitefish, MT: Kessinger Rare Prints, 2004.

———. *The Elements of Law, Natural and Politic*. 1640. Online: http://www.constitution.org/th/elements.htm.

———. *Leviathan or the Matter, Forme, and Power of a Common Wealth Ecclesiasticall and Civil*. Edited by Michael Oakeshott. New York: Simon and Schuster, 1962.

Horne, Gerald. *The Counter Revolution of 1776: Slave Resistance and the Origins of the United States of America*. New York: New York University Press, 2014.

Hughes, Langston. *The Collected Poems of Langston Hughes*. Edited by Arnold Rampersad and David Roessel. New York: Penguin Classics, 1994.

Human Rights Watch. "Punishment and Prejudice: Racial Disparities in the War on Drugs." May 2000, https://www.hrw.org/reports/2000/usa/.

Huxley, Aldous. *Brave New World*. New York: HaperPerenial, 1946.

Ingraham, Christopher. "Our Infant Mortality Rate Is a National Embarrassment." *Washington Post*, September 29, 2014, https://www.washingtonpost.com/news/wonk/wp/2014/09/29/our-infant-mortality-rate-is-a-national-embarrassment/?utm_term=.43821b60bb02.

Jefferson, Thomas. "Letter to William Fleming." March 20, 1764. https://founders.archives.gov/documents/Jefferson/01-01-02-0009.

———. "Notes on the State of Virginia." 1785. http://avalon.law.yale.edu/18th_century/jeffvir.asp.

Jennings, Willie. *The Christian Imagination: Theology and the Origins of Race*. New Haven, CT: Yale University Press, 2010.

Johnson, Lyndon B. Commencement Address at Howard University: "To Fulfill These Rights." June 4, 1965. http://teachingamericanhistory.org/library/document/commencement-address-at-howard-university-to-fulfill-these-rights/.

———. Remarks to Members of the Southern Baptist Christian Leadership Seminar. March 25, 1964. https://www.presidency.ucsb.edu/documents/remarks-members-the-southern-baptist-christian-leadership-seminar.

———. Remarks on the Accomplishments of the 89th Congress. October 15, 1966. https://www.presidency.ucsb.edu/documents/remarks-the-accomplishments-the-89th-congress.

———. State of the Union Address. January 8, 1964. http://www.let.rug.nl/usa/presidents/lyndon-baines-johnson/state-of-the-union-1964.php.

Katznelson, Ira. *Fear Itself: The New Deal and the Origins of Our Time*. New York: Liveright, 2013.

———. *When Affirmative Action Was White: An Untold History of Racial Inequality in Twentieth-Century America*. New York: Norton, 2005.

Kendi, Ibram X. *Stamped from the Beginning: The Definitive History of Racist Ideas in America*. New York: Nation, 2016.

Kennedy, John F. Address at Rice University, Houston, Texas, September 12, 1962. Online: https://er.jsc.nasa.gov/seh/ricetalk.htm.

Ketcham, Ralph. *James Madison: A Biography*. Charlottesville: The University of Virginia Press, 1990.

King, Martin Luther, Jr. "Beyond Vietnam: A Time To Break Silence Speech." Speech delivered at Riverside Church, New York, NY, April 4 1967.

———. *A Testament of Hope: The Essential Writings and Speeches of Martin Luther King Jr.* Edited by James M. Washington. New York: HarperSanFrancisco, 1986.

———. "The Three Evils of Society." Address Delivered at the National Conference on New Politics, Chicago, IL, August 31, 1967.

Kotz, Nick. *Judgment Days: Lyndon Johnson, Martin Luther King Jr., and the Laws that Changed America*. New York: Houghton Mifflin, 2005.

Kuhn, Thomas S. *The Structure of Scientific Revolutions*. Chicago: The University of Chicago Press, 2012.

Levingston, Steven. *Kennedy and King: The President, The Pastor, and the Battle Over Civil Rights*. New York: Hachette, 2017.

Lincoln, Abraham. *Letter to Horace Greenly*. August 22, 1862. Online: http://www.abrahamlincolnonline.org/lincoln/speeches/greeley.htm.

Locke, John. *An Essay Concerning Human Understanding*. Edited by Roger Woolhouse. New York: Penguin, 1997.

———. *Essay on the Poor Law and Working Schools*. 1697. In *Political Essays*, edited by Mark Goldie, 182–98. New York: Cambridge University Press, 1997.

———. *John Locke: Selected Correspondence*. Edited by Mark Goldie. New York: Oxford University Press, 2002.

———. *Political Writings*. Edited by David Wotton. Indianapolis: Hackett, 2003.

———. *The Reasonableness of Christianity with A Discourse of Miracles and Part of A Third Letter Concerning Toleration*. Edited by I. T. Ramsey. Stanford: Stanford University Press, 1958.

———. *Some Thoughts on Education and Of the Conduct of Understanding*. Edited by Ruth W. Grant and Nathan Tarcov. Indianapolis: Hackett, 1996.

Marmor, Theodore R., et al. *America's Misunderstood Welfare State: Persistent Myths, Enduring Realities*. New York: Basic, 1990.

Marsden, George. *Jonathan Edwards: A Life*. New Haven, CT: Yale University Press. 2003.

Martinich, A. P. *Hobbes: A Biography*. New York: Cambridge University Press, 1999.

———. *The Two Gods of Leviathan: Thomas Hobbes on Religion and Politics*. New York: Cambridge University Press, 1992.

McCullough, David. *John Adams*. New York: Touchstone, 2001.

McFeely, William S. *Grant: A Biography*. New York: Norton, 1981.

Meacham, Jon. *Thomas Jefferson: The Art of Power*. New York: Random House, 2012.

Montero, David. "A Changing of the Guard at Houston's Disciplinary School." *PBS: Frontline*, September 27, 2012, https://www.pbs.org/wgbh/frontline/article/a-changing-of-the-guard-at-houstons-disciplinary-school.

Moyers, Bill D. *What a Real President was Like. The Washington Post*, November 13, 1988, https://www.washingtonpost.com/archive/opinions/1988/11/13/what-a-real-president-was-like/d483c1be-doda-43b7-bde6–04e10106ff6c/?utm_term=.08813b7ae19f.

Muthu, Sankar, ed. *Empire and Modern Political Thought*. New York. Cambridge University Press, 2012.

Nester, William. *A Short History of American Industrial Policies*. New York: St. Martin, 1998.

Nixon, Richard. Address Accepting the Presidential Nomination at the Republican National Convention in Miami Beach, Florida. August 8, 1968. https://www.c-span.org/video/?4022-2/richard-nixon-1968-acceptance-speech.

Noll, Mark A. *America's God: From Jonathan Edwards to Abraham Lincoln*. New York: Oxford University Press, 2002.

———. *God and Race in American Politics: A Short History*. Princeton, NJ: Princeton University Press, 2008.

Pager, Devah. "The Mark of a Criminal Record." *American Journal of Sociology* 108 (2003) 937–75.

Perlstein, Rick. *Nixonland: The Rise of a President and the Fracturing of America*. New York: Scribner, 2008.

Perone, James E. *Woodstock: An Encyclopedia of the Music and Art Fair*. Santa Barbara, CA: Greenwood, 2005.

Phillipson, Nicholas. *Adam Smith: An Enlightened Life*. New Haven, CT: Yale University Press, 2010.

Pinkerton, James. "Bullet Proof Part I: Unarmed and Dangerous," *Houston Chronicle*, November 25, 2013, https://www.houstonchronicle.com/local/investigations/item/Bulletproof-Part-1-Unarmed-and-Dangerous-24419.php.

Piven, Frances Fox, and Richard A. Cloward. *Regulating the Poor: The Functions of Public Welfare*. New York: Vintage, 1993

Powell, Michael. "Following Months of Criticism, Obama Quits His Church." *New York Times*, June 1, 2008, https://www.nytimes.com/2008/06/01/us/politics/01obama.html.

Putnam, Robert. *Bowling Alone: The Collapse and Revival of American Community*. New York: Simon and Schuster, 2000.

Rae, John. *The Life of Adam Smith*. New York: Cosmio, 2006.

Rand, Ayn. *Atlas Shrugged*. New York: Signet, 1957.

———. *Philosophy: Who Needs It?* New York: Signet, 1984.

Reagan, Ronald. "The President's News Conference." August 12, 1986, made available online by Gerhard Peters and John T. Wooley, *The American Presidency Project*, http://presidency.proxied.lsit.ucsb.edu/ws/index.php?pid=37733&st=&st1=.

Rowe, C. Kavin. *One True Life: The Stoics and Early Christians as Rival Traditions*. New Haven, CT: Yale University Press, 2016.

Russell, Bertrand. *The History of Western Philosophy*. New York: Touchstone, 1972.

Scalia, Antonin. "The Disease as Cure: 'In Order to Get Beyond Racism, We Must First Take Account of Race.'" *Washington University Law Review*, issue 1 (1979) 147–57.

Shelton, Jason, and Michael O. Emerson. *Blacks and Whites in Christian America: How Racial Discrimination Shapes Religious Convictions.* New York: New York University Press, 2012.

Smith, Jean Edward. *Eisenhower: In War and Peace.* New York: Random House, 2013.

Smith, Adam. *Correspondence of Adam Smith.* Edited by E. C. Mossner and J. S. Ross. Indianapolis: Liberty Fund, 1987.

———. *Correspondence of Adam Smith.* Edited by Earnest Campbell Mosner and Ian Simpson Ross. New York: Oxford University Press, 1987.

——— . *Essays on Philosophical Subjects.* Edited by W. P. D Wightman. Indianapolis: Liberty Fund, 1982.

——— . *Lectures on Jurisprudence.* Edited by R. L. Meek, D. D. Raphael, and P. G. Stein. Indianapolis: Liberty Fund, 1982.

——— . *Lectures on Rhetoric and Belles Lettres.* Edited by J. C. Bryce. Indianapolis: Liberty Fund, 1985.

——— . *The Theory of Moral Sentiments.* Edited by D. D. Raphael and A. L. Macfie. Indianapolis, IN: Liberty Fund, 1982.

———. *The Wealth of Nations.* Edited by Edwinn Cannan. New York: The Modern Library. 2000.

Sorrell, Tom, ed. *The Cambridge Companion to Hobbes.* New York: Cambridge University Press, 1996.

Spinoza, Benedictus de. *On the Improvement of the Understanding: The Ethics; Correspondence.* New York: Dover, 1977.

———. *A Political Treatise.* New York: Exercere Cerebrum, 2016.

Stampp, Kenneth M. *The Peculiar Institution: Slavery in Ante-Bellum South.* New York: Vintage, 1956.

Stewart, Dugald. *Account of the Life and Writings of Adam Smith, LL.D.: From the Transactions of the Royal Society of Edinburgh.* Edinburgh, 1794.

Stinson, Susan. "The Other Side of the Paper: Jonathan Edwards as Slave-Owner." *Valley Advocate Online*, April 5, 2012, http://valleyadvocate.com/2012/04/05/the-other-side-of-the-paper-jonathan-edwards-as-slave-owner/.

Taft, William Howard. Inaugural Address. March 4, 1909. Online: http://avalon.law.yale.edu/20th_century/taft.asp.

Tolkien, J. R. R. *On Fairy Stories.* 1939. In *The Monsters and the Critics, and Other Essays*, edited by Christopher Tolkien, 109–61. Boston: Houghton Mifflin, 1984.

Trattner, Walter I. *From the Poor Law to Welfare State: A History of Welfare in America.* New York: The Free Press, 1999.

Tyson, Timothy B. *Blood Done Sign My Name.* New York: Broadway, 2004.

Valls, Andrew, ed. *Race and Racism in Modern Philosophy.* London: Cornell University Press, 2005.

Wacker, Grant. *America's Pastor: Billy Graham and the Shaping of a Nation.* Cambridge, MA: The Belknap Press of Harvard University Press, 2014.

Wall Street Journal. "President-Elect Obama." *Wall Street Journal*, November 5, 2008, https://www.wsj.com/articles/SB122586244657800863.

Washington Post Staff. "Transcript: Obama delivers eulogy for Charleston pastor, the Rev. Clementa Pinckney." *The Washington Post*, June 26, 2015, https://www.washingtonpost.com/news/post-nation/wp/2015/06/26/transcript-obama-delivers-eulogy-for-charleston-pastor-the-rev-clementapinckney/?noredirect=on&utm_term=.1d585d382b71.

West, E. G. *Adam Smith: The Man and His Works*. Indianapolis: Liberty Fund, 1976.

Wittgenstein, Ludwig. *Remarks on Frazer's Golden Bough*. Atlantic Highlands, NJ: Humanities, 1979.

White, Theodore H. "For President Kennedy: An Epliogue." *Life Magazine*, December 6, 1963, 158–59.

Wise, Timothy. *Between Barack and a Hard Place: Racism and White Denial in the Age of Obama*. San Francisco: City Lights, 2009.

Wolfe, Thomas. *You Can't Go Home Again*. New York: Scribner, 1940.

Wolin, Sheldon. *Democracy Incorporated: Managed Democracy and the Specter of Inverted Totalitarianism*. Princeton, NJ: Princeton University Press, 2008.

———. *Politics and Vision: Continuity and Innovation in Western Political Thought*. Expanded edition. Princeton, NJ: Princeton University Press, 2004.

X, Malcolm. *The Autobiography of Malcolm X*. With the assistance of Alex Haley. New York: Grove, 1965.

Zelizer, Julian E. *The Fierce Urgency of Now: Lyndon Johnson, Congress and the Battle for the Great Society*. New York: Penguin, 2015.

Zinn, Howard. *A People's History of the United States: 1492–Present*. New York: HarperPerennial Modern Classics, 1999.

Index